The Heart Of Pittsburgh II

Sacred Heart Elementary School

Parent Teacher Guild

♥♥

By the **Parent Teacher Guild of**

Sacred Heart Elementary School

Additional copies may be obtained at the cost of $17.95,

plus $2.50 postage and handling, each book.

Pennsylvania residents add $1.26 sales tax, each book.

Send check or money order, along with your name and address, to:

Sacred Heart Elementary School PTG

c/o Cookbook Committee

325 Emerson Street

Pittsburgh, PA 15206

(See order form in back of book.)

❤❤

Proceeds from the sale of

The Heart of Pittsburgh II

will provide funding for continual advancement in the science and technology

curriculums at Sacred Heart Elementary School

Copyright © 2004, Sacred Heart Elementary School PTG

Pittsburgh, Pennsylvania

First Printing, December, 2004–5,000 copies

Second Printing, January, 2009–5,000 copies

ISBN 978-0-9667438-1-4

LCCCN 2004093987

WIMMER
COOKBOOKS

A CONSOLIDATED GRAPHICS COMPANY

800.548.2537   wimmerco.com

The Heart of Pittsburgh II is a repeat performance. Inspired by the response to the original *Heart of Pittsburgh*, this new edition continues to celebrate the city's cultural diversity and rich ethnic heritage. Designed as a fundraiser for Sacred Heart Elementary, the book has taken on a life of its own. To our delight, the original book has sold beyond our expectations. The Sacred Heart community, local vendors and national book chains are all helping to promote the book. Our cookbook committee takes the book on the road for tastings and demonstrations. We are always elated to receive praise for our book from transplanted Pittsburghers from across the country, as well as from people who have never seen our great city.

Proceeds from the original book made the completion of a state-of-the-art library and computer lab for the school a reality. The success of the *Heart of Pittsburgh,* and encouragement from our vendors, prompted the committee to once again roll up our shirt sleeves and begin to collect recipes. Proceeds from this book will allow for continued advancement in the school's science and technology curriculums assuring students the greatest opportunity for education in these very important areas.

Sacred Heart Elementary is often called the "United Nations of Pittsburgh" because of its international student body. To celebrate our diversity, *The Heart of Pittsburgh II* contains numerous recipes submitted by the school's international families. These recipes add a colorful flavor to the book. In keeping with the original, this book again contains thirteen neighborhood historical sketches. We hope you enjoy the reading as well as the wonderful recipes included in this second edition. Enjoy learning about the history of Observatory Hill, Homewood or Regent Square. Then treat yourself to some tried and true hometown recipes, many with an international taste from a far-away homeland.

The Heart of Pittsburgh II took over two years to prepare. A dedicated committee solicited and tested all of the recipes, wrote and edited the text, designed the graphics and photographed the city. No contribution to the effort went unappreciated. It has truly been a labor of love for a talented group of school volunteers. We again thank Bishop William J. Winter, pastor of Sacred Heart Parish, Sister Patricia Laffey, principal of Sacred Heart Elementary, and the Sacred Heart Parent Teacher Guild for their encouragement and support.

Lastly, we thank the local organizations in our *Uniquely Pittsburgh* section of this book. Representing a cross section of the city, we highlight dedicated individuals and organizations who strive to make Pittsburgh an even better place to live. Whether a fire station, library or ethnic food festival, our city is filled with caring people who give Pittsburgh its unique flavor and its reputation for friendly neighborhood living.

We dedicate *The Heart of Pittsburgh II* to all of the families and friends of Sacred Heart — past, present and future.

♥♥

The Cookbook Committee

$\mathcal{A}$cknowledgments
♥♥

Chief Editor: Diane DeNardo

Assistant Editor: Karen Raffensperger

Graphic Design: Marcie McGuire, McGuire Anderson Design

Historical Copy Research: Anne McCafferty

Marketing & Public Relations: Diane DeNardo & Connie Kramer

Photography: Karen Raffensperger

Recipe Testing Coordinator: Kelly Runco

The Heart of Pittsburgh Committee
Co-chairs: Karen Raffensperger & Mary Roberge

Michelle Bisceglia	Barbara Dickson	Joanne Redondo
Toni Black	Connie Kramer	Kelly Runco
Valerie Buckley	Terry Laskowski	Nora Runco
Donna Caliguiri	Anne McCafferty	Beth Saxon
Michelle Cromer	Ellen McCormick	Amy Spence
Lila Decker	Marcie McGuire	Sylvia Stehlik
Diane DeNardo	Denise O'Conner	Andrea Wearden
Maria DeRenzo	Colleen Powell	

The committee wishes to extend its sincere thanks to the following people for their contribution of time and effort in assisting us with the task of testing recipes included in *The Heart of Pittsburgh II*:

Ellen Borge	Amy Kissell	Janet Peterson
Lynn Cauley	Jean Laird	Cathy Rosfeld
Wendy Chapman	Mary Ann Lasky	Marge Runco
Holly Dolan	Donna Linnelli	Tony Piccoli
Betty Ferons	Jane Lucchino	Angie Sassos
Kathy Fine	Francine Marthens	Tina Stacey
Anne Franks	Deborah McCarthy	Molly Thayer
Sue Hamilton	Karen Mitchell	Anne Thomasmeyer
Marty Harkins	Kelly Morgano	Bernadette West
Dee Hughes	Judi Owen	Jackie Wolfe
Alice Johnston	Susan Parente	

Sincere thanks are extended to the Pittsburgh Neighborhood Alliance and Wendell Jordon, under whose leadership numerous community leaders created the *Pittsburgh Neighborhood Atlas*, Pittsburgh, PA, originally published in 1976. This book provided neighborhood historical data for our cookbook.

Our thanks would not be complete without acknowledging the children and their families, as well as the Sacred Heart teaching and ancillary staffs, whose enthusiam in recipe collection and support throughout this project helped *The Heart of Pittsburgh II* reach beyond the walls of our Sacred Heart community.

♥♥

The Cookbook Committee wishes to extend their sincere thanks and appreciation to McGuire Anderson Design for so generously donating their time and talents to the cover and page design of *The Heart of Pittsburgh II.*

McGuire Anderson continues to remain a loyal friend to the Sacred Heart Community and to Catholic school education.

$\mathcal{E}$lementary education is a cornerstone in the development of every child, serving as the foundation for so many of life's important endeavors. Born in 1873 of the educational and spiritual needs of the then predominantly Irish immigrants of Pittsburgh's East End, Sacred Heart Elementary School has been dedicated to developing moral and academic excellence for more than 125 years.

The first Sacred Heart Church, situated on what is now Centre Avenue, originally served as both church and school. The school opened in 1873 under the direction of parishioners Misses Barry and White and moved into its own four-room brick building adjacent to the church in 1874. Enrollment grew rapidly, and, in December, 1874, seven Sisters of Charity came from Altoona to staff the school. The sisters and lay teachers have provided guidance and tutelage to our students ever since.

Responding to continued parish growth, a three-story school building was completed in 1884, and Sacred Heart High School was established in one room of that building in 1913. A new eight-room school building on Sheridan Avenue was completed in 1923. The following year, construction of a new church on Shady and Walnut streets was begun, and, in 1947, the current Sacred Heart Elementary School, on Walnut and Emerson streets, was dedicated. Sacred Heart High School moved to a new Alder Street location in 1950, where it served the East End until 1989.

Today, Sacred Heart Elementary School provides an academically enriched program that includes reading and English, mathematics, algebra, science, art, religion, social studies, health and physical education, Spanish, music, and computer applications. Because of well-developed study habits, the involvement of parents, and dedicated teachers, our students consistently demonstrate significant achievement in language and mathematics that is well above the national average. As one of the largest elementary schools in the Roman Catholic Diocese of Pittsburgh, our school continues to offer our students the highest caliber of education and moral guidance.

After 125 years of existence, Sacred Heart Elementary School is a stellar example of the adage, "Great beginnings last a lifetime."

The Cookbook Committee

$\mathcal{T}$able of Contents

♥♥

Carrick

*O*ne of Pittsburgh's southern-most neighborhoods, Carrick is just a quick trolley ride away from downtown Pittsburgh. First settled in 1791 by John Wilson and his family, the area was originally called Engleartville after the Engleartville Glass Company which was located there.

In 1818, Noble Calhoun purchased a little more than 1000 acres of what is now called Carrick for $5,000. He made a tidy profit in 1842 when he sold the land to William Noble. William Noble in turn quickly sold 100-acre plots to coal mine operators. Coal, mined for Jones & Laughlin Company, provided Carrick residents with a steady source of employment.

The area was christened Carrick in 1853 when Dr. John O'Brien, a local doctor who had emigrated from Ireland, suggested the name for the first post office. For the doctor, the name evoked nostalgic memories of his hometown of Carrick-on-Suir in Ireland's Count Tipperary.

Most of Carrick's early settlers were coal miners and farmers. One early prominent citizen was John Wilson, Jr., the grandson of Carrick's first settler and the town's wagon-maker and postmaster for 19 years. In 1890, John Phillips, founder of the Pennsylvania Game Conservation, built a home on Brownsville Road and soon organized a campaign to have it paved. From this humble beginning, Brownsville Road evolved to become an important transportation artery and commercial strip for local residents.

Although Brownsville Road and the Castle Shannon Railroad provided access to Pittsburgh, Carrick remained largely rural until the Pittsburgh and Castle Shannon trolley line opened the area to development in 1904. Carrick quickly grew into a lovely suburban residential community. Residents built attractive homes with spacious lawns, flower gardens, shrubbery, greenhouses and paved walkways. Phillips Park, named for John Phillips, served as a "trolley park." It was an amusement park built at the end of the trolley line to entice passengers to ride to the end of the line and to increase fare revenue on the weekends.

With Brownsville Road as its business district, and a well-maintained housing stock, Carrick continues to attract city residents who want to enjoy a suburban environment with convenient access to downtown Pittsburgh and its amenities. Carrick's picturesque elevation and active civic and recreational organizations make it a perfect example of a vibrant and engaged urban neighborhood. ♥♥

Russian Tea

4 cups water
15 whole cloves
1 tea bag (1-cup size)
1½ cups freshly squeezed orange
 juice, approximately 3 oranges
2-3 tablespoons freshly squeezed
 lemon juice, approximately
 3 lemons
1 (32-ounce) can pineapple juice
1 cup sugar

In a medium pot, bring the water to a boil. Add cloves; boil for 5 minutes. Remove from heat. Add tea bag; steep for 10 minutes. Strain mixture into a 3 to 4-quart container. Add orange and lemon juices; mix well. Stir in pineapple juice and sugar, stirring until sugar dissolves. Serve warm.

Note: Store unused tea in refrigerator.

Yield: Approximately 10 cups
Georgia Moncada

Champagne Punch

1 (16-ounce) package frozen
 strawberries in syrup, thawed
¼ cup sugar
2½ cups orange juice
2 tablespoons lemon juice
1 (750-milliliter) bottle
 Champagne

Place strawberries with syrup in a blender. Purée until smooth. Add sugar; blend well. Pour mixture into a 2-quart container. Stir in the orange and lemon juices. Cover and chill mixture in refrigerator until ready to serve. Just prior to serving, pour mixture into a punch bowl and slowly stir in the Champagne.

Note: Any sparkling white wine may be used in place of the Champagne.

Variation: For a non-alcoholic punch, use ginger ale in place of the Champagne.

Yield: Approximately 2 quarts
Susan Stager-Pavlick

John's Christmas Slush

1 (12-ounce) can lemonade
  concentrate
1 (12-ounce) can orange juice
  concentrate
1 cup sugar
5 cups water
2 cups whiskey
1 (2 -quart) bottle 4-percent soda

In a 3-quart plastic, sealable container, mix together the first 5 ingredients. Seal container and freeze for 48 hours. To serve, use a 3:1 ratio of slush to soda. Scoop slush into chilled serving glasses; add soda. *Enjoy!*

Yield: 10 cups of slush; approximately 20 servings

John Malinak

Eggnog

12 eggs, separated
1 cup sugar
1 quart milk
2 cups whiskey
1 cup rum
1 quart heavy cream, whipped
1 tablespoon vanilla extract,
  optional
Nutmeg, to taste

In a large bowl, beat egg whites until stiff; set aside. In a separate large bowl, beat together the egg yolks and sugar. Add the milk, whiskey and rum; mix well. Using a spatula, fold in the egg whites and whipped cream. Stir in the vanilla extract. Serve well-chilled topped with a dash of nutmeg.

Note: Store in refrigerator for up to 4 days. Recipe contains raw eggs. Pasteurized eggs may be substituted.

Yield: 32 (5-ounce) servings; approximately 5 quarts

Georgia Moncada

Kahlúa

A Coffee Liqueur

1 cup very strong brewed espresso
   or dark roast coffee
2 cups sugar
1 pint (80-proof) vodka
1 vanilla bean, halved
4 (2½-pint) bottles

In a small saucepan, over medium heat, bring the espresso to a boil. Add the sugar. Boil until sugar is completely dissolved; remove from heat. When mixture is cooled, stir in the vodka. Place one vanilla bean half in each of 2 bottles. Using a funnel, pour ½ of the liquid into each bottle. Cap with airtight bottle sealers. Place in a cool, dark cupboard; let brew for 3 weeks. Before serving, shake each bottle to loosen sediment. Using a cheese cloth and a funnel, strain liquid into 2 clean (2½-pint) bottles. Add 1 shot of Kahlúa to coffee as an after-dinner drink or serve over ice mixed with cream as an apéritif.

Variation: Use dark rum in place of vodka. Mixture will resemble Tia Maria, another delicious coffee liqueur.

Yield: 5 cups

Marcia Storb

Orange-Cranberry Toddy

6 whole cloves
6 cups orange juice
2 cups cranberry juice cocktail
1 stick of cinnamon
1 cup dark rum
2 oranges, sliced

Place cloves in a tea ball or cheese cloth. In a large saucepan, over medium heat, mix together the orange juice, cranberry juice cocktail and cinnamon. Place cloves in pan. Bring to a boil, stirring continuously. Remove from heat; stir in rum. Remove cloves. Serve warm in mugs garnished with orange slices.

Yield: 8 servings

Francine Marthens

Peach-Reisling Sangria

1 (750-milliliter) bottle dry
    Reisling wine
1½ cups white cranberry-peach
    drink
½ cup peach schnapps
3 tablespoons fresh lemon juice
2 tablespoons sugar
½ vanilla bean, split lengthwise
2 (½-inch thick) lemon slices
2 (½-inch thick) orange slices
2 peaches, peeled, cut into wedges
10 fresh raspberries
3 cups ice cubes

Place first 5 ingredients in a large clear glass pitcher. Scrape vanilla bean seeds into pitcher. Add vanilla bean; stir to blend. Gently stir in the fruit. Cover pitcher and chill overnight. Add ice just prior to serving. *This sangria makes an elegant presentation.*

Yield: 8 servings

Joanne Redondo

Mango-Pineapple Smoothie

1 (8-ounce) container plain yogurt
¼ cup orange juice
¼ cup pineapple juice
2 tablespoons honey
1 cup frozen mango chunks
1 cup frozen pineapple chunks
1 cup frozen banana slices
1 cup cubed or crushed ice

Place all ingredients in a blender in the order listed. Blend until smooth. Serve in frosted glasses garnished with additional fruit, if desired. *For a quick healthy breakfast on the go, take a chilled smoothie with you in a thermos.*

Note: To freeze fruit, wash, peel and chop any fresh fruit into bite-size chunks. (Canned fruit may also be used.) Place 1-cup portions of fruit into individual zip-top plastic bags. Seal and freeze in batches to always have frozen fruit on hand. The riper the fruit, the more intense the flavor, so freeze over-ripe bananas instead of discarding them.

Variation: Try combining other fruits, fruit juices and yogurts to create your own favorite smoothie. Pour any leftover smoothie into popsicle molds and freeze for a healthy summer treat.

Yield: 4 servings

Antonia DeNardo Piccoli

My Sister's Spaghetti Sauce

Olive oil
6 ribs of celery with leaves,
    coarsley chopped
3 medium onions, coarsley
    chopped
2 cloves garlic, coarsley chopped
2 carrots, peeled, coarsley
    chopped
2 (29-ounce) cans tomato purée
2 (29-ounce) cans tomato sauce
2 cups water
2 tablespoons dried parsley
1 tablespoon dried basil
Salt and ground black pepper,
    to taste

Place an 8-quart or larger stockpot over low heat. Add enough olive oil to cover bottom ¼ to ½-inch deep. Add the celery, onions, garlic and carrots to pot. Cover and simmer for 1 hour, stirring occasionally. Add the remaining ingredients to pot. Cover and simmer, stirring occasionally, for 4 hours. Allow sauce to cool slightly. Using a food processor or blender, purée sauce in batches.

Note: This is a thick sauce which freezes well.

Yield: 4½ quarts

Amy Spence

Charred Tomato Sauce

1 large onion, unpeeled
1 whole bulb of garlic, unpeeled
3 pounds ripe plum tomatoes,
    halved
½ cup finely chopped fresh basil
    or cilantro
Salt and ground black pepper,
    to taste

Preheat oven to 350 degrees. Wrap the onion and garlic bulb in aluminum foil. Bake for 1 to 1½ hours, or until very soft. Set aside to cool. Turn on oven broiler. Arrange the tomatoes in a single layer, skin side up, on a baking sheet. Broil, rotating pan so that skins blacken evenly. Continue broiling until skins completely char, approximately 10 to 15 minutes. Peel the cooled onion. Cut top off garlic bulb; gently squeeze out individual cloves. Using a food processor, purée the charred tomatoes, onion, garlic cloves and basil. Season with salt and pepper. Swirl the sauce on individual dinner plates and top with your favorite broiled or pan-seared poultry or fish dish.

Yield: 3 cups

Bernadette West

Spicy Peanut Dipping Sauce

1 cup raw peanuts, chopped
2 tablespoons honey
2 tablespoons rice vinegar
3 tablespoons soy sauce
2 teaspoons sesame oil
1 tablespoon olive oil
1 clove garlic, minced
3 tablespoons freshly squeezed
　lemon juice
3 tablespoons freshly squeezed
　lime juice

Preheat oven to 375 degrees. Spread peanuts on a baking sheet with sides. Roast for 3 to 5 minutes. Using a food processor or blender, combine the honey, vinegar, soy sauce, sesame oil, olive oil and garlic. Process until smooth, approximately 30 seconds. Add the peanuts; continue processing until sauce becomes the consistency of a chunk-style peanut butter, approximately 30 seconds. Add lemon and lime juices; process just until blended. Refrigerate until ready for use. Use as a dipping sauce for chicken and seafood or as a spread for bread.

Note: Unsalted, unroasted peanuts are found at natural food stores or in specialty grocery stores.

Yield: 1½ cups

Cynthia Taibbi Kates

Easy Oil and Garlic Pasta Sauce

½ cup olive oil
2 cloves garlic, minced
½ cup water
2 tablespoons chopped fresh
　parsley
2 tablespoons chopped fresh basil
⅛ teaspoon ground black pepper

In a heavy skillet, over medium heat, heat the olive oil. Add garlic; sauté for 30 seconds. (Do not brown.) Lower heat and slowly stir in the water. Add the parsley, basil and pepper. Simmer for 10 minutes. Serve over your favorite pasta.

Yield: 1 cup

Diane Norkus

Raisin Sauce for Ham

½ cup light brown sugar
1 teaspoon dry mustard
2 tablespoons cornstarch
2 tablespoons white vinegar
2 tablespoons fresh lemon juice
¼ teaspoon grated lemon peel
1½ cups water
½ cup golden raisins

In a small bowl, mix together the brown sugar, mustard and cornstarch; set aside. In a medium saucepan over low to medium heat, warm the vinegar, lemon juice and peel, water and raisins. Add the brown sugar mixture; heat slowly, stirring, until thickened. Serve warm sauce over ham.

Yield: 2½ cups

Cindy McKenna

Curried Pineapple Chutney

3 tablespoons vegetable oil
½ large red onion, chopped
1 red bell pepper, seeded, chopped
3 tablespoons minced jalapeño chilies
1½ tablespoons curry powder
2 (20-ounce) cans crushed pineapple, drained
¾ cup orange juice
¾ cup cider vinegar
¾ cup packed light brown sugar

In a large, heavy pot, over medium to high heat, heat the oil. Add red onion and bell pepper; sauté until softened, approximately 8 minutes. Add chilies and curry powder; cook, stirring, for 2 minutes. Add pineapple, orange juice, vinegar and brown sugar. Cook, stirring, until mixture boils. Decrease heat to low. Cover and simmer for 1 hour, stirring frequently, until mixture thickens and reduces to approximately 4 cups. Remove from heat; allow to cool completely. Refrigerate until use. *Delicious served with grilled tuna, swordfish or chicken.*

Note: Chutney may be made 2 to 3 days ahead.

Yield: Approximately 4 cups

Rebecca Lando

Till's Chicken Marinade

2 cups white vinegar
1 cup vegetable oil
3 tablespoons ground black
 pepper
3 tablespoons poultry seasoning
2 teaspoons Tabasco sauce,
 optional
2 teaspoons onion powder,
 optional
2 teaspoons garlic powder,
 optional

In a large glass bowl, mix together all marinade ingredients. Pour marinade over chicken pieces. Cover and marinate overnight in refrigerator. Discard marinade after use.

Yield: 3¼ cups; enough for 2 pounds of chicken

Till Kennon

Jamaican Jerk Rub

½ cup sugar
2 tablespoons paprika
2 tablespoons dried basil
2 tablespoons garlic powder
2 tablespoons celery salt
2 tablespoons coriander
2 tablespoons onion powder
1 tablespoon ground cumin
1 tablespoon ground black pepper
1 tablespoon crushed red pepper
 flakes, or to taste, optional
1 tablespoon cayenne pepper, or
 to taste, optional

In a small bowl, mix together all rub ingredients. Store at room temperature in a sealed container. Use as a seasoning rub for poultry, pork, beef or fish. Using your hands, spread rub over entire meat or fish portions. Let marinate for at least 20 minutes before cooking.

Yield: 1⅓ cups

Cathy Rosfeld

The Captain's Salad Dressing

1¼ cups canola oil
¾ cup apple cider vinegar
1 teaspoon sea salt or coarse
 kosher salt
1 teaspoon seasoned-salt flavor
 enhancer
1 teaspoon freshly ground black
 pepper
1-2 tablespoons minced garlic,
 to taste

Place all dressing ingredients in a 2-cup container with lid. Shake well. Prepare 1 hour before serving to allow flavors to blend. Serve over your favorite salad greens or vegetables.

Note: Refrigerate unused dressing.

Yield: 2 cups

Dr. David Spence (In Memory)

Traditional Caesar Salad Dressing

⅓ cup freshly squeezed lemon
 juice
¼ cup freshly grated Parmesan
 cheese
1 egg
1 egg white
4 anchovy fillets, chopped,
 optional
1 tablespoon Worcestershire sauce
1 clove garlic, minced
1 teaspoon freshly ground black
 pepper, and to taste
½ teaspoon salt, and to taste
½ cup vegetable oil
1½ cups olive oil

Using a food processor or blender, pulse together all ingredients except the vegetable and olive oils. Process until smooth, approximately 1 minute. With food processor running, add the vegetable and olive oils in a slow, steady stream. Continue blending until thickened, approximately 30 to 60 seconds. Season with additional salt and pepper, if desired. Cover and refrigerate. Allow dressing to stand at room temperature for 30 minutes before use.

Note: Recipe contains raw eggs. Pasteurized eggs may be substituted. Recipe may be made 1 day in advance.

Yield: 3 cups

Alex Black

Herb Vinaigrette

½ cup olive oil
½ cup red wine vinegar
½ cup finely chopped fresh basil
2 tablespoons finely chopped fresh oregano
½ teaspoon sugar
2 large cloves garlic, minced
½ teaspoon seasoned salt
½ teaspoon crushed red pepper flakes

In a medium bowl, whisk together all vinaigrette ingredients. Transfer to a 2-cup container; cover and refrigerate for 1 to 2 hours. Allow vinaigrette to come to room temperature before serving.

Note: Refrigerate unused dressing.

Yield: 1¾ cups dressing

Patty Just

Honeyed Hot Salsa

2 tablespoons red wine vinegar
2 tablespoons olive oil
1 tablespoon brown sugar
2 cloves garlic, minced
1 tablespoon honey
1 (28-ounce) can chopped tomatoes, drained
½ cup minced onion
½ cup finely chopped green bell pepper
2 tablespoons minced fresh cilantro
½ teaspoon dried oregano
½ teaspoon cayenne pepper
¼ teaspoon cumin

In a small saucepan, over low to medium heat, bring the vinegar, olive oil, brown sugar and garlic to a boil. Allow to boil, stirring, until reduced by half. Stir in the honey; remove from heat. Allow to cool slightly. In a medium bowl, mix together all remaining ingredients. Add honey mixture to bowl; mix well. Cover and refrigerate overnight. Serve salsa with tortilla chips or as a topping for poultry or seafood.

Yield: 4 cups

Francine Marthens

Allegheny West

Strolling down the streets of Allegheny West, one sees ornate architectural details, finely carved stonework, European-style gardens, herringbone-patterned cobblestone sidewalks, magnificent churches, and majestic shade trees. The opulence and detail highlight the rich history of this North Side neighborhood and still greet visitors today.

Allegheny West takes its name literally from its geographic location relative to the former city of Allegheny. Allegheny City sat across the Allegheny River from the larger city of Pittsburgh. In 1788, what is today Allegheny West was farm area around the Allegheny Commons, then public land used by the urban residents to graze their animals.

The population grew rapidly and expanded to the surrounding farmlands. Allegheny West became a neighborhood of Allegheny City and town officials designated the Commons area as a public park to ensure green space for the expanding urban community.

By 1860, large exclusive residences began to line Brighton Road, Beech Avenue, and much of the area south of Western Avenue. By 1884, Ridge Avenue and Brighton Road were home to the rich and socially prominent. Churches and schools including Calvary Methodist, Emmanuel Episcopal and the Allegheny Preparatory School helped to secure Allegheny West as a desirable community. The early 1900's were the highpoint for Allegheny West's reputation as the wealthiest neighborhood in the city.

By the 1930's, however, pollution, increasing population density and the availability of automobiles, encouraged the wealthiest families to move to homes beyond the city limits. Landlords and small business owners bought up the housing stock.

In the 1960's and 70's, major changes took place in Allegheny West. The campus of the Community College of Allegheny County was built on the site of several demolished mansions and construction of Three Rivers Stadium (now demolished and replaced with Heinz Field) led to the razing of other residential areas to create parking lots.

Countervailing forces in the form of citizen preservation groups staved off further residential encroachment. Concerted restoration and renovation efforts succeeded in recreating Allegheny West as, once again, one of the city's most desirable neighborhoods. ♥♥

Baked Garlic with Roquefort and Rosemary

6 whole garlic bulbs
3 tablespoons chilled butter, cut
    into 6 even slices
¼ cup olive oil
1 (14½-ounce) can chicken broth
¼ cup dry white wine
2 teaspoons chopped fresh
    rosemary
4 fresh rosemary sprigs, divided
Freshly ground black pepper, to
    taste
8 ounces Roquefort cheese,
    crumbled
Crusty French bread, sliced

Preheat oven to 375 degrees. Cut ½ inch off top end of each garlic bulb exposing the tops of cloves (do not cut off root end). Remove and discard any loose papery outer skin. Place each garlic bulb, cut side up, in a glass baking dish. Top each bulb with 1 slice of butter. Drizzle olive oil evenly over each bulb. Add the chicken broth and white wine to baking dish. Sprinkle chopped rosemary over bulbs. Place 2 rosemary sprigs in baking dish. Season with pepper. Bake, uncovered, basting every 15 minutes with pan juice, until garlic is tender, approximately 1 hour and 15 minutes. Add Roquefort cheese to baking dish and continue baking until cheese is almost melted, approximately 10 minutes. Discard cooked rosemary sprigs. To serve, gently squeeze each garlic bulb to remove individual cloves. Discard casings. Place cloves, softened cheese and pan juices in a serving dish. Garnish with the 2 remaining fresh rosemary sprigs. Dip bread slices into juice. Spread with the roasted garlic and softened Roquefort cheese.

Note: Add additional chicken broth to baking dish during roasting, if needed, to maintain enough juice for basting. Recipe may be prepared up to 8 hours prior to baking. Cover and refrigerate; bake as directed.

Yield: Serves 12

Diane Norkus

Yakitori

A Japanese Grilled Chicken Appetizer

20 ounces boneless, skinless dark chicken meat, cut into bite-size pieces
Bamboo skewers, soaked in salted water

Sauce
4 tablespoons sugar
½ cup mirin
½ cup soy sauce

Lemon wedges or slices

Prepare outdoor grill or heat broiler. Lightly brush grill rack or broiler pan with oil to prevent sticking. Place 4 pieces of chicken lengthwise on each bamboo skewer, so that skewers will lay flat on grill surface. To prepare the sauce, combine all ingredients in a small saucepan. Boil sauce, stirring, until reduced by ⅓. Lightly coat chicken pieces with sauce. Grill or broil skewered chicken, turning once, until cooked through, approximately 3 to 4 minutes. Re-coat chicken with the sauce 2 to 3 times during cooking. Serve warm with lemon wedges.

Note: Mirin, a rice cooking wine, is found in Asian food markets or in the specialty section of your grocery store. Metal skewers may be used in place of bamboo skewers.

Yield: 6 to 8 appetizers

Yukiko Yasue

Artichoke Hors D'Oeuvres

1 cup light mayonnaise
1 (14-ounce) can artichokes,
   drained, chopped
1 cup freshly grated Parmesan
   cheese
1 cup shredded mozzarella cheese
1 teaspoon minced garlic
6 English muffins

Preheat oven to 400 degrees. In a medium bowl, combine the first 5 ingredients; mix well. Cut each muffin in half. Spread mixture on muffin halves. Cut each muffin half into 4 pieces; place on a baking sheet. Bake for 15 to 20 minutes or until tops begin to brown. Serve warm.

Note: Prepared Artichoke Hors D'Oeuvres may be frozen before baking. Thaw at room temperature; bake as directed.

Yield: 48 hors d'oeuvres

Dorianne DiGregorio

Cocktail Reubens

8 slices Swiss cheese
Thousand Island salad dressing
36 slices party rye or
   pumpernickel bread
4 ounces corned beef, thinly sliced
1 (14-ounce) can sauerkraut,
   drained

Preheat oven to 400 degrees. Line a baking sheet with aluminum foil; set aside. Cut each slice of Swiss cheese into 4 to 6 pieces to fit size of the bread; set aside. Spread a small amount of salad dressing on each bread slice; place on prepared baking sheet. Lay 1 slice of corned beef atop each bread slice. Place 1 teaspoon of sauerkraut atop each corned beef slice. Top with 1 piece of Swiss cheese. Bake reubens for 6 to 8 minutes, until heated through and cheese melts. *Simple and delicious.*

Yield: 36 appetizers

Donna Linnelli

Tortellini with Parmesan Lemon Dip

Dip
1 cup sour cream
½ cup freshly grated Parmesan cheese
Juice of 2 lemons
Grated zest of 2 lemons
3 cloves roasted garlic, peeled, crushed

1½ pounds cheese or meat tortellini
1 tablespoon olive oil
1 package (6-inch) wooden skewers
Parsley sprigs, optional

To prepare the dip, in a small bowl, combine the sour cream, Parmesan cheese, lemon juice, zest and garlic; mix well. Place in a small serving bowl; set aside. Prepare tortellini, according to package directions, until just tender; do not overcook. Drain; toss with the olive oil. To assemble, put two tortellini on one skewer, repeat until all tortellini are used. Arrange tortellini skewers around the dip on a serving tray. Garnish dip with parsley sprigs. Serve tortellini warm or at room temperature.

Variation: Cut red bell peppers into chunks; boil just until tender. When assembling the skewers, alternate peppers with the tortellini.

Yield: 1¼ cups dip; 40 appetizers
Kelly Runco

Fresh Herb and Goat Cheese Dip

8 ounces premium fresh goat cheese, softened
3 tablespoons extra-virgin olive oil
3 tablespoons plain yogurt
2 tablespoons chopped fresh chives
2 tablespoons chopped fresh sage
2 tablespoons chopped fresh thyme
2 tablespoons chopped fresh tarragon
2 tablespoons chopped fresh rosemary
Salt and freshly ground black pepper, to taste
Edible flowers, optional

Using a food processor, blend the goat cheese, olive oil and yogurt just until smooth. Add the fresh herbs. Pulse processor a few times until herbs are evenly distributed. Season with salt and pepper. Transfer dip to a serving bowl. Cover and refrigerate until flavors have blended and dip is cold, approximately 3 hours. Garnish with edible flowers. Serve dip with toasted baguette slices, crackers or raw vegetables.

Note: Dip may be made 1 day ahead; cover and refrigerate.

Yield: 1½ cups

Diane DeNardo

Artichoke Dip

1 (14-ounce) can artichokes, drained, finely chopped
1 cup Hellmann's mayonnaise
½ teaspoon garlic powder
1 (10-ounce) package frozen chopped spinach, thawed, drained
1 (8-ounce) package cream cheese, softened
1 small onion, chopped
½ cup freshly grated Parmesan cheese, or to taste

Preheat oven to 350 degrees. Spray an 8x8-inch shallow baking dish with a nonstick vegetable oil cooking spray; set aside. In a large bowl, combine the artichokes, mayonnaise, garlic powder, spinach, cream cheese and onion; mix well. Spread mixture evenly into prepared baking dish; sprinkle Parmesan cheese over top. Bake for 25 to 30 minutes until browned on top. Serve warm from the oven with crackers or home baked pita chips.

Variation: Substitute Asiago cheese for the Parmesan cheese.

Yield: Serves 6 to 8

Cecelia Morello

Tuna Ball

2 (6-ounce) cans of tuna, packed
   in water, drained
2 (8-ounce) packages cream
   cheese, softened
1 tablespoon dry onion flakes
1-2 tablespoons horseradish,
   to taste
2 cups chopped walnuts

In a large bowl, flake the tuna. Add the cream cheese; mix well. Add the onion flakes and horseradish. Mix until smooth. Cover and refrigerate for 4 hours. Shape mixture into a ball. Spread walnuts on waxed paper; roll tuna ball in the nuts until completely covered. Serve with your favorite crackers.

Yield: Serves 10 to 15

Tookie Wozniak

Sweet and Sour Sausage Balls

4 pounds bulk sweet Italian pork
   sausage
1½ cups fresh breadcrumbs
4 eggs, lightly beaten

Sauce
3 cups ketchup
½ cup white vinegar
½ cup soy sauce
¾ cup brown sugar

Line a large tray or baking sheet with waxed paper. To prepare the sausage balls, in a large bowl, mix together the sausage, breadcrumbs, and eggs. Roll mixture into 1-inch balls. Place sausage balls on tray. In a large skillet, over low to medium heat, brown sausage balls in batches; set aside on paper towels to drain. To prepare the sauce, in a large pot, mix together the ketchup, vinegar, soy sauce and brown sugar; bring to a simmer over low to medium heat. Add sausage balls; cover and simmer for 30 minutes, stirring occasionally. Transfer to a serving dish; serve warm. *Great for parties.*

Yield: Approximately 150 appetizers

Kay Raffensperger

Spicy Barbecue Meatballs

1½ pounds ground turkey or
    extra-lean ground beef
¾ cup quick-cooking oats
1 cup finely chopped onion
1½ teaspoons minced fresh garlic
1 teaspoon dried oregano
1½ teaspoons beef bouillon
    granules
½ teaspoon ground black pepper
2 egg whites

Sauce
3 tablespoons Dijon mustard
1¼ teaspoons chili powder
½ teaspoon Tabasco sauce, or
    to taste
1 (8-ounce) can unsalted tomato
    sauce
3 tablespoons honey

Preheat oven to 350 degrees. Coat a baking sheet with nonstick vegetable oil cooking spray; set aside. To prepare the meatballs, in a large mixing bowl, combine all meatball ingredients; mix well. Shape the meatball mixture into 1-inch balls; place on baking sheet. Bake until thoroughly cooked, approximately 25 minutes. Transfer cooked meatballs to a heated chafing dish, crock-pot or casserole; keep warm. To prepare the sauce, in a small saucepan, combine all sauce ingredients. Simmer over low to medium heat until hot. Pour the sauce over meatballs; toss gently. Serve warm. *A delicious low-fat, heart-healthy appetizer.*

Yield: 60 appetizers

Angela Stead

Pesto Pinwheels

1 sheet frozen puff pastry
⅓ cup prepared pesto sauce
⅔ cup freshly grated Parmesan
    cheese
1 egg beaten with 1 teaspoon
    water

Thaw puff pastry for 20 minutes. Preheat oven to 400 degrees. Line a baking sheet with parchment paper; set aside. Unfold the pastry. On a lightly floured surface, roll the pastry to approximately 10x12-inches. Spread pesto sauce over top; sprinkle with the Parmesan cheese. Starting with a long edge, roll up the pastry, jelly-roll fashion. Cut into ½-inch slices. Place slices on the prepared baking sheet. Brush tops with the egg mixture. Bake for 8 to 10 minutes or until golden brown. Serve warm. *A buffet favorite.*

Yield: 24 appetizers

Toni Marra

Deviled Eggs Florentine

**12 large eggs, hard-boiled, peeled,
  cut into halves**
**1 (10-ounce) package frozen
  spinach**
1 tablespoon sour cream
¼ teaspoon salt
Dash of nutmeg
Dash of cayenne pepper
3-4 tablespoons mayonnaise
1 teaspoon prepared mustard
**Salt and freshly ground black
  pepper, to taste**
Paprika

Place egg yolks in a small mixing bowl; set aside. Place egg white halves on a serving plate; cover and refrigerate to chill. Cook spinach according to package directions; drain thoroughly. Using a blender or food processor, combine the spinach, sour cream, salt, nutmeg and cayenne pepper. Purée until smooth, scraping down sides of blender 2 to 3 times as needed; set spinach mixture aside. Using a blender or fork, mash egg yolks with the mayonnaise, mustard, salt and pepper. Spoon spinach mixture into each egg white half. Using a decorating bag, pipe a small amount of yolk mixture on top of spinach filling. Sprinkle with paprika before serving. *Served with black olives, cherry tomatoes and carrot curls, this flavorful recipe makes a festive presentation.*

Yield: 24 appetizers

Barbara Dickson

Toni's Red Pepper Spread

2 cloves garlic, peeled, chopped
1 tablespoon olive oil
1 tablespoon balsamic vinegar
**1 (15-ounce) can garbanzo beans,
  drained**
**1 (12-ounce) jar roasted red
  peppers, with juice**
¼ teaspoon salt
**1 tablespoon chopped fresh
  parsley or tarragon**

In a small bowl, stir together the garlic, olive oil and balsamic vinegar. Using a food processor or blender, purée the garbanzo beans while slowly adding the olive oil mixture in a steady stream. Add the red peppers with juice, salt and parsley; purée until smooth. Serve chilled or at room temperature with crackers, vegetables, pita chips or crusty bread.

Yield: Approximately 2 cups

Toni Black

Holiday Cheese Puffs

1 sheet frozen puff pastry
⅓ cup frozen spinach, thawed, well-drained
½ cup crumbled blue cheese
¼ cup crumbled cooked bacon
1 (2-ounce) jar diced pimentos, drained
2 tablespoons ranch-style dressing

Preheat oven to 400 degrees. Line a baking sheet(s) with parchment paper; set aside. While puff pastry is frozen, cut into 24 (2x2-inch) squares. Place squares on baking sheet. In a medium bowl, combine all other ingredients; mix well. Place 2 teaspoons of spinach mixture on the center of each pastry square. Bake for 20 minutes or until golden brown.

Variation: Substitute feta cheese for the blue cheese.

Yield: 24 appetizers

Janice Burgett

Inarizushi

A Japanese Sushi Appetizer

Vinegared Rice
2 cups cooked sushi rice (short-grain Japanese-style rice), hot
2-3 tablespoons Mitsukan Susizu (seasoned rice vinegar), to taste

16 Misuzu Oinarisan (teriyaki-seasoned pouches of deep-fried tofu)

To prepare the vinegared rice, using a shamoji or spatula, spread the cooked hot rice on a sushi-oke or large plate. Sprinkle the Mitsukan Susizu over the rice and quickly fold rice with the spatula being careful not to smash it. Rice will begin to cool; cool only enough that hot rice can be handled. (The rice will have a shiny appearance.) Using your hands, shape 2 tablespoonfuls of the sushi rice into small ovals; press each rice oval into a Misuzu Oinarisan. Fold the open side to close each pouch. Place on a serving platter. Serve at room temperature.

Note: The ingredients for Inarizushi are found at Asian food markets.

Yield: 16 appetizers

Miwa Tokuda

Bean Salsa

1 (14-ounce) can diced tomatoes, drained
1 (14-ounce) can black beans, rinsed, drained
1 (14-ounce) can black-eyed peas, rinsed, drained
1 (14-ounce) can whole-kernel corn, drained
½ large green bell pepper, seeded, diced
1 small onion, diced
1 cup of zesty Italian dressing

In a large bowl, combine all ingredients; mix well. Cover; chill for four hours before serving. Serve with tortilla chips. *Also a delicious accompaniment to grilled chicken or fish.*

Variation: For a tasty alternative, substitute pinto beans and kidney beans for the black beans and black-eyed peas.

Yield: Approximately 8 cups

Maria DiGregorio

Black Bean & Corn Salsa

1 (16-ounce) can black beans, rinsed, drained
1 (7-ounce) can shoepeg corn, drained
½ cup Italian salad dressing
2 cloves garlic, minced
3 tablespoons finely chopped cilantro
½ teaspoon Tabasco sauce
¾ teaspoon chili powder
1 medium tomato, chopped
½ green, orange or red bell pepper, seeded, diced
½ red onion, diced
Tortilla chips

In a medium mixing bowl, combine the black beans, corn, salad dressing, garlic, cilantro, Tabasco sauce and chili powder; toss well. Cover and marinate in refrigerator for at least 1 hour. Before serving, add the tomato, bell pepper and onion; re-toss. Serve with tortilla chips.

Yield: 3½ to 4 cups

Teresa Adams

Our Favorite Salsa

¼ cup canola or vegetable oil
2 tablespoons cider or red wine
  vinegar
1 teaspoon salt, or to taste
3 large ripe tomatoes, finely
  chopped
1 medium sweet onion, finely
  chopped
1 medium green bell pepper,
  seeded, finely chopped
1 rib of celery, finely chopped
1 (4.5-ounce) can chopped chilies,
  drained
1 banana pepper, seeded, finely
  chopped, optional
1-2 tablespoons chopped fresh
  cilantro, to taste, optional

In a large bowl, whisk together the oil, vinegar and salt. Add the remaining salsa ingredients. Toss well to thoroughly combine. Cover; refrigerate for 24 hours. Serve with tortilla chips. *Great for a boat ride on the Monongahela, Ohio and Allegheny Rivers.*

Yield: Approximately 5 cups

Denise Orlando

Mexican Taco Dip

1 (8-ounce) package cream cheese,
  softened
1 (8-ounce) container sour cream
1 (1.25-ounce) package taco
  seasoning mix
3 teaspoons mild taco sauce, or
  to taste
⅓ cup sliced black olives, or
  to taste
½ cup shredded Cheddar cheese,
  or to taste
½ cup chopped tomatoes, or
  to taste
Tortilla chips

Place the cream cheese, sour cream, taco seasoning mix and taco sauce in a blender. Blend until combined. Transfer to a serving bowl; top with the olives, Cheddar cheese and tomatoes. Serve with tortilla chips.

Yield: Approximately 3 cups

Pam D'Alessandro

Korean Pan-Fried Dumplings

Filling

1 cup finely chopped cabbage
1 teaspoon salt, divided
½ teaspoon sugar
1 cup unpeeled, finely chopped
  zucchini
½ pound ground beef, cooked,
  well-drained
1 cup finely chopped scallions
  (whites and small amount of
  green)
½ cup finely chopped carrots
1 egg, lightly beaten
2 tablespoons sesame oil
1 tablespoon soy sauce
3½ tablespoons white cooking
  wine
½ teaspoon ground black pepper
½ teaspoon garlic salt
2 tablespoons sesame seeds,
  toasted

1 (12-ounce) package wonton
  wrappers
1 egg yolk mixed with
  1 tablespoon water
Cooking oil

To prepare the filling, place cabbage in a small bowl. Sprinkle with ½ teaspoon of the salt and the sugar. Allow to stand for 1 minute. Using your hands, squeeze out excess liquid from cabbage; transfer to a large bowl. Place zucchini in a separate small bowl; sprinkle with ½ teaspoon of the salt. Allow to stand for 1 minute. Again using your hands, squeeze out excess liquid from zucchini; place in bowl with cabbage. Gently mix together the cabbage and zucchini, ground beef, scallions and carrots. Add the egg; mix well. In a small mixing bowl, whisk together the sesame oil, soy sauce, cooking wine, pepper, garlic salt and sesame seeds. Add to the meat mixture; mix well. Place wonton wrappers on a baking sheet with sides. Using a pastry brush, coat edges of the wonton wrappers with egg yolk mixture. Place 1 to 2 teaspoons of filling mixture in center of each wonton wrapper. Gather edges of wonton wrappers together to form a triangle; pinch edges to seal. In a large, heavy skillet, heat 2 to 3 tablespoons of cooking oil until a drop of water in oil sizzles. Fry dumplings in batches, turning once, until lightly browned, approximately 2 to 3 minutes on each side. Add additional oil as needed to continue frying all dumplings. Drain well on paper towels before serving. *A crowd pleaser.*

Yield: 50 dumplings

Seung Jin Choi

Layered Shrimp Spread

12 ounces cream cheese, softened
1 small onion, finely chopped
1 tablespoon Worcestershire
sauce, or to taste
2 tablespoons mayonnaise
1 tablespoon lemon juice
Dash of garlic salt
½ cup cocktail sauce
½ pound peeled shrimp, cooked,
chopped

Using a blender or electric mixer, combine the cream cheese, onion, Worcestershire sauce, mayonnaise, lemon juice and garlic salt until smooth. Spread cream cheese mixture evenly on a 12-inch round serving plate. Spread cocktail sauce over top of cream cheese mixture. Layer shrimp pieces over top. Serve with crackers.

Note: Recipe may be prepared 1 day ahead. Cover tightly and refrigerate.

Variation: 1 (6½-ounce) can of crabmeat may be substituted for the shrimp. Drain, flake and pick through the crabmeat for pieces of shell.

Yield: Serves 8 to 10

Ann Van Wassen

Creamy Shrimp Dip

2 tablespoons finely chopped
onion
1 cup mayonnaise
½ cup sour cream
2 tablespoons ketchup
½ teaspoon Worcestershire sauce
⅛ teaspoon cayenne pepper
1 (6-ounce) package cooked
shrimp, rinsed, drained,
chopped

In a large bowl, mix together all dip ingredients except the shrimp. Gently fold in the shrimp. Transfer to a serving bowl. Serve with crackers or vegetables.

Yield: 2 cups

Pat Knavish

Toasted Almond Spread

⅓ cup sliced almonds
1-2 teaspoons butter
1 (8-ounce) package cream cheese, softened
6 ounces shredded Swiss cheese, approximately 1½ cups
⅓ cup mayonnaise-style salad dressing
2 tablespoons chopped scallions (white part and small amount of green)
⅛ teaspoon nutmeg
⅛ teaspoon ground black pepper

Preheat oven to 350 degrees. Lightly coat a 9-inch glass pie plate with nonstick vegetable oil spray; set aside. In a small skillet, over medium heat, sauté almonds in the butter until lightly toasted. Place all remaining ingredients in a mixing bowl. Using an electric mixer, blend until creamy. Fold in the almonds. Spread into prepared pie plate. Bake for 8 minutes. Stir and continue baking for an additional 7 minutes. Transfer to a serving dish. Serve with crackers or sliced French bread. If desired, garnish with additional toasted almonds.

Yield: 2 cups

Margie Snodgrass

Crabmeat Pie

1 (16-ounce) can crabmeat, drained, picked through for pieces of shell
1 cup finely chopped celery
1½ teaspoons finely chopped onion
1 cup finely chopped red or green bell pepper
¼ teaspoon salt
¾ cup mayonnaise
1 teaspoon lemon juice
25 round butter crackers, rolled into crumbs, 2 tablespoons reserved
½ cup shredded extra-sharp Cheddar cheese

Preheat oven to 350 degrees. Butter a 9 or 10-inch glass pie plate; set aside. In a large mixing bowl, combine the crabmeat, celery, onion, bell pepper, salt, mayonnaise, lemon juice and crackers; mix well. Spread crabmeat mixture into prepared pie plate; sprinkle top with cheese and the reserved 2 tablespoons of cracker crumbs. Cover pie plate with foil; bake for 20 minutes. Remove foil and bake for an additional 15 minutes, or until browned on top. Let rest for 10 minutes. Serve with crackers.

Yield: Serves 20

Marie Malczak

Stuffed Mushrooms

16 large white mushrooms,
  cleaned
2 slices of bacon, cooked crisp,
  crumbled
4 ounces cream cheese, softened
2 tablespoons Worcestershire
  sauce

Preheat oven to 350 degrees. Line a baking sheet with foil; set aside. Remove stems from mushrooms; finely chop. In a medium bowl, combine the chopped mushroom stems, bacon, cream cheese and Worcestershire sauce; mix well. Place 1 teaspoon of the mixture in each mushroom cap; place on baking sheet. Bake for 15 to 20 minutes; serve hot.

Yield: 16 appetizers

Georgia Moncada

Spinach Dip

2 (10-ounce) packages frozen
  chopped spinach, thawed, well-
  drained
2 cups non-fat plain yogurt
2 (1-ounce) packages ranch-style
  salad dressing mix
½ cup finely chopped scallions
  (white part and small amount
  of green)
1 large onion, finely chopped, or
  to taste
½ teaspoon salt
½ teaspoon ground black pepper
1 cup Hellmann's mayonnaise

In a large bowl, combine all ingredients; mix well. Cover and refrigerate dip for 2 hours before serving. Transfer to a serving bowl. Serve with vegetables, crackers or toasted pita wedges. *A delicious dip for parties.*

Yield: 6 cups

Francine Marthens

Stuffed Banana Peppers with Béchamel Sauce

8-10 medium to large (hot or sweet) banana peppers, stemmed, seeded

Filling
1 cup chopped walnuts
1½ cups cooked (hot or sweet) bulk sausage, well-drained
1 (7 to 10-ounce) ball fresh mozzarella cheese, cubed

¼ cup olive oil

Béchamel Sauce
1 cup chicken broth
⅓ cup finely diced onions
1 carrot, finely diced
6 whole black peppercorns
3 tablespoons butter
3 tablespoons flour
1 cup milk
½ teaspoon salt
1 egg yolk, beaten

Tomatoes, thinly sliced, optional
Parsley sprigs, optional

Preheat oven to 300 degrees. Place banana peppers in a pot of boiling water for approximately 5 minutes to soften; drain and set aside to cool. To prepare the filling, in a medium bowl, mix together all filling ingredients. Stuff banana peppers with the filling. Place stuffed peppers on a baking sheet; drizzle with the olive oil. Bake for 20 minutes. To prepare the Béchamel Sauce, in a small saucepan, bring the broth to a boil. Add the onion, carrot and peppercorns; lower heat and simmer for 10 minutes. Strain the broth, discarding the vegetables and peppercorns. Set broth aside. In the same saucepan, over low to medium heat, whisk together the butter and flour until smooth. Slowly return the broth to the saucepan, stirring continuously. Add the milk and salt. Cook over medium heat, stirring continuously, until the sauce thickens and boils. Add 1 tablespoon of the hot sauce to the egg yolk; add to the saucepan stirring vigorously. Cook, stirring, over low heat for 1 additional minute; do not boil. Transfer the stuffed peppers to a serving platter; ladle the sauce over top. Garnish with the tomatoes and parsley.

Note: The stuffed peppers may also be grilled. Grill for 20 minutes. Do not allow peppers to char. ·

Yield: 8 to 10 appetizers; 1½ cups Béchamel Sauce

Ellen McCormick

Lawrenceville

Lawrenceville, one of Pittsburgh's largest neighborhoods, is an urban community that has it all—parks, a variety of housing types, unique shops and galleries in a vibrant business district, industry, and easy access to downtown. It has become a destination point for both city residents and tourists who admire its European village ambiance.

Long before this modern development, Delaware Indians had settled along the riverbank location. Its long shoreline along the Allegheny River provided them easy access to water transportation. William B. Foster, father of the American composer Stephen Foster, established Lawrenceville in 1814. He named it after Captain James Lawrence, hero of the War of 1812, who was famous for his dying words, "Don't Give Up The Ship!"

Lumber and boat-building were important industries prior to the Civil War. The manufacture of military equipment was also important and at its heart was the Allegheny Arsenal. In 1814, Foster sold thirty acres (between today's 39th and 40th Streets) for $12,000 to the U.S. Government for an arsenal. Lawrenceville was an excellent site for this because of its accessibility to river transportation and its proximity to what was then the country's only iron producing district. In 1862, a disastrous explosion occurred when a horse's shoe ignited gunpowder scrapings in the driveway. Seventy-nine workers, mostly young girls, died and the force of the explosion destroyed houses and shattered windows for miles around.

Most of Lawrenceville's growth and development occurred between 1860 and 1900. Immigrants built their houses on the hillsides, close to work yet removed from the constant mill smoke. Germans arrived first and were soon followed by Poles, Croatians, Slovenes, and Slovaks. Many worked in manufacturing plants that provided long-term employment—Heppenstall, Crucible Steel, the Schiffler plant of U.S. Steel and McConway/Torley. The Pittsburgh Brewing Company, a consolidation of a number of old Pittsburgh brewing companies including Iron City Brewery, still operates here today.

Allegheny Cemetery, a notable landmark, opened in 1844. It is the resting-place of many famous Pittsburghers including the city's first mayor, Ebeneezer Denny, the actress Lillian Russell Moore, composer Stephen Foster, and the victims of the Allegheny Arsenal explosion. Designed as a rural cemetery with a park-like setting, it remains a serene oasis, although now nestled within a vibrant bustling city. ♥♥

Escarole, Sausage and White Bean Stew

1 teaspoon extra-virgin olive oil, and to taste

10 ounces bulk (sweet or hot) Italian sausage, broken into 1-inch chunks

5 large cloves garlic, minced

½ teaspoon crushed red pepper flakes, or to taste

1 head of escarole, cleaned, dried, chopped into 2-inch pieces

3 cups cooked or canned white beans, drained

3 cups chicken broth

4 tablespoons unsalted butter

½ cup freshly grated Parmigiano-Reggiano cheese, and to taste

2 ripe plum tomatoes, diced or 1 (14½-ounce) can chopped tomatoes, drained

2 tablespoons chopped fresh parsley, divided

Kosher salt and freshly ground black pepper, to taste

In a heavy soup pot, over medium to high heat, heat the olive oil. Add the sausage; cook, stirring, until browned, approximately 10 to 15 minutes. Drain and return sausage to pot. Add the garlic and red pepper flakes; sauté until garlic softens, approximately 2 minutes. Add the escarole; stirring, cook until wilted, approximately 2 minutes. Add the beans; cook, stirring, for 1 additional minute. Add the chicken broth and bring to a gentle boil. Add the butter, grated cheese, tomatoes and 1 tablespoon of the parsley. Cook, stirring, just until butter melts and soup is heated through. (Do not overcook or cheese may begin to clump.) Season with salt and pepper. Ladle soup into individual serving bowls. Prior to serving, drizzle additional olive oil over top of soup and sprinkle with additional grated cheese. Garnish with the remaining parsley.

Note: Freshly grated Romano cheese may be used in place of, or in combination with, the Parmigiano-Reggiano cheese.

Yield: 4 servings

Beth Bergman

Roasted Vegetable Soup

2 medium eggplants, unpeeled
2 small yellow onions, unpeeled
1 bulb of garlic, unpeeled
1 large tomato
2 red bell peppers
2 tablespoons olive oil
20 fresh basil leaves, divided
Leaves from 1 sprig of fresh
    oregano
Salt and freshly ground black
    pepper, to taste
3-4 cups chicken broth
1 cup freshly grated Parmesan
    cheese, or to taste
2 tablespoons unsalted butter

Preheat oven to 350 degrees. Cover 2 baking sheets (with sides) with heavy-duty aluminum foil. Prick eggplants several times with a fork; place on a prepared baking sheet. Place onions, garlic and tomato on the second prepared baking sheet. Roast vegetables for 30 minutes. Remove tomato from baking sheet; set aside to cool. Continue roasting eggplant, onion and garlic for an additional 30 minutes, until soft. Transfer to a large bowl to cool. Using a heavy, long-tined fork, roast bell peppers directly over an open gas flame until skins blacken. Place roasted peppers in a brown paper bag; set aside to steam until cool. Peel eggplant and cut in half. Remove and discard seed strips. Chop eggplants into large pieces; set aside. Peel onions; cut into large pieces; set aside. Slice bulb of garlic ½-inch from top and squeeze out roasted cloves; set aside. Peel tomato and squeeze out seeds; set aside. Peel and seed roasted peppers. In a large pot, over medium heat, heat the olive oil. Add the roasted peppers, eggplant, onion, garlic, tomato, 10 basil leaves and oregano to pot. Season with salt and pepper. Cook, uncovered, over low to medium heat for approximately 30 minutes, stirring often. Add 3 cups of broth; simmer, covered, for 30 minutes. Cool for 15 minutes. Using a food processor or blender, filled ¼ to ½ full, purée soup in batches. Pour puréed soup into a clean pot and re-heat to a simmer. If soup is too thick, thin with additional broth to desired consistency. Reduce heat to low; stir in cheese until melted, approximately 10 minutes. Stir in butter just prior to serving. Season with additional salt and pepper. Chop the remaining basil leaves and use as a garnish over individual serving bowls.

Note: To omit the step of roasting peppers over an open flame, use store-bought roasted red peppers. Although this soup may be eaten the day it is prepared, the flavor improves overnight.

Yield: 8 servings
Marcella Karvellis McGuire

Tortellini Spinach Soup

1 tablespoon olive oil or vegetable oil
1 cup thinly sliced carrots
½ cup chopped onion
1 clove garlic, minced
3 (14½-ounce) cans chicken broth
1 (9-ounce) package fresh cheese-filled tortellini
1 (10-ounce) package frozen chopped spinach, thawed, drained
½ teaspoon dried oregano
Salt and ground black pepper, to taste
½ cup shredded mozzarella cheese or grated Parmesan cheese

In a large soup pot or Dutch oven, over medium to low heat, heat the oil. Add the carrots, onion and garlic; sauté until onions are tender. Add broth to pot; bring to a boil. Add tortellini. Boil gently until tortellini are almost tender, approximately 4 to 5 minutes. Add spinach, oregano, salt and pepper. Simmer 2 to 3 minutes, stirring occasionally, until spinach is tender. Ladle into individual serving bowls and sprinkle with cheese.

Note: Cheese-filled tortellini are found in the refrigerator section of the grocery store.

Yield: 6 cups; 4 servings

Kelly Runco

Lentil Soup

1½ cups dried lentils
1 large carrot, peeled, diced
1 large rib of celery, diced
1 small onion, finely chopped
1 whole clove of garlic
1 bay leaf
2 tablespoons minced fresh parsley
½ cup olive oil
Salt and ground black pepper, to taste
1-2 tablespoons balsamic vinegar, to taste

Place lentils in a 4-quart pot of water. Bring to a boil. Allow to boil for 5 minutes; drain pot. Add enough fresh water to pot to cover lentils. Add the vegetables, garlic, bay leaf, parsley and olive oil. Simmer, covered, over low to medium heat for 1 hour. Remove bay leaf and garlic clove. Before serving, season with salt, pepper and balsamic vinegar.

Variation: For a richer tasting soup, substitute beef or chicken broth in place of the fresh water.

Yield: 4 to 6 servings

Alexandra Davides

Navy Bean Soup

1 pound dried navy beans
⅓ pound of bacon (approximately
   5-6 slices), diced
3 cloves garlic, minced
2 cups diced celery
2 cups diced onion
2 cups diced carrots
3 smoked ham hocks or 1 ham
   bone with meat
2 bay leaves
4 quarts chicken broth
3 cups peeled, diced uncooked
   potatoes
1 cup diced tomatoes
Salt and ground black pepper,
   to taste

Soak navy beans overnight; discard beans that float. Drain beans; set aside. In a heavy soup pot, fry bacon until cooked but not crisp. Add garlic; sauté for 3 minutes. Add celery, onion and carrots to pot; cover and cook for 5 minutes. Add navy beans, ham hocks, bay leaves and chicken broth. Simmer, uncovered, for 1½ hours. Remove approximately ⅓ of the navy beans from pot; finely chop or mash. Return chopped beans to pot. Add potatoes and tomatoes. Continue cooking until potatoes are tender. Season with salt and pepper. Remove and transfer ham hocks to a work surface. Cut ham from the bone and add to soup pot. Remove bay leaves before serving. *Serve with kaoli (whole-grain crispbread) or a loaf of French bread for a real treat on a rainy day.*

Note: If soup is too thin, thicken with a flour-butter roux. If soup is too thick, thin with additional chicken broth. The quick method of bean preparation may be used; follow package directions.

Yield: 4 quarts

Marcella Karvellis McGuire

Corn Chowder

½ cup water
2 cups peeled, diced potatoes
1 cup diced celery or carrots
1 teaspoon salt
¼ teaspoon ground black pepper
1 (14½-ounce) can creamed corn
1½ cups milk
2 cups shredded Cheddar cheese

Place first 5 ingredients in a 3-quart pot over low to medium heat. Cover and simmer until potatoes and vegetables are soft, approximately 10 to 20 minutes. Add creamed corn; simmer for 5 additional minutes. Add milk and cheese; simmer, stirring, until cheese melts and chowder is hot (do not boil). Serve immediately.

Yield: 4 servings

Dorianne DiGregorio

Potato, Cabbage and Ham Soup

8 tablespoons butter
8-10 medium potatoes, peeled,
    diced
5 medium carrots, peeled, diced
1 medium to large onion, diced
¼ cup plus 2 tablespoons flour
8 cups chopped cabbage
4 cups water
2 (14½-ounce) cans chicken broth
½ teaspoon dried dill
2 pounds cooked ham, diced
Freshly ground black pepper,
    to taste
Chicken bouillon granules,
    to taste

In a large Dutch oven or 10-quart soup pot, melt the butter over medium heat. Add potatoes, carrots and onion; cook, stirring, for 5 minutes. Add the flour; cook, stirring, for 1 minute. Add cabbage, water, chicken broth, dill, and ham. Season with pepper. Bring to a boil over medium to high heat. Decrease heat to low. Add bouillon. Cover pot; simmer for 20 minutes, stirring occasionally. *A very hearty soup that gets rave reviews.*

Yield: 6 to 8 servings

Victoria Gazzo

Carrot Soup

2 pounds of carrots, peeled
3 large onions
3 tablespoons butter
2 medium to large red potatoes,
    peeled, quartered
1 bay leaf
6 cups chicken broth
Salt and ground black pepper,
    to taste

Using a food processor, finely chop the carrots and onions. In a 6-quart soup pot, over low heat, melt the butter. Add carrots and onions; sauté until tender, approximately 10 minutes. Add potatoes, bay leaf and broth; simmer, covered, for 45 minutes. Remove bay leaf. Using a food processor, purée soup in small batches until smooth. Season with salt and pepper.

Note: Using larger potatoes will result in a thicker soup.

Yield: 8 servings

Alexandra Davides

Italian Tortellini Soup

2 tablespoons olive oil
½ pound bulk hot Italian sausage
½ pound bulk sweet Italian
  sausage
2 large onions, chopped
3 ribs of celery, chopped
3 carrots, peeled, chopped
2 (28-ounce) cans crushed
  tomatoes with liquid
1 (40-ounce) can white beans,
  rinsed, drained
3 tablespoons tomato paste
6 cups beef broth
1½ cups red wine
1 tablespoon paprika
2 tablespoons dried basil
½ cup chopped fresh parsley
Chopped fresh oregano, to taste
1 pound dried tortellini pasta
Freshly grated Parmesan cheese,
  to taste

In a large soup pot, over medium heat, heat the olive oil. Add sausage; cook, stirring, until browned. Add onions, celery and carrots; cook, stirring, until tender. Add all remaining ingredients except the tortellini and Parmesan cheese. Cook for 2 hours over medium heat, stirring occasionally. Add tortellini during the last 15 minutes of cooking. Serve in individual bowls, topped with the Parmesan cheese. *Delicious served with crusty Italian bread.*

Variation: Omit the wine and increase beef broth from 6 cups to 7½ cups.

Yield: 8 to 10 servings

Karen Mitchell

Meatball Soup

1 (28-ounce) can whole tomatoes,
  drained, chopped (juice
  reserved)
3½ cups water
1 pound of carrots, peeled,
  chopped
6-7 medium potatoes, peeled,
  cubed

Meatballs
1½ pounds extra-lean ground beef
1 teaspoon salt
½ teaspoon ground black pepper
2 tablespoons dried parsley

Place tomatoes with juice, water, carrots and potatoes in a soup pot. Cook, over medium heat, until vegetables are tender, approximately 40 minutes. To prepare the meatballs, in a medium bowl, using your hands, mix together all meatball ingredients. Shape mixture into ¾ to 1-inch balls; set aside. When vegetables are tender, slowly drop meatballs into soup. Cover and cook until meatballs are cooked through, approximately 15 to 20 additional minutes. Do not overcook.

Yield: 8 to 12 servings

Dorianne DiGregorio

Two Bean Soup with Sun-Dried Tomatoes

¼-½ cup sun-dried tomatoes,
    to taste
2 tablespoons olive oil
1 cup chopped onion
1 carrot, peeled, diced
1 cup chopped red bell pepper
1 jalapeño pepper, seeded, finely
    chopped
2 cloves garlic, finely chopped
1 teaspoon ground cumin
½ teaspoon dried oregano
2 cups chicken broth
1 (14-ounce) can black beans,
    rinsed, drained
1 (14-ounce) can red kidney
    beans, rinsed, drained
1 (28-ounce) can whole tomatoes
    with juice
Salt and ground black pepper,
    to taste

Place sun-dried tomatoes in a small bowl. Cover with warm water and allow to soak for 2 minutes until softened. Drain, chop and set aside. In a large soup pot, heat the olive oil over low to medium heat. Add onion, carrot, bell and jalapeño peppers; cook, stirring, until slightly softened. Add garlic; cook 1 minute. Add cumin and oregano; cook, stirring, for 1 additional minute. Add sun-dried tomatoes, chicken broth, black beans, kidney beans and whole tomatoes with juice. Using a wooden spoon, gently break up whole tomatoes against side of pot. Simmer over low heat, stirring occasionally, for 20 to 25 minutes. Season with salt and pepper.

Yield: 6 servings

Lorraine Raffensperger

Jan's Bean Soup

1-1½ pounds dried great Northern
    beans or white beans of choice
1 ham bone with meat
1 (29-ounce) can diced tomatoes
    with juice
1 (10¾-ounce) can tomato soup
2-3 potatoes, peeled, diced
2-3 carrots, peeled, sliced
1 large onion, chopped
2 large cloves garlic, chopped
1-2 bay leaves
1 tablespoon finely chopped fresh
    parsley
1 tablespoon finely chopped fresh
    dill
1 tablespoon finely chopped fresh
    oregano
1 head of escarole, endive,
    swisschard or other greens,
    chopped, optional

Rinse beans well; place in large pot. Cover beans with water and bring to a boil. Remove pot from heat; cover and let stand for 1 hour. Drain beans; set aside. Place ham bone in a 6 to 8-quart pot. Fill pot with water to 1-inch from top. Cook ham bone over medium heat for 1 hour. Remove ham bone from pot; set aside to cool. Strain liquid and return to pot. Add beans and all remaining soup ingredients, except ham bone and greens, to pot. Cook over low to medium heat until beans are tender, approximately 1½ to 2 hours. Remove ham from bone. Add ham and the greens during the last 30 minutes of cooking. Remove bay leaves before serving. *A hearty soup which is delicious with crusty bread and a salad.*

Note: For a thicker soup, transfer some of the cooked beans to a blender. Purée and return to pot. Increasing the cooking time will also thicken the soup.

Yield: 10 to 12 servings

Jan Stayianos

Potato and Barley Soup

3 tablespoons olive oil
2 cups chopped onion
6 carrots, peeled, thinly sliced
2 ribs of celery, thinly sliced
1 cup sliced mushrooms
2 medium to large potatoes, peeled,
    chopped into ½-inch cubes
1 cup barley
8 cups chicken or vegetable broth
Salt and ground black pepper,
    to taste
Freshly grated Parmesan cheese
3 slices of cooked bacon, crumbled
Chopped fresh parsley

In a large stock pot or saucepan, heat the olive oil over medium heat. Add the onion, carrots, celery, and mushrooms; sauté for 10 minutes. Add the potatoes, barley, broth, salt and pepper. Simmer for 1 hour or until the barley is tender and the soup thickens. If soup is too thick, add small amounts of water or broth. Ladle the soup into individual bowls; sprinkle with the Parmesan cheese, bacon and parsley.

Yield: 6 to 8 servings; 10 cups

Cynthia Taibbi Kates

Etruscan Peasant Soup

1 tablespoon olive oil
1 pound sweet Italian sausage
  links, cut into ½-inch pieces
½ pound boneless, skinless chicken
  breasts, cut into ½-inch pieces
¾ cup chopped onion
2 cloves garlic, minced
2 cups coarsely chopped spinach
1 (15-ounce) can cannellini beans,
  rinsed, drained
1 (14½-ounce) can diced, seasoned
  tomatoes with juice
1 (14½-ounce) can chicken broth
½ teaspoon crushed red pepper
  flakes, optional
1 cup red wine
Freshly grated Parmesan cheese

In a large saucepan or Dutch oven, over medium heat, heat the olive oil. Add the sausage, chicken, onion and garlic. Cook, stirring, until the sausage is no longer pink and chicken is cooked through. Add the spinach, beans, tomatoes, broth, red pepper flakes and wine; bring to a boil. Reduce heat; simmer for 20 minutes or until heated through. Sprinkle the Parmesan cheese over individual servings. Serve with fresh Italian or garlic bread.

Variation: Omit the wine and add 1 additional cup of chicken broth to the soup.

Yield: 6 to 8 servings

Mike Troyan

Seaweed Soup

2 ounces dried seaweed
10 cups warm water
2 tablespoons sesame oil
½ pound lean ground beef
5 cups chicken or beef broth
¼-½ teaspoon garlic powder,
  to taste

Soak the dried seaweed in the warm water for 30 minutes. Rinse well; drain in a colander. Using kitchen shears, or by hand, cut or tear the seaweed into bite-sized pieces. In a large, heavy pot, over medium heat, heat the sesame oil. Add the ground beef; cook, stirring, until browned, approximately 10 minutes. Add the seaweed; cook, stirring continuously, for 2 minutes. Add the broth; boil for 5 minutes. Season with the garlic powder; boil for an additional 2 minutes. Serve immediately.

Note: Dried seaweed is found in Asian food stores or at specialty groceries.

Variation: Chopped clams may be substituted for the ground beef.

Yield: 4 servings

Sing Lim Choi

Miso Soup

A Japanese Soup

5½ cups water, divided
1 sheet thin deep-fried tofu
3-4 tablespoons miso paste
6 ounces firm tofu, cut into ½-inch
    cubes
4 strips of dried wakame
1 teaspoon dashinomoto, optional
1 scallion (white part and small
    amount of green), chopped

In a large pot, over high heat, bring the water to a boil. Place the deep-fried tofu in a bowl; cover with ½ cup of the boiling water to remove any excess oil. Drain and cut in half lengthwise. Cut each half into ½-inch strips. Place deep-fried tofu strips into the pot of boiling water. Add the miso paste; stir to dissolve. Add the firm tofu cubes, dried wakame and dashimomoto. Bring to a second boil; immediately remove pot from heat. Remove dried wakame strips and discard. Ladle soup into serving bowls; garnish with the scallions.

Note: Miso, made from soybeans, is protein-rich. Miso soup accompanies most Japanese meals. Ingredients are found at Asian food stores or specialty groceries.

Variation: Miso soup has many variations. Vegetables, including potatoes, daikon, seaweed, snow peas, onions or eggplant, may be added. Vegetables needing a longer cooking time should be put in the boiling water prior to adding the miso. Seasonings, including shiso leaves, ginger, sesame seed, nori, sprouts, juzu or citron peel, are all flavorful additions to the soup.

Yield: 4 servings

Eriko Sasaki

Poppy Seed, Onion and Cheddar Cheese Bread

3 tablespoons poppy seeds
4 cups unbleached flour
2 tablespoons baking powder
1 teaspoon baking soda
1½ teaspoons salt
6 green onions (white part and small amount of green), finely chopped
2 cups grated sharp Cheddar cheese
4 eggs
2 cups buttermilk

Place poppy seeds in a small bowl. Cover with a small amount of boiling water. Allow seeds to soak until they sink, approximately 10 minutes. Drain well. Wring seeds dry in a kitchen towel; set aside. Preheat oven to 375 degrees. Grease 3 (9x5x3-inch) loaf pans; set aside. In a large bowl, combine the flour, baking powder, baking soda and salt. Stir in the poppy seeds, onions and cheese. In a separate bowl, whisk the eggs until frothy. Whisk buttermilk into the eggs. Make a well in the center of flour mixture. Pour egg mixture into the well. Using a wooden spoon, quickly incorporate egg mixture into the flour mixture. (Do not over-mix; batter should be lumpy.) Divide batter equally into the prepared pans. Bake until a cake tester inserted in center of bread comes out clean, approximately 35 minutes. Remove pans from oven to wire racks; cool to room temperature before serving. *Our recipe testers loved this bread.*

Variation: Batter may also be used to make muffins. Bake in paper-lined tins for 25 minutes.

Yield: 3 loaves

Amy Gordon

51

Beer Waffles

2 cups flour
4 teaspoons baking powder
¼ teaspoon salt
1½ cups milk
1 cup beer
2 eggs, separated
½ cup butter, melted, cooled

Preheat waffle iron. Lightly coat with nonstick vegetable oil cooking spray. In a large mixing bowl, combine all dry ingredients. Add milk, beer, egg yolks and butter. Using an electric mixer, blend until smooth. In a separate bowl, beat the egg whites to form soft peaks; gently fold into batter. Prepare waffles according to waffle iron directions.

Yield: 8 waffles

Lila Decker

Fabulous French Toast

2 cups orange juice
2 cups milk
2 tablespoons orange liqueur
½ teaspoon vanilla extract
4 eggs, lightly beaten
1 tablespoon cinnamon, and to
   taste
¼ cup sugar, optional
1 loaf of French bread, cut into
   1 to 1½-inch thick slices
Butter
Powdered sugar

Preheat oven to 325 degrees. In a medium bowl, mix together the juice, milk, liqueur, vanilla extract, eggs, cinnamon and sugar; blend well. In batches, dip bread slices in egg mixture to thoroughly coat. (Do not allow bread to become soggy.) Using a nonstick skillet, over medium heat, melt a small amount of butter. Cook bread slices, in batches, until golden brown, approximately 4 to 5 minutes on each side. Transfer French toast to an ovenproof dish; keep warm in oven. Prior to serving, dust bread slices with powdered sugar and additional cinnamon. Serve with maple syrup.

Variation: Egg bread may be substituted for the French bread.

Yield: 4 to 6 servings

Alexandra Davides

French Puffs

¾ cup sugar, divided
2 teaspoons cinnamon
1½ cups flour
1½ teaspoons baking powder
½ teaspoon salt
½ teaspoon nutmeg
⅓ cup shortening
1 egg, lightly beaten
½ cup milk
Melted butter, to taste

Preheat oven to 400 degrees. Place paper liners in a (12-tin) muffin pan; set aside. In a small bowl, mix together ¼ cup of the sugar and the 2 teaspoons cinnamon; set aside. In a separate small bowl, combine the flour, baking powder, salt and nutmeg; set aside. In a large mixing bowl, cream together the shortening and the remaining ½ cup sugar. Add the egg; mix well. Stir in the milk. Slowly add the flour mixture; mix to thoroughly combine. Spoon batter into muffin tins to ½-¾ full. Bake for 12 to 15 minutes, until lightly browned. Remove from oven; cool for 10 minutes. Remove puffs from muffin tins. While still warm, brush tops of puffs with the melted butter. Dip tops in the cinnamon-sugar mixture. Serve warm. *Delicious served for breakfast or brunch.*

Note: Puffs are scone-like muffins.

Yield: 12 puffs

Sonja Hissom-Braun

Romano Garlic Bread

1 long loaf of sour dough bread
½ cup butter, softened
¼-1 teaspoon minced garlic,
    to taste
4 teaspoons chopped fresh parsley,
    divided
1 cup mayonnaise
1 tablespoon lemon juice
3 cups coarsely grated Romano
    cheese

Preheat oven to 400 degrees. Cut bread in half lengthwise. Cut each bread length in half widthwise; set aside. In a small bowl, mix together the butter, garlic and 1 teaspoon of the parsley. Spread butter mixture evenly onto cut sides of each bread piece; set bread slices aside on a baking sheet. In a medium bowl, mix together the mayonnaise, lemon juice, Romano cheese and the remaining 3 teaspoons of parsley. Spread cheese mixture evenly onto tops of buttered bread pieces. Bake for 8 to 10 minutes until golden brown.

Yield: 4 servings

Diane Norkus

Golden Zucchini Bread

4 eggs, beaten
2 cups sugar
1 cup vegetable oil
1½ teaspoons baking soda
1½ teaspoons salt
¾ teaspoon baking powder
1 teaspoon cinnamon
1 teaspoon vanilla extract
3½ cups flour
1 cup chopped walnuts
2 heaping cups peeled, shredded
    zucchini

Preheat oven to 350 degrees. Grease and flour 2 (9x5x3-inch) loaf pans; set aside. In a large bowl, mix together the eggs, sugar and oil. Add the baking soda, salt, baking powder, cinnamon and vanilla extract; mix well. Gradually add the flour; mixing until thoroughly combined. Stir in the walnuts and zucchini. Pour mixture evenly into prepared pans. Bake for 1 hour, or until golden. Remove from oven; cool on wire racks.

Note: This zucchini bread is different from most because of its very appealing golden color.

Yield: 2 loaves

Patty Molchan

Michele's Favorite Pineapple Casserole

3 eggs, beaten
1 tablespoon flour
½ cup sugar
1 (20-ounce) can crushed
    pineapple, drained
6 (1-inch) slices of Italian bread,
    cubed (crust optional)
4 tablespoons butter, melted

Preheat oven to 350 degrees. Lightly grease a 9x9-inch baking dish; set aside. In a medium bowl, mix together the eggs, flour and sugar. Stir in the pineapple. Add bread cubes; toss to coat. Spread mixture evenly into the prepared pan. Pour the melted butter over top of pineapple mixture. Bake, uncovered, for 50 to 60 minutes until top is lightly browned. *Serve hot as a delicious accompaniment to many meals.*

Note: Recipe may be made ahead. Re-heat before serving.

Variation: For a dessert treat, serve warm with vanilla ice cream.

Yield: 6 to 8 servings

Michele Chaballa-Storb

Irish Soda Bread

2 cups flour
⅓ cup sugar
1½ teaspoons baking powder
¼ teaspoon baking soda
¼ teaspoon salt
1 cup raisins
1 teaspoon caraway seeds
1 cup buttermilk

Preheat oven to 375 degrees. In a large bowl, sift together the flour, sugar, baking powder, baking soda and salt. Stir in the raisins and caraway seeds. Add the buttermilk and mix until a soft dough forms. On a lightly floured surface, knead the dough briefly until stickiness disappears. Form dough into a flat round loaf. Place loaf in the center of an 8 or 9-inch round or square glass baking dish. Cut an X into the top of loaf. Bake for 10 minutes. Reduce oven temperature to 350 degrees and bake for an additional 40 to 45 minutes. Remove from oven; let bread cool completely in baking dish before slicing and serving. *Delicious plain or toasted, topped with your favorite jam.*

Yield: 8 to 10 servings

Margaret O'Connell Jones

Blueberry Quick Bread

5 cups flour
1½ cups sugar
2 tablespoons baking powder
½ teaspoon salt
¾ cup butter or margarine, softened
1½ cups chopped walnuts
4 eggs, lightly beaten
2 cups milk
2 teaspoons vanilla extract
3 cups fresh blueberries, rinsed, drained

Preheat oven to 350 degrees. Grease and lightly flour 2 (9x5x3-inch) loaf pans; set aside. In a large bowl, mix together the flour, sugar, baking powder and salt. Using a pastry blender, cut the butter into flour mixture to form fine crumbs. Stir in the walnuts. In a small bowl, mix together the eggs, milk and vanilla extract. Stir the egg mixture into flour mixture until just moistened. (Do not overmix.) Gently fold in the blueberries. Spoon equal amounts of batter into prepared pans. Bake for 1 hour and 20 minutes, or until a cake tester inserted in center of bread comes out clean. Cool bread in pans on wire racks for 10 minutes.

Yield: 2 loaves

Pat Knavish

Challah

Jewish Braided Bread

1¼ cups plus 1 tablespoon water, divided
3 tablespoons vegetable oil
1 teaspoon salt
2 tablespoons sugar
Pinch of saffron
1 (¼-ounce) package active yeast
4-6 cups flour, divided
2 eggs, beaten
Poppy seeds

In a small saucepan, over high heat, bring 1¼ cups of the water to a boil. Add oil, salt, sugar and saffron, stirring until sugar dissolves. Remove from heat; allow to cool to lukewarm. Transfer water mixture to a large bowl. Add yeast and 3 cups of the flour; beat to thoroughly combine. Cover bowl with a dish towel and set aside for 10 minutes. Reserve 2 tablespoons of the beaten egg; set aside. Add the remaining egg to flour mixture. Slowly add the remaining flour, using only enough for the dough to be easily handled. (All flour may not be used.) Turn out dough onto a lightly floured surface and knead for 10 minutes. Grease a separate large bowl. Place dough in prepared bowl; set aside until dough doubles in size. Punch down dough and turn out onto work surface. Divide dough in fifths. Roll each dough piece into a 12-inch rope, approximately 1 to 2 inches wide. Braid 4 ropes together to form 1 large loaf; place on a greased baking sheet. Divide last rope piece into thirds. Roll each piece to ½ to 1 inch in width. (Rope will lengthen a bit.) Braid rope pieces and place on top of large loaf. Cover loaf with dish towel and let rise again until doubled in size. Preheat oven to 350 degrees. In a small bowl, mix the reserved 2 tablespoons of egg with the remaining 1 tablespoon of water. Brush egg mixture over top of bread loaf; sprinkle with poppy seeds. Bake for 40 to 50 minutes, or until golden brown.

Note: The amount of flour used is at the discretion of the baker. The braiding sequence is always under 2 strands and over 1 strand. Bread freezes well.

Variation: Divide dough in half and make 2 smaller loaves. Bake for 30 to 40 minutes.

Yield: 1 loaf

Maura Petrone

Stuffed French Toast

1 (8-ounce) package cream cheese,
   softened
1½ teaspoons vanilla extract,
   divided
½ cup chopped walnuts
1 loaf of French or Italian bread,
   cut into 6 slices, 1½ to 2-inches
   thick
4 eggs
1 cup whipping cream
½ teaspoon nutmeg
Butter
1 (12-ounce) jar apricot preserves
½ cup orange juice

Preheat oven to 170 degrees. In a small bowl, mix together the cream cheese and 1 teaspoon of vanilla. Using an electric mixer, or by hand, beat until fluffy. Stir in the walnuts. Using a serrated knife, cut a deep pocket in each bread slice, cutting from top toward bottom of slice. Spoon 1½ tablespoons of the cream cheese mixture into each bread pocket; set aside. In a medium mixing bowl, beat together the eggs, whipping cream, nutmeg and the remaining ½ teaspoon of vanilla. Using tongs, gently dip each bread slice in egg mixture to coat. Using the butter, lightly grease a griddle and place over medium to high heat. Cook bread slices, in batches, until golden brown on both sides. Re-butter griddle as needed. Transfer French toast slices to a baking sheet; keep warm in oven. In a small saucepan, over low heat, mix together the preserves and juice; drizzle over warm *Stuffed French Toast*.

Yield: 6 servings

Pat Knavish

Blueberry Waffles at the Appletree Inn

½ cup whole-wheat pastry flour
1½ cups all-purpose flour
1 teaspoon baking powder
½ teaspoon ground ginger
½ teaspoon ground cinnamon
¼ teaspoon salt
4 tablespoons butter, melted
2 eggs, separated
1½ cups milk
1½ cups blueberries, rinsed, drained

Prepare waffle iron. In a large bowl, mix together the flours, baking powder, ginger, cinnamon and salt. In a small bowl, mix together the butter, egg yolks and milk. Add to the flour mixture. Using a fork, mix until lightly combined. Fold in the blueberries. Using a hand beater or an electric mixer, beat egg whites to stiff peaks; gently fold into batter. Ladle batter onto hot waffle iron (amount depends on waffle iron). Cook until lightly browned. Serve warm with maple syrup and top with additional fresh blueberries.

Yield: 6 to 8 waffles

The Appletree Inn, Shadyside neighborhood, Pittsburgh, PA

Cranberry-Apple Bread

1½ cups flour
1½ teaspoons baking powder
1 teaspoon cinnamon
½ teaspoon baking soda
2 cups peeled, cored, coarsley chopped apples
¾ cup sugar
2 teaspoons vegetable oil
1 egg, lightly beaten or ¼ cup pasteurized artificial egg product
1 cup fresh cranberries
½ cup chopped walnuts, optional

Preheat oven to 350 degrees. Grease a 9x5x3-inch loaf pan; set aside. In a small bowl, mix together the flour, baking powder, cinnamon and baking soda; set aside. In a large bowl, toss the apples with the sugar and vegetable oil. Stir in the egg. Add flour mixture to the apples; stir until just moistened (batter will be thick). Stir cranberries and walnuts into the batter. Spread batter evenly into prepared pan. Bake for 50 to 60 minutes, or until a cake tester inserted in center of the bread comes out clean.

Yield: 1 loaf

Bill Connelly, owner, Dubblebbees Dog Grooming Studio, Highland Park neighborhood, Pittsburgh, PA

Meal-in-a-Muffin

1 large apple, peeled, cored,
   quartered
1 medium carrot, peeled
½ cup vegetable oil
2 large eggs
⅓ cup sugar
2 teaspoons vanilla extract
½ cup flaked, sweetened, dried
   coconut
½ cup raisins
⅓ cup chopped pecans or walnuts
¾ cup flour
½ cup rolled oats (not quick-
   cooking)
3 tablespoons wheat germ
¾ teaspoon ground cinnamon
¼ teaspoon ground ginger
⅛ teaspoon ground nutmeg
½ teaspoon baking powder
¼ teaspoon salt

Preheat oven to 375 degrees. Grease or place paper liners in a (12-tin) muffin pan; set aside. Using a food processor or blender, shred the apple and carrot. Transfer to a bowl; set aside. Add the oil, eggs, sugar and vanilla extract to processor. Process until well blended, approximately 30 seconds. Using a spatula, scrape down sides of processor bowl. Add the shredded apple, carrot and all remaining ingredients. Pulse until just combined, approximately 6 to 8 times. (Do not over-process.) Divide batter evenly into prepared muffin tins. Bake for 20 minutes or until edges brown and muffins are firm to the touch. *Great for breakfast on the run.*

Yield: 12 muffins

Anne McCafferty

Never-Fail Crescent Rolls

2¼ teaspoons dry active yeast
1 cup warm milk
½ cup vegetable oil
3 eggs, lightly beaten
1 teaspoon salt
½ cup sugar
4¾ cups flour

In a small bowl, stir yeast into the warm milk to dissolve. Allow yeast mixture to sit until foam forms on top. Add the vegetable oil and eggs. In a large bowl, combine the salt, sugar and flour. Add yeast mixture to flour mixture; stir to combine. Cover and let rise in a warm spot until double in size, approximately 2½ hours. Grease 2 baking sheets; set aside. Divide dough into 3 equal parts. (Dough will be sticky; do not add more flour.) On a lightly floured surface, roll out each dough third into a 9-inch round. Cut dough round, pizza style, into 8 triangles. Roll each triangle up from large end to the point to form a crescent shape. Place crescents on prepared baking sheets. Repeat for remaining dough thirds. Let rise on baking sheets until double in size, approximately 1 hour. Preheat oven to 350 degrees. Bake for 10 to 12 minutes, until golden. *Served warm, these are a delicious addition to any meal.*

Note: The longer the crescents are allowed to rise, the less baking time that is required.

Yield: 24 rolls

Amy Spence

Cherry Pecan Bread

2 cups flour
1 teaspoon baking soda
½ teaspoon salt
¾ cup sugar
½ cup butter or margarine,
  softened
2 eggs
1 cup buttermilk
1 teaspoon vanilla extract
1 (10-ounce) jar maraschino
  cherries, drained, cut into small
  pieces
1 cup chopped pecans

Glaze (optional)
½ cup powdered sugar
Water

Preheat oven to 350 degrees. Grease a 9x5x3-inch loaf pan; set aside. In a small bowl, sift together the flour, baking soda and salt; set aside. In a large mixing bowl, using an electric mixer, cream together the sugar, butter and eggs. Slowly add dry ingredients to sugar mixture, alternating with the buttermilk; beat until well blended. Stir in the vanilla, cherries and pecans. Pour batter into prepared pan. Bake for 50 to 60 minutes, or until a cake tester inserted in center of bread comes out clean. Cool on a wire rack. To prepare the glaze, in a small bowl, mix together powdered sugar with small amounts of water to a drizzling consistency. Drizzle glaze over cooled bread.

Note: For a moister bread, increase the butter to ¾ cup.

Variation: Substitute walnuts for the pecans.

Yield: 1 loaf

Pat Knavish

Scallion and Goat Cheese Muffins

1 cup whole or 2 percent milk, divided
4 ounces mild goat cheese, softened
1½ cups flour
1 tablespoon baking powder
1½ teaspoons sugar
½ teaspoon salt
6 tablespoons unsalted butter, melted, cooled
1 large egg
1 bunch scallions (white part and small amount of green), finely chopped (approximately 1 cup)

Preheat oven to 400 degrees. Lightly grease a (12-tin) muffin pan; set aside. In a small bowl, mix together 2 tablespoons of milk and the goat cheese; set aside. In a large bowl, sift together the flour, baking powder, sugar and salt. In a separate small bowl, whisk together the butter, the remaining milk and egg. Stir butter mixture and scallions into the flour mixture until just combined. Divide half of the batter evenly into muffin tins. Top each batter-filled tin with 2 teaspoons of the goat cheese mixture. Ladle remaining batter evenly over tops of the goat cheese mixture. Bake until golden, approximately 20 minutes, or until a cake tester inserted into center of a muffin comes out clean. *These muffins are always a favorite on the brunch buffet.*

Yield: 12 muffins

Diane Norkus

Blueberry Muffins

2 cups flour
1 cup sugar
2 teaspoons baking powder
½ cup butter, softened
2 eggs, lightly beaten
¾ cup milk
1 teaspoon vanilla extract
2 cups fresh blueberries, rinsed, drained, lightly floured

Preheat oven to 375 degrees. Grease and flour or place paper liners in a (12-tin) muffin pan; set aside. In a large bowl, mix together the flour, sugar, baking powder and butter with a fork until crumbly. Add the eggs, milk and vanilla extract; stir well to combine. Gently fold in the blueberries. Fill muffin tins to ¾ full; bake for 30 minutes.

Note: Out of season, use frozen blueberries. Thaw and drain well before use.

Variation: Substitute a 13x9-inch cake pan for the muffin pan; bake cake for 30 minutes.

Yield: 12 muffins

Barb Dunn

Homewood

𝒫rior to the 1860's, Homewood was a swampy rural area that connected with Pittsburgh via the Pennsylvania Railroad and the Greensburg Turnpike, today's Penn Avenue. Homewood was named for the Honorable William Wilkins (1779-1865), a prominent Pittsburgh jurist, U.S. Congressional Representative, U.S. Senator, Minister to Russia under President Andrew Jackson, and Secretary of War under President John Tyler. In 1839, he constructed a stately mansion in the area, which he called "Homewood."

At a time when Pittsburgh was a town of only 21,500 people, "Homewood" was built in the middle of a pristine forest. Situated on 650 acres, the mansion and estate stood slightly north of today's Homewood cemetery at what is now Reynolds Street and South Murtland Avenue. The estate's long entrance drive began on Penn Avenue. Wilkins Avenue was then a private road leading from Judge Wilkins' home to Oakland. For sixty years, the estate had the reputation of being the most fashionable and aristocratic home in Western Pennsylvania.

In 1868, Judge Thomas Mellon, founder of Mellon National Bank, acquired land on Hamilton Avenue and built a home that adjoined the Homewood Avenue Railroad Station. James Kelly, another large property owner at the time, owned much of the acreage known as "Brushton" that adjoined the Mellon and Wilkins' estates. At the time, mostly middle and upper middle class Protestant families of English, Scot-Irish and German descent lived in Homewood. Beyond the railroad tracks, at the southern edge of Homewood, wealthy captains of industry also built lavish homes and gardens.

Pittsburgh annexed Homewood in 1868 and the Borough of Brushton in 1894. In 1871, Homewood's first grocery store, John Harbaugh's Grocery, opened. Industry also located in the neighborhood including three brickyards, a clay pot factory and a lead factory.

From 1941 to 1962, Homewood was home to the National Negro Opera Company, a renowned traveling company founded by Mary Caldwell Dawson. Today, Homewood continues its vibrant legacy as a strong African-American community and is a literary landmark of John Edgar Wideman. Wideman, an internationally acclaimed writer who grew up in Homewood, memorialized the neighborhood's stories and experiences in his fictional writings including "The Homewood Trilogy". The Carnegie Library-Homewood, a grand and inviting facility, serves as a community center. The neighborhood is home to several prominent African-American churches, musical and cultural organizations. ♥♥

Tri-Color Squash Salad

1 butternut squash,
approximately 4 pounds,
peeled, halved, seeded

Dressing
⅓ cup tarragon vinegar
¼ cup olive oil
2 tablespoons honey
2 tablespoons Dijon mustard
2 cloves garlic, minced
½ teaspoon salt, or to taste
½ teaspoon dried basil
¼ teaspoon dried tarragon
Freshly ground black pepper,
to taste

1 red bell pepper, seeded, diced
1 green bell pepper, seeded, diced
½ red onion, coarsely chopped
¼ cup chopped fresh parsley

Preheat oven to 375 degrees. Coat the bottom of a 13x9x2-inch baking pan with nonstick vegetable oil cooking spray; set aside. Cut squash into 1-inch square pieces. Place on prepared pan. Bake for approximately 45 minutes, until tender. (Do not overbake.) Set aside in a large bowl to cool. To prepare the dressing, in a small bowl, whisk together all dressing ingredients; set aside. Place red and green bell peppers, onion and parsley in bowl with squash; toss gently. Add dressing; toss to coat. Cover and marinate at room temperature or in refrigerator for 1 to 2 hours before serving.

Yield: 10 to 12 servings

Christine Salvi

Mushroom Salad

¾ cup vegetable or olive oil
½ cup white vinegar
¼ cup water
2 teaspoons garlic powder
2 teaspoons salt
¼ teaspoon ground black pepper
1 pound mushrooms, sliced
1½ cups thinly sliced carrots
1 cup diced green bell pepper
½ cup sliced onion
1 cup pimentos, drained, sliced
Chopped fresh basil, to taste

In a large saucepan, combine the oil, vinegar, water, garlic powder, salt and pepper. Over medium heat, bring mixture to a boil. Reduce heat to low, cover and simmer for 5 minutes. Add mushrooms, carrots, bell pepper and onion. Re-cover and simmer for an additional 3 minutes. Remove from heat; stir in pimentos and basil. Transfer to a large bowl. Cover and refrigerate for 1 day before serving.

Note: Recipe must be made a day ahead.

Yield: 8 to 10 servings

Donna Linnelli

Apple Salad with Celery Seed Dressing

Celery Seed Dressing
½ cup sugar
1 teaspoon dry mustard
1 teaspoon salt
2 teaspoons celery seeds
1 tablespoon minced onion
1 cup vegetable or canola oil
⅓ cup cider vinegar

4-5 Granny Smith apples, peeled, cored, thinly sliced
2 heads of Romaine lettuce, cleaned, torn into bite-size pieces

To prepare *Celery Seed Dressing,* place all dressing ingredients in a blender or food processor. Blend or pulse until thoroughly combined. Place apples in a medium bowl. Pour dressing over apples; toss to coat. Cover and refrigerate for 1 to 2 hours, until well-chilled. Serve apples atop the lettuce.

Yield: 6 to 8 servings

Patricia Mickelson

Pear and Walnut Salad

Dressing
½ cup vegetable or canola oil
3 tablespoons cider vinegar
¼ cup sugar
½ teaspoon celery seeds
¼ teaspoon salt

¼ cup walnuts
4 cups torn lettuce
1 ripe pear, peeled, cored, finely chopped
2 ounces blue cheese, crumbled

Combine all dressing ingredients in a 1-cup container with lid. Shake well to blend; refrigerate until ready to use. Preheat oven to 375 degrees. Place walnuts on a baking sheet. Bake for 3 to 5 minutes until lightly toasted. Remove from oven and coarsley chop. Place lettuce, pear, blue cheese and walnuts in a large salad bowl; toss to combine. Pour dressing over salad; re-toss to evenly coat.

Yield: 4 servings

Denise Orlando

Roast Beef Salad

1 pound shaved or chipped, lean
   premium roast beef
1 medium red onion, quartered,
   thinly sliced
½ cup chopped fresh parsley
½ cup Italian dressing
1½ teaspoons Dijon mustard

In a medium bowl, combine the roast beef and onion. In a small bowl, whisk together the parsley, Italian dressing and mustard. Add dressing mixture to roast beef and onions; toss well to coat. Marinate, covered, in the refrigerator for 1 to 2 hours. Serve chilled with crusty French bread.

Note: Shaved or chipped roast beef is found in the deli section of most grocery stores.

Yield: 3 to 4 servings

Chrissy Ranalli

Bacon and Egg Salad

6 hard-boiled eggs, coarsely
   chopped
3 ounces thick-cut bacon
   (approximately 3 slices), cut
   into ¼-inch pieces
Salt and freshly ground black
   pepper, to taste
½ cup real mayonnaise
1 teaspoon ketchup

Place eggs in a medium bowl; set aside. In a small nonstick skillet, cook bacon until crisp and browned, approximately 4 to 5 minutes. Using a slotted spoon, transfer bacon to paper towels to drain. Add bacon to the eggs. Season with salt and pepper; toss well. In a small bowl, mix together the mayonnaise and ketchup. Add to the eggs and bacon; mix well. Serve with crackers or over a fresh bed of lettuce.

Variation: Fresh, chopped herbs are a delicious addition to this salad.

Yield: 4 servings; approximately 2 cups

Elizabeth McKenna (In Memory)

Tuna and White Bean Salad

1 (12½-ounce) can solid white
    tuna, drained, flaked
1 (15-ounce) can cannellini beans,
    rinsed, drained
1 large tomato, diced
¼ cup chopped red onion
1 tablespoon fresh lemon juice
2 teaspoons Dijon mustard
2 cloves garlic, minced
¼ cup olive oil
¼ cup chopped fresh basil
Salt and freshly ground black
    pepper, to taste
4 large lettuce leaves
Fresh basil leaves

In a large bowl, combine the tuna, beans, tomato and onion; set aside. In a small bowl, whisk together the lemon juice, mustard and garlic. Gradually whisk in the olive oil. Add lemon juice mixture to tuna mixture; toss to coat. Gently stir in the chopped basil; season with salt and pepper. To serve, line individual plates with 1 to 2 lettuce leaves. Spoon salad onto lettuce. Garnish with fresh basil leaves.

Yield: 2 main course; 4 side dish servings

Toni Black

Nutty Spinach Salad

1 (8-ounce) bag baby spinach
1 (16-ounce) bag coleslaw
4 scallions, sliced
1 pound mushrooms, sliced
½ cup slivered almonds, toasted
2 tablespoons sesame seeds,
    toasted
2 (3½-ounce) packages Ramen
    noodles without seasoning,
    broken up

Dressing
¾ cup vegetable or canola oil
1 teaspoon seasoned-salt flavor
    enhancer
2 teaspoons salt
2 teaspoons ground black pepper
6 tablespoons rice vinegar

In a large serving bowl, toss together the spinach, coleslaw, scallions, mushrooms, almonds, sesame seeds and Ramen noodles; set aside. In a small bowl, whisk together all dressing ingredients. Add dressing to salad; toss to coat. Top with additional almonds, if desired.

Yield: 10 to 12 servings

Vicky Nychis

Southwestern Chicken and Bean Salad

Dressing

3 tablespoons lemon juice
1 tablespoon coarse-grain
   mustard
¼ cup olive oil
¼ cup salsa
½ teaspoon ground cumin

2 boneless, skinless chicken breast
   halves
1 large carrot
1 avocado, peeled, cut into ½-inch
   slices
½ medium cucumber (peeling
   optional), thinly sliced
½ cup frozen corn kernels, thawed
1 (14½-ounce) can kidney or black
   beans, rinsed, drained
1 small head of Romaine lettuce,
   rinsed, drained

To prepare the dressing, in a small non-reactive bowl, whisk together the lemon juice and mustard. Gradually whisk in the oil and salsa. Whisk in the cumin; set aside, reserving 2 tablespoons of the dressing. Place chicken breast halves in a glass dish. Coat chicken with the reserved 2 tablespoons of dressing. Cover and let sit at room temperature for 30 minutes. Prepare barbecue grill or turn oven to broil. Cook chicken 4 inches from heat source, turning once, until juices run clear, approximately 8 to 10 minutes. Cut chicken into ½-inch slices; set aside. Using a vegetable peeler, cut carrot into ribbon-thin strips; place in a large bowl. Add avocado, cucumber, corn and beans to bowl; toss gently. Line a platter with lettuce leaves. Tear remaining lettuce into bite-size pieces and lay over lettuce leaves. Spoon vegetable mixture over lettuce and top with chicken slices. Drizzle dressing over top of salad.

Note: Chicken coated with the 2 tablespoons of dressing may sit overnight. Cover and refrigerate the chicken and the unused dressing.

Yield: 4 servings

Kathleen Meyer

Oriental Chicken Salad

2 whole chicken breasts
Salt and freshly ground black
   pepper, to taste
1 head of lettuce, chopped
4 scallions, sliced
1 tablespoon sesame seeds,
   toasted, optional

Dressing
½ cup vegetable or canola oil
½ cup white vinegar
2 tablespoons sesame seed oil
½ cup sugar
2 teaspoons salt
2 teaspoons seasoned-salt flavor
   enhancer

1 (5-ounce) can chow mein noodles

Preheat oven to 350 degrees. Place chicken breasts in a shallow baking dish. Season with salt and pepper. Bake for 40 to 45 minutes until cooked through and juices run clear. Thinly slice and set aside to cool. In a large serving bowl, toss together the chicken, lettuce, scallions and sesame seeds; set aside. Place all dressing ingredients in a 2-cup container with lid. Shake vigorously to mix. Pour dressing over salad; toss to coat. Top with chow mein noodles.

Note: To toast sesame seeds, in a small skillet over medium heat, stir sesame seeds until lightly browned. Allow to cool before adding to the salad.

Yield: 4 servings

Donna Linnelli

South Pacific Chicken Salad

Dressing
3 cups mayonnaise
1 tablespoon curry powder
2 tablespoons soy sauce
2 tablespoons lemon juice

Salad
8 cups cubed cooked chicken
   breast, approximately 8 chicken
   breast halves
1 (8-ounce) can sliced water
   chestnuts, drained
1 (20-ounce) can pineapple
   chunks, drained
1 pound seedless green grapes,
   halved
2 cups diced celery
1 cup sliced almonds, optional

Salad greens

To prepare the dressing, in a medium bowl, whisk together all dressing ingredients; set aside. In a large bowl, mix together all salad ingredients. Add dressing to salad; toss well. Refrigerate for 3 to 4 hours. Serve over salad greens topped with additional sliced almonds, if desired.

Note: If doubling recipe, use only 1½ the amount of dressing.

Variation: Turkey may be used in place of the chicken.

Yield: 12 to 16 servings

Marlene Prince

Greek Potato Salad

3 small (1-inch diameter)
    zucchinis, unpeeled
3 tablespoons olive oil
3 tablespoons wine or cider
    vinegar
Salt and freshly ground black
    pepper, to taste
3 medium potatoes, peeled, diced
    into 1-inch pieces, boiled until
    just tender
1½ pounds fresh green beans, cut
    in half, steamed until just
    tender
1 (15-ounce) can butter beans,
    rinsed, drained
4-5 scallions, chopped, or to taste

Place a steamer rack in a large pot. Add water to a 1-inch level. Place zucchinis on rack. Over medium to high heat, steam until just tender, approximately 8 to 10 minutes. Let the zucchinis cool; peel and slice into 1-inch pieces. In a small bowl, whisk together the olive oil and vinegar. Season with the salt and pepper. Place the zucchini, potatoes, green beans, butter beans, and scallions in a large serving bowl. Coat with the olive oil and vinegar mixture. *This salad was served by Spiro's grandmother on the Greek island of Lefkas in the Ionian Sea.*

Variation: For a tasty summertime salad, use baby new potatoes and add ripe grape or cherry tomato halves.

Yield: 8 to 10 servings

Jan and Spiro Stayianos

Italian Potato Salad

4 pounds red potatoes, cooked,
    quartered or halved

Marinade
3 cloves garlic, minced
⅔ cup olive oil
⅓ cup white wine vinegar
1 teaspoon salt
1 teaspoon ground black pepper

1 (10-ounce) package frozen peas,
    thawed, drained
1 red bell pepper, seeded, finely
    chopped
1 cup chopped fresh basil

Allow potatoes to cool slightly; place in large serving dish. Place all marinade ingredients in a 2-cup container with lid; shake vigorously to combine. Pour marinade over potatoes. Allow to marinate for 15 minutes at room temperature or until potatoes cool completely. Add peas, bell pepper and basil to potatoes; toss gently. Cover and refrigerate overnight. Serve chilled. *A delicious side dish for meat or seafood.*

Yield: 10 to 12 servings

Bunny Conte

Layered Chopped Salad

Dressing

⅓ cup vegetable broth
¼ cup red wine vinegar
2 tablespoons olive oil
1 teaspoon sugar
½ teaspoon salt
½ teaspoon dried Italian
    seasoning
¼ teaspoon freshly ground black
    pepper
3 cloves garlic, minced

Salad

4 cups finely chopped Romaine
    lettuce
2 cups finely chopped iceberg
    lettuce
½ cup finely chopped radicchio
½ cup thinly sliced Belgian endive
1½ cups finely chopped cucumber,
    peeling optional
½ cup finely chopped celery
1 cup shredded carrot
1¾ cups finely chopped red bell
    pepper
1 cup seeded, diced plum
    tomatoes, approximately
    4 whole tomatoes
1 cup finely chopped red onion
½ cup thinly sliced scallions
2 cups diced, cooked beets
3 hard-boiled eggs, finely chopped
1 tablespoon chopped fresh
    flat-leaf parsley

To prepare the dressing, in a small bowl, whisk together all dressing ingredients; set aside. To prepare the salad, arrange the Romaine lettuce in the bottom of a 2-quart glass bowl or trifle dish. Lay the iceberg lettuce over top of Romaine. Layer, in order, the radicchio, endive, cucumber, celery, carrot, bell pepper, tomatoes, red onion and scallions. Drizzle dressing over top. Do not mix. Cover and chill 4 hours or overnight. Before serving, arrange beets over scallion layer. Top with eggs and garnish with parsley. *This colorful salad easily feeds a crowd.*

Note: Serve leftover salad in a pita pocket or tortilla wrap for a delicious low-calorie, vegetarian lunch entrée.

Yield: 10 servings

Connie Kramer

Tortellini Salad

1 cup almonds, toasted
¼ cup dried basil
1½ cups bottled zesty vinaigrette
 dressing, or to taste
10 grape tomatoes, halved
1 small red onion, chopped
1 cup pitted black olives, chopped
1¼ pounds cheese tortellini,
 cooked al dente, cooled
1¼ pounds spinach tortellini,
 cooked al dente, cooled

Using a food processor, pulse together the almonds and basil. Slowly add dressing in a steady stream. Place tomatoes, onion and black olives in a large serving bowl. Pour dressing over top; toss well. Add cheese and spinach tortellinis; toss to evenly coat. *A nice salad for picnics or lunch boxes.*

Note: Salad will keep for 3 to 4 days in the refrigerator.

Variation: For even more color, use tri-color tortellini.

Yield: 10 to 12 servings

MeLynne Storb

Green Salad with Cranberry Vinaigrette

1 cup sliced almonds

Vinaigrette
3 tablespoons red wine vinegar
⅓ cup olive oil
2 tablespoons water
1 tablespoon Dijon mustard
¼ cup fresh cranberries
½ teaspoon minced garlic
½ teaspoon salt
½ teaspoon freshly ground black
 pepper

1 pound mixed salad greens, torn
 into bite-size pieces
½ red onion, thinly sliced
4 ounces blue cheese, crumbled

Preheat oven to 375 degrees. Arrange sliced almonds in a single layer on a baking sheet. Toast in oven until light brown in color, approximately 5 minutes; set aside. To prepare the vinaigrette, in a food processor or blender, pulse together the vinegar, olive oil, water, mustard, cranberries, garlic, salt and pepper until smooth. In a large bowl, toss together the salad greens, red onion, blue cheese and almonds. Just prior to serving, pour vinaigrette over top of salad; toss to thoroughly coat.

Note: If fresh cranberries are unavailable, substitute with dried cranberries.

Yield: 6 to 8 servings

Rosa Vaccarello

Italian Leafy Green Salad

Salad

**2 cups torn Romaine lettuce,
approximately ⅓ of a head**
1 cup torn radicchio
1 cup torn escarole
1 cup torn red leaf lettuce
**¼ cup chopped scallions (white
part and small amount of green)**
½ red bell pepper, sliced into rings
½ green bell pepper, sliced into rings
12 cherry tomatoes, stemmed

Dressing

¼ cup grape-seed oil
¼ cup balsamic vinegar
**2 tablespoons freshly squeezed
lemon juice**
2 tablespoons chopped fresh basil
**Salt and freshly ground black
pepper, to taste**

In a large salad bowl, combine all salad ingredients; toss well. In a small bowl, whisk together all dressing ingredients. While whisking, pour dressing over salad. Toss to thoroughly coat. Serve immediately.

Note: Grape-seed oil, the secret to this recipe, is found in specialty food markets. Olive oil may be used in place of the grape-seed oil.

Yield: 6 servings

Maria DeRenzo

Black Bean Salad

**1 (15-ounce) can black beans,
rinsed, drained**
**1 scallion (white and small
amount of green), chopped**
½ red onion, sliced
**1 jalapeño pepper, seeded,
chopped**
**2 tablespoons chopped fresh
cilantro, or to taste**
Juice of 1 lime
3 tablespoons olive oil
**Salt and ground black pepper,
to taste**

In a large bowl, toss together all salad ingredients. Serve chilled or at room temperature. *Black Bean Salad* also makes a great salsa for tortilla chips.

Yield: 2 cups

Toni Marra

Corn Salad

2 cups freshly cooked corn
  kernels, approximately 4 ears
  of corn
¼ cup diced red bell pepper
¼ cup chopped Vidalia onion
1 tablespoon minced fresh dill

Dressing
⅓ cup vegetable oil
2 tablespoons Dijon mustard
2 tablespoons white wine vinegar
2 tablespoons sugar
½ teaspoon salt

In a large bowl, combine the corn, bell pepper, onion and dill; set aside. To prepare the dressing, in a small saucepan over medium heat, bring the oil, mustard, vinegar, sugar and salt to a simmer, stirring. Slowly pour ½ of the warm dressing over the corn mixture; toss to coat. Slowly add more dressing to desired consistency (not all dressing may be used). Serve warm, at room temperature, or cover and refrigerate for several hours to serve chilled.

Note: Frozen, thawed corn kernels may be used in place of fresh.

Yield: 4 servings

Joseph Parente

Till's Tantalizing Potato Salad

1 cup mayonnaise
2 tablespoons white vinegar
1-2 teaspoons salt, to taste
¼ teaspoon ground black pepper
6 cups cooked, cubed potatoes,
  cooled
1 cup chopped onion
1 cup chopped celery
2 hard-boiled eggs, chopped
Fresh tomato slices
Parsley sprigs or snipped fresh
  basil, optional

In a small bowl, whisk together the mayonnaise and vinegar. Add salt and pepper; mix well. In a large bowl, combine potatoes with the onion, celery and eggs. Add mayonnaise mixture to potato mixture; toss well to coat. Layer tomato slices over top. Garnish with parsley. Serve cold.

Yield: 10 to 12 servings

Till Kennon

Bean and Olive Salad

Dressing
¾ cup olive oil
⅓ cup red wine vinegar
2 tablespoons lemon juice
3 cloves garlic, minced
¾ teaspoon salt
½ teaspoon dried basil
¼ teaspoon dried oregano

2 pounds fresh green beans, ends
   trimmed, rinsed
1 (14-ounce) can garbanzo beans,
   rinsed, drained
1 (14-ounce) can kidney beans,
   rinsed, drained
1 (6-ounce) can large, pitted black
   olives, well-drained, sliced
1 medium sweet onion, thinly
   sliced
¼ cup chopped fresh parsley
Freshly ground black pepper,
   to taste

Combine all dressing ingredients in a 2-cup container with lid. Shake vigorously to blend; set aside. Place a steamer rack in a large pot filled with 1 inch of water. Place green beans on rack. Cover pot; steam over high heat for 5 minutes. Drain beans; set aside to cool. In a large serving bowl, combine the green beans, garbanzo and kidney beans, olives, and onions. Pour dressing over top; toss well to evenly coat. Sprinkle salad with parsley and black pepper. Serve at room temperature. *A very pretty salad that is a wonderful addition to a summer barbecue.*

Yield: 8 servings

Regina Black

Carolina Black-Eyed Pea Salad

Dressing
2 tablespoons extra-virgin olive oil
2 tablespoons red wine vinegar
2 teaspoons Dijon mustard
2 teaspoons salt
2 teaspoons ground black pepper

2 (15½-ounce) cans black-eyed
   peas, rinsed, drained
3 medium-size ripe tomatoes, cut
   into chunks
½ cup thinly sliced red onion
1 (10-ounce) bag spinach, stems
   removed, leaves chopped
4 strips of bacon, cooked crisp,
   crumbled
½ cup pecan halves, toasted,
   coarsley chopped

In a small bowl, whisk together all dressing ingredients. In a large bowl, combine the black-eyed peas, tomatoes and onion. Add dressing; toss gently. Cover and refrigerate. Just prior to serving, add the spinach; toss to coat. Sprinkle bacon and pecans over top of salad. *Great to bring on a picnic.*

Note: Dressing may be prepared up to 8 hours ahead; cover and refrigerate. To toast pecans, place in a nonstick skillet. Cook, stirring, over medium to low heat until lightly toasted, approximately 5 to 6 minutes.

Yield: 8 servings

Donna Caliguiri

Potato Salad Niçoise

3 cups green beans, steamed to
    crisp-tender
6 tomatoes, peeled, quartered
½ cup vinaigrette dressing, and
    to taste
1 clove garlic
3 cups new potatoes, unpeeled
½ cup white wine, warmed
Salad greens
Pitted black olives, optional

In a large bowl, gently combine the beans and tomatoes. Add vinaigrette dressing; toss to coat. Cover and marinate in refrigerator until use. Place potatoes in a medium, heavy pot. Cover with water. Add garlic clove to pot. Cook over medium to high heat just until potatoes are fork-tender. Drain and allow to cool slightly. Quarter, halve or slice potatoes; transfer to a medium bowl. While potatoes are still warm, sprinkle with the wine. Let stand at room temperature for 1 hour. To serve, place salad greens on a large serving platter. Mound potatoes over greens. Using a slotted spoon, place bean and tomato mixture atop potatoes. Add additional dressing over top of beans and tomatoes, if desired. Garnish with black olives.

Note: A ¼ cup of wine vinegar mixed with a ¼ cup of meat stock may be substituted for the white wine.

Variation: Capers or anchovy fillets may be added to, or used in place of, the black olives.

Yield: 4 to 6 servings

Donna Linnelli

Manchester

*M*anchester, one of Pittsburgh's North Side neighborhoods, received its name from early English immigrants after the industrial city of their homeland. The neighborhood has had an interesting and varied history. Until the late eighteenth century, the area known as Manchester belonged to the Shawnee and Delaware Indians. When all Indian lands were declared to be the property of the State, the native Americans lost their communities along the Ohio River. Ohio is from the Delaware Indian word "Ohiopeekhanne," meaning "the main stream, with water whitened by the froth."

In 1787, the land was surveyed and distributed as compensation to Pennsylvania veterans of the Revolutionary War. As larger parcels of land were subdivided into smaller tracts, the community developed its grid pattern that is still in place today. By 1843, Manchester became a borough and, in 1867, it merged with the City of Allegheny across the river from the larger city of Pittsburgh. Manchester grew as a prosperous middle-class neighborhood, attracting residents who desired its suburban-like environment and low population density.

By the late 1800's, Manchester's development as an important industrial center mirrored that of its English namesake, an irony not lost on early residents and business owners. The community's industrial and river wharf economy was centered on the banks of the Ohio River with a neighborhood commercial district along Beaver Avenue. Several factories scattered throughout the area added to its economic base.

In 1907, Allegheny was annexed to the City of Pittsburgh and Manchester became a city neighborhood. Today it is mostly residential and boasts some of the finest examples of Victorian architecture in the city. A stroll along its streets offers views of Italianate, French Second Empire, Richardsonian Romanesque and Queen Anne styles of architecture. Ornate cornices, porches, transom windows and ironwork grace the stylish homes.

Many of Manchester's finest homes have been restored due to ongoing joint efforts that began in the 1970's among Pittsburgh History and Landmarks Foundation, the Manchester Citizens Corporation, the Pittsburgh Urban Redevelopment Authority and private developers.

Today, Manchester also serves as home to the Bidwell Training Center and to the Manchester Craftsmen's Guild, which brings local and world-renowned jazz musicians to Pittsburgh for its concert series. ♥♥

Puffed Apple Pancakes

½ cup butter, melted
2 Granny Smith apples, peeled, cored, thinly sliced
7 eggs
2 cups milk
1¼ cups flour
3 tablespoons sugar
2 teaspoons vanilla extract
½ teaspoon salt
½ teaspoon cinnamon
4 tablespoons brown sugar

Preheat oven to 400 degrees. Pour equal amounts of melted butter into 2 (9-inch) pie pans. Arrange the slices from 1 apple in the bottom of each pie pan. Bake until butter sizzles, approximately 5 minutes. Using a blender, combine the eggs, milk, flour, sugar, vanilla extract, salt and cinnamon. Pour equal amounts of egg mixture into the 2 pie pans over top of hot apples. Sprinkle 2 tablespoons of brown sugar over tops of each egg mixture. Bake, uncovered, for 20 to 25 minutes or until puffed and brown.

Variation: For a summertime breakfast or brunch, substitute fresh ripe peaches for the apples.

Yield: 2 to 4 servings

Toni Marra

Breakfast Soufflé

1 pound bulk beef, pork or turkey sausage
6 eggs
2 cups milk
1 cup shredded sharp Cheddar cheese
2 slices of bread with crust, cubed
¼ teaspoon salt, or to taste
1 teaspoon dry mustard

Grease an 8x8-inch or 9x5-inch glass baking dish; set aside. In a large skillet, brown the sausage; drain well. In a large mixing bowl, beat together the eggs and milk. Stir in the cheese, bread, salt, mustard and sausage. Pour the egg mixture into prepared dish; cover and refrigerate overnight. Remove baking dish from refrigerator 30 minutes prior to baking. Preheat oven to 350 degrees. Bake, uncovered, for 55 to 60 minutes; let stand for 5 minutes before serving. *Easy and delicious.*

Note: Recipe must be prepared the day before.

Yield: 6 servings

Annette Browning

Egg and Corn Quesadilla

2 tablespoons olive oil
1 medium onion, chopped
1 green bell pepper, seeded,
    chopped
1 clove of garlic, minced
3 cups frozen (thawed) or canned
    corn, drained
1 teaspoon dried chives
½ teaspoon dried parsley
½ teaspoon salt
¼ teaspoon ground black pepper
4 eggs, beaten
4 (10-inch) flour tortillas
½ cup salsa
1 cup sour cream
1 cup shredded Cheddar cheese
1 cup shredded mozzarella cheese

Preheat oven to 350 degrees. Lightly grease a baking sheet; set aside. In a large skillet, over medium heat, heat the olive oil. Add the onion, bell pepper and garlic; sauté until onion and bell pepper are tender. Add the corn, chives, parsley, salt and pepper to skillet; cook for 3 minutes or until heated through. Stir in the eggs; cook until completely set, stirring occasionally. Remove skillet from heat. Place 1 tortilla on the prepared baking sheet. Top with ⅓ of the egg mixture, ⅓ of the salsa and ⅓ of the sour cream. Sprinkle top with ¼ cup each of the Cheddar and mozzarella cheeses. Place another tortilla on top and repeat the layering two times. Top with the remaining tortilla. Sprinkle on the remaining cheeses. Bake for 10 minutes or until cheese is melted. To serve, cut the quesadilla into wedges. Serve with additional salsa and sour cream.

Yield: 6 to 8 servings

Georgia Moncada

Monterey Jack Casserole

6 eggs
1 cup milk
½ cup flour
16 ounces small-curd cottage
  cheese
3 ounces cream cheese, cut into
  small cubes, softened
¼ cup butter or margarine,
  softened
1 tablespoon sugar
1 teaspoon baking powder
½ teaspoon salt
Dash of Worcestershire sauce
Dash of paprika
¼ teaspoon dried dill
1 pound Monterey Jack cheese,
  cut into small cubes
2-3 cups chopped cooked ham,
  to taste

Preheat oven to 350 degrees. Lightly grease a 13x9-inch baking dish; set aside. In a large mixing bowl, using an electric mixer, beat the eggs until frothy. Slowly add the milk, flour, cottage cheese, cream cheese and butter; mix well. Add the sugar, baking powder, salt, Worcestershire sauce, paprika and dill; mix well. Using a spatula, fold in the Monterey Jack cheese and ham. Pour egg mixture into prepared baking dish. Bake, uncovered, for 1 hour.

Variation: Substitute 1 pound of crumbled cooked bacon for the ham.

Yield: 8 to 12 servings

Rita Pompeo

Baked Vegetable Frittata

An Italian Baked Egg Dish

2 pounds fresh asparagus, ends trimmed, cut into 2-inch pieces
1 tablespoon butter
2 large red, orange or yellow bell peppers, seeded, thinly sliced
4 shallot cloves, minced
12 eggs
½ cup half & half
4 tablespoons chopped fresh parsley
1½ teaspoons salt
½ teaspoon freshly ground black pepper
1 medium zucchini, thinly sliced, (peeling optional)
3 scallions (white part and small amount of green), thinly sliced
¾ cup freshly grated Asiago cheese
Parsley sprigs, optional

Preheat oven to 350 degrees. Coat a 13x9-inch glass baking dish with nonstick vegetable oil cooking spray; set aside. Place the asparagus in boiling water for 1 minute to blanch. Drain and place under cold running water to stop cooking; set aside. In a large skillet, over medium heat, melt the butter. Add the bell peppers and shallots. Sauté until peppers soften; set aside. In a large bowl, whisk together the eggs, half & half, parsley, salt and pepper. Add the asparagus, bell pepper mixture, zucchini and scallions to bowl; mix well. Pour into the prepared dish. Sprinkle the Asiago cheese evenly over top. Bake, uncovered, for 30 to 35 minutes or until set and golden. Allow the frittata to cool slightly and slide onto a serving platter. Garnish with parsley sprigs. *A beautiful addition to the brunch table.*

Note: Frittata may be prepared the night before. Cover and refrigerate. To serve, bring to room temperature. Warm in a 300 degree oven.

Yield: 12 to 14 servings

Denise O'Connor

Palachinke

Serbian Cheese-Filled Crêpes

Crêpes
¾ cup flour
1 tablespoon sugar
1 teaspoon baking powder
½ teaspoon salt
2 eggs
1 cup milk
Butter or vegetable oil

Filling
1 pound small-curd cottage cheese
2 eggs, beaten

Topping
1 cup sour cream
1 tablespoon sugar

Orange or lemon peel, optional

Preheat oven to 350 degrees. To prepare the crêpes, in a large mixing bowl, sift together the flour, 1 tablespoon of sugar, baking powder and salt. In a separate bowl, beat together the eggs and milk. Add egg mixture to dry ingredients; mix well. Heat an 8 or 9-inch crêpe pan or nonstick skillet over medium heat. Brush bottom of pan with a small amount of the butter. Pour ¼ cup of batter into skillet and quickly tilt with a circular motion to spread batter into a thin crêpe. Cook for approximately 1 to 2 minutes, flipping once, to brown lightly on both sides. Brush skillet with additional butter as needed and continue cooking crêpes. To prepare the filling, in a small bowl, mix together the cottage cheese and eggs. Spoon 2 to 3 tablespoons of the filling into center of each crêpe and roll up. Lay crêpes side by side in a 15x10x2-inch baking dish; set aside. To prepare the topping, in a small bowl, combine sour cream and 1 tablespoon of sugar. Spread topping over each crêpe. Bake, uncovered, for 20 minutes. Garnish with the orange peel.

Yield: 10 to 12 palachinke

Maura Petrone

Make Ahead Brunch

Butter or margarine, softened,
  to taste
16 thin slices of French bread,
  with or without crust
1 pound Cheddar cheese, grated
1 pound Monterey Jack cheese,
  grated
1 pound of bacon, cooked,
  crumbled
1 cup sliced mushrooms
½ cup chopped onion
½ green bell pepper, seeded,
  chopped
½ red bell pepper, seeded,
  chopped
14 eggs
1 cup half & half
1 cup milk
1 teaspoon salt
½ teaspoon freshly ground black
  pepper
1 teaspoon paprika
½ teaspoon dry mustard

Butter a 4-quart casserole. Spread butter on both sides of the bread slices. Place 8 of the slices on bottom of prepared casserole. Sprinkle ½ of the Cheddar and Monterey Jack cheeses and ½ of the bacon over bread slices. Top with the remaining 8 slices of bread. Sprinkle on the remaining cheeses and bacon. Layer the mushrooms, onion, and bell peppers over top of cheese and bacon. In a large mixing bowl, beat the eggs. Add the half & half, milk, salt, black pepper, paprika and dry mustard; beat well to combine. Pour the egg mixture over casserole. Cover; refrigerate for 24 hours. Preheat oven to 350 degrees. Bake, uncovered, for 1½ hours.

Note: Recipe must be prepared the day before.

Yield: 10 to 12 servings

Toni Marra

Quiche Lorraine

1 (9-inch) unbaked pie crust
½ small onion, minced
½ green bell pepper, seeded, finely chopped
¼ pound mushrooms, finely chopped
4 slices of bacon, crisply cooked, crumbled, fat reserved
4 eggs, lightly beaten
¾ cup milk
¾ cup light cream
¼ teaspoon salt
Freshly ground black pepper, to taste
2 cups shredded Swiss cheese mixed with 2 tablespoons flour

Preheat oven to 350 degrees. Line a 9-inch round quiche pan or pie plate with the piecrust; set aside. In a medium skillet, over medium heat, sauté the onion, bell pepper and mushrooms in reserved bacon fat until soft. Remove from heat; drain off any excess fat. In a large bowl, combine the eggs, milk, cream, salt, pepper, sautéed vegetables and bacon. Stir in the cheese and flour mixture. Pour filling into pie crust; bake, uncovered, for 60 to 70 minutes or until set and golden brown on top. Remove from oven; let sit for 5 minutes before cutting. *Serve with salad and fresh fruit for a delicious brunch, luncheon or light supper.*

Note: To prepare Quiche Lorraine for a crowd, prepare enough dough for 2 (9-inch) pie crusts. Roll dough to fit an 11x7-inch glass baking dish. Double all ingredients and follow directions above. Bake for 1 hour and 15 minutes.

Yield: 6 to 8 servings

Margaret Jones

My Mom's Quick Zucchini Quiche

2 cups diced zucchini,
    approximately 1 small zucchini
    (peeling optional)
1 small onion, finely chopped
1½ cups shredded Cheddar cheese
1 cup biscuit-making mix
1 teaspoon salt
1 teaspoon dried oregano
¼ teaspoon ground black pepper
6 eggs
⅓ cup vegetable oil
2 tablespoons grated Parmesan
    cheese, or to taste

Preheat oven to 350 degrees. In a large mixing bowl, combine the zucchini, onion, Cheddar cheese, biscuit-making mix, salt, oregano, and pepper. Spread mixture into a 9 or 10-inch square baking dish. In the same bowl, beat the eggs and oil together; pour over the zucchini mixture. Sprinkle with the Parmesan cheese. Bake, uncovered, for 35 to 40 minutes.

Yield: 4 to 6 servings

Annette Browning

A Neapolitan Breakfast

Eggs Purgatory

2 tablespoons olive oil
1 small onion, finely chopped
Pinch of crushed red pepper
    flakes, or to taste
¼ teaspoon dried marjoram or
    oregano
1 (14-ounce) can crushed tomatoes
Salt and freshly ground black
    pepper, to taste
6 eggs
Freshly grated Parmesan cheese
Italian bread

In a large skillet, over medium heat, heat the olive oil. Add the onion, red pepper flakes and marjoram. Sauté until the onion is translucent, approximately 4 minutes. Add the tomatoes; stir well to combine. Simmer until sauce begins to thicken, approximately 7 to 10 minutes. Season with salt and pepper. Break eggs directly into skillet over top of sauce. Cook eggs until whites are set and yolks are to desired consistency. Transfer eggs and sauce to individual plates. Serve with Parmesan cheese and crusty Italian bread.

Note: Recipe may also be made with leftover or prepared tomato sauce. Heat the sauce in a skillet. Cook the eggs as directed.

Yield: 2 to 3 servings

Anthony Conte

Sacred Heart Parish Epiphany Breakfast

18 eggs
1 cup plus 2 tablespoons
    half & half
3 tablespoons butter
1 (10¾-ounce) can cream of
    mushroom soup
2 (3-ounce) jars sliced
    mushrooms, drained
1¼ cups shredded sharp Cheddar
    cheese
8-10 slices of crisp-fried bacon,
    crumbled

Preheat oven to 250 degrees. Grease a 3-quart casserole or baking dish; set aside. In a large mixing bowl, beat together the eggs and half & half. In a large skillet, over medium heat, melt the butter. Add the egg mixture; scramble until cooked through. Remove skillet from heat. Stir in the cream of mushroom soup, mushrooms and cheese. Pour into prepared casserole; top with the bacon. Bake for 1 hour.

Note: Recipe may be prepared the day before; cover tightly and refrigerate. Bring to room temperature before baking.

Yield: 8 to 10 servings

Betty Hannigan

Rustic Potato Omelet

2 tablespoons unsalted butter,
    divided
2 tablespoons olive oil, divided
1 medium onion, diced
3 cloves of garlic, minced
4 medium potatoes, peeled, diced
8-10 slices of bacon, crisp-fried,
    drained, crumbled
6 eggs, beaten
Salt and freshly ground black
    pepper, to taste
½ cup grated Gruyère cheese,
    optional

In large skillet or omelet pan, over medium heat, heat 1 tablespoon of the butter with 1 tablespoon of the olive oil. Add the onion; sauté until soft. Add the garlic; sauté for 2 additional minutes. Transfer onion and garlic to a plate. Add the remaining butter and olive oil to skillet. Add the potatoes; sauté until potatoes are crisp on the outside but soft when pierced with a fork, approximately 20 minutes. Add the bacon, onion and garlic to skillet. Pour the eggs evenly over potato mixture. Season with salt and pepper. Cook over medium heat until omelet is set on the bottom. Cover the skillet; continue cooking until top is set, approximately 2 to 3 minutes. Sprinkle the cheese over top; allow to melt. Fold omelet in half. Slide onto a plate; serve immediately. *Add fresh fruit and crusty French bread for a delicious hearty meal any time of the day.*

Yield: 2 to 4 servings

Diane DeNardo

Quiche Provençale

Filling

1 small eggplant, peeled, cut into
½-inch cubes
2 teaspoons salt, divided
4 tablespoons olive oil, divided
1 cup finely minced onion
1 garlic clove, minced
1 green bell pepper, seeded, finely
chopped
3 ripe tomatoes, peeled, seeded,
chopped
¼ teaspoon ground white pepper
2 tablespoons chopped fresh or
½ teaspoon dried basil
1 teaspoon dried oregano

Sauce

3 tablespoons butter
4 tablespoons flour
2 cups warm milk
Salt and ground black pepper,
to taste
Pinch of nutmeg
2 egg yolks, beaten

1 (9-inch) unbaked pie shell
4 tablespoons freshly grated
Parmesan cheese

To prepare the filling, place eggplant cubes in a colander; sprinkle with 1½ teaspoons of the salt and allow to drain for at least 1 hour. Dry eggplant with paper towels; set aside. Preheat oven to 375 degrees. In a large skillet, over medium heat, heat 2 tablespoons of the olive oil. Sauté the onions and garlic until onion is soft and lightly browned. Add the bell pepper to skillet; sauté until soft. Add the tomatoes; cook until mixture becomes a stiff purée, approximately 10 minutes. Stir in the remaining ½ teaspoon of salt, white pepper, basil and oregano. In a separate skillet, heat the remaining 2 tablespoons of olive oil. Add the eggplant; sauté until evenly browned. Dry with paper towels. Stir dried eggplant into tomato mixture. To prepare the sauce, melt the butter in a heavy saucepan over low heat. Add the flour and cook for 1 to 2 minutes stirring continuously to avoid browning. Add the warm milk. Stir continuously until mixture comes to a boil and thickens. Season with the salt, black pepper and nutmeg. Remove pan from heat; whisk in the egg yolks. Pour eggplant filling into the pie shell. Pour sauce over top; sprinkle with Parmesan cheese. Bake, uncovered, for 35 to 40 minutes or until lightly browned on top. Let quiche sit for 5 minutes before serving. *A real treat with fresh fruit and a glass of French wine.*

Variation: For a different taste, try adding anchovies, flaked tuna or crabmeat to the filling.

Yield: 5 to 6 servings

Anne McCafferty

Brookline

$\mathcal{B}$rookline is thought to take its name from Brookline, Massachusetts, the birthplace of U.S. President John F. Kennedy. The terrain was similar to its Massachusetts namesake in that it was "well watered." A spring ran at Berkshire Avenue, a brook flowed adjacent to Edgebrook Avenue, Saw Mill Run Creek was a major presence, another creek flowed along West Liberty Avenue, and a large duck pond was located near McNeily Road.

Brookline, as we know it today, is actually a real estate composition of parts of the old West Liberty Borough, former Lower St. Clair Township, and part of Baldwin Township. The community originally belonged to Washington County, PA. In 1788, Allegheny County was formed and Brookline fell within its newly drawn boundary lines.

Brookline was settled by farmers who migrated from southeastern Pennsylvania and Maryland after the Revolutionary War. In search of land tracts that they could permanently settle, they developed a prosperous farming district in Brookline that led to further commercial enterprises.

Pioneer Avenue was constructed in 1897 and served as an important section of the state road between Pittsburgh and Washington, PA. With this dirt wagon trail, commercial development soon followed. Grain was ground at Boggs Grist Mill, near the city end of Pioneer Avenue, and Espy's Tanyards produced leather for harnesses, boots and saddles.

In 1904, the opening of a streetcar tunnel through Mount Washington was a transportation breakthrough for the southern communities that heretofore had to depend solely on unpredictable dirt roads to reach downtown Pittsburgh. The streetcar cut miles and hours off an arduous trip and in turn jump-started real estate and housing development in the area.

In 1905, the West Liberty Improvement Company began to sell lots in Brookline. By 1908, the area had attracted so many residents that it was annexed to the City of Pittsburgh. The population grew quickly and another tunnel was designed to provide even easier access to downtown. Slightly more than a mile long, the Liberty Tunnel, familiarly called "the Tubes," opened in 1924 to great fanfare.

Today, Brookline is a vibrant residential community with an attractive business district. It continues to thrive as a welcoming and diverse city neighborhood due to its many active church and civic organizations that sponsor recreational, cultural and family-oriented programs. ♥♥

Mark's Boston Fettuccini

¼ **pound of bacon, diced**
4 scallions with greens, chopped
3 medium cloves of garlic, minced
12 ounces mushrooms, chopped
1 tablespoon extra-virgin olive oil
Salt and freshly ground black
pepper, to taste
1 tablespoon chopped fresh thyme
1 teaspoon chopped fresh oregano
¼ **pound sliced domestic**
prosciutto, chopped

Sauce
1½ **cups heavy cream or**
half & half
10 tablespoons unsalted butter
12 ounces Pecorino Romano or
Parmigiano-Reggiano cheese,
freshly grated

1 pound dry or fresh fettuccini
(see note)
Fresh basil, cut in thin strips to
equal 2 tablespoons

In a large, nonstick skillet, sauté bacon until just crisp. Using a slotted spoon, remove bacon and drain on paper towels. Drain skillet reserving 1 tablespoon of bacon fat. Add the scallions and garlic to reserved bacon fat in skillet. Sauté until the onions are translucent. Do not allow garlic to brown. Add the mushrooms, olive oil, salt and pepper; sauté until mushrooms cook down and liquid is absorbed. Add thyme, oregano, bacon and prosciutto. Mix well; cover and keep warm. To prepare the sauce, place cream and butter in a heavy saucepan. Cook over low to medium heat until butter melts. Do not boil. Slowly add the cheese, whisking until incorporated. Do not boil. Drain fettuccini; return to pot. Add the mushroom and bacon mixture to fettuccini. Add the sauce; mix well. Transfer fettuccini to a serving platter and garnish with basil. Serve immediately. *A delicious indulgence.*

Note: If using dry fettuccini, cook according to package directions while sauce is being prepared. If using fresh fettuccini, cook when sauce preparation is completed.

Yield: 4 to 6 servings

Mark Flaherty

Orecchiette with Turkey Sausage and Broccoli Rabe

2 bunches of broccoli rabe,
    washed, stems removed
1 pound orecchiette pasta
¼ cup plus 3 tablespoons olive oil,
    divided
1 pound bulk Italian-style turkey
    sausage
3 cloves of garlic, minced, or
    to taste
⅛ teaspoon crushed red pepper
    flakes, optional
¼ cup freshly grated Parmesan
    cheese

In a large pot of salted boiling water, cook the broccoli rabe just until crisp-tender, approximately 3 minutes. Using a slotted spoon, transfer the broccoli rabe to a large bowl of ice water; allow to cool. (Ice bath will retain the color of the broccoli rabe.) Transfer to a colander to drain. Bring the salted water back to a boil. Place pasta in the boiling water; cook according to package directions. Drain and transfer to a serving bowl. Toss pasta with ¼ cup of the olive oil; cover and set aside. In a large, heavy skillet, over medium heat, heat the remaining 3 tablespoons of olive oil. Add the sausage, breaking into small pieces with a spoon. Cook until browned, approximately 5 to 10 minutes. Add the garlic and red pepper flakes; sauté for 2 minutes. Add broccoli rabe to skillet; toss with the sausage. Add the pasta and Parmesan cheese; toss well. Serve immediately.

Yield: 6 to 8 servings

Susan Parente

My Mom's Skipper's Linguine

6 slices of bacon, cut into ½-inch
    pieces, or to taste
¼ cup sliced green onion (white
    part and small amount of green)
2 cloves of garlic, minced
6 tablespoons butter
2 (6½-ounce) cans minced clams,
    drained
1 (6½-ounce) can white tuna,
    drained, flaked
1 (2¼-ounce) can sliced, pitted
    ripe olives, drained
¼ cup chopped fresh parsley
⅛ teaspoon ground black pepper
12 ounces linguine
1 lemon, cut into wedges
Freshly grated Parmesan cheese

In a large skillet, fry the bacon until crisp. Remove bacon and drain, reserving ¼ cup of the bacon fat. Using the same skillet, sauté onion and garlic in the reserved fat until tender; do not brown. Add the butter; stir until melted. Stir in the bacon, clams, tuna, olives, parsley and pepper. Heat thoroughly. Set aside, covered, to keep warm. Prepare linguine according to package directions. Drain linguine and place in a warm serving bowl. Toss linguine with the warm skillet mixture. Serve with lemon wedges and Parmesan cheese.

Yield: 4 to 6 servings

Belle Moldovan

Baked Farfalle with Tomatoes, Crimini Mushrooms and Prosciutto

2 cups finely chopped onion
3 large cloves of garlic, minced
¼ teaspoon crushed red pepper
  flakes, or to taste
½ teaspoon freshly ground black
  pepper, and to taste
1 teaspoon dried basil
1 teaspoon dried oregano
2 tablespoons olive oil
1 pound fresh Crimini
  mushrooms, sliced
8 tablespoons unsalted butter,
  divided
6 tablespoons flour
4 cups milk
2 (28-ounce) cans Italian peeled,
  whole tomatoes, drained well,
  chopped
¼ pound prosciutto, thinly sliced
⅔ cup minced fresh parsley leaves
¼ pound Italian fontina cheese,
  grated, approximately 1 cup
½ cup crumbled Gorgonzola
  cheese
1½ cups freshly grated Parmesan
  cheese, divided
1 pound farfalle pasta
Salt, to taste

Preheat oven to 450 degrees. Grease a 4-quart casserole dish; set aside. In a large skillet, over medium to low heat, sauté the onion, garlic, red pepper flakes, ½ teaspoon black pepper, basil and oregano in the olive oil until onion is soft, approximately 5 minutes. Add the mushrooms; cook over medium heat, stirring continuously, for 10 to 15 minutes or until mushrooms are tender; set aside. In a medium saucepan, over low heat, melt 6 tablespoons of the butter. Whisk in the flour; cook, whisking continuously, for 3 minutes to create a roux. Add the milk in a slow stream, whisking continuously. Simmer, still whisking, for an additional 10 to 15 minutes or until thickened. Pour sauce over the mushroom mixture. Add the tomatoes, prosciutto, parsley, fontina and Gorgonzola cheeses, and 1¼ cups of the Parmesan cheese. Toss well to combine; set aside. In a large pot of salted water, boil the farfalle for 5 minutes; drain well (pasta will not be tender). Add farfalle to the mushroom mixture. Season with salt and pepper. Toss well to thoroughly combine; transfer to prepared casserole. Sprinkle with the remaining Parmesan cheese. Dot with the remaining butter. Bake, uncovered, in middle of the oven for 30 minutes, or until top is golden and farfalle is tender. *A nice combination of flavors.*

Note: Farfalle are large bow-tie shaped pasta. Recipe may be prepared and refrigerated over night. Bring to room temperature prior to baking.

Yield: 8 to 10 servings

Joanne Redondo

Cold Sesame Noodles with Cucumber

1 pound Asian noodles, capellini
   or thin spaghetti
3 tablespoons sesame oil
2 tablespoons soy sauce
2 tablespoons rice wine vinegar or
   white vinegar
1 teaspoon sugar
½ teaspoon chili paste or crushed
   red pepper flakes
2 tablespoons toasted sesame
   paste or peanut butter
1 carrot, finely grated, optional
1 large cucumber, peeled, seeded,
   cut into long thin strips
4 scallions, with 1-inch of green,
   minced, divided
2 tablespoons toasted sesame
   seeds (see note), divided

Cook noodles according to the package directions. Drain; rinse with cold water. Transfer well-drained noodles to a serving platter. In a medium mixing bowl, whisk together the sesame oil, soy sauce, rice wine vinegar, sugar, chili and sesame pastes. Stir in the carrot, cucumber, ⅓ of the scallions, and 1½ tablespoons of the sesame seeds. Pour over noodles; toss to combine. Garnish with remaining scallions and sesame seeds.

Note: To toast sesame seeds, place in a skillet over medium heat. Shaking the skillet frequently, toast until brown, approximately 5 to 8 minutes.

Yield: 4 entrée servings; 6 to 8 side dish servings

Diane DeNardo

Atomic Pasta

1½ pounds medium shrimp,
   shelled, deveined; shells
   reserved
3 tablespoons butter, divided
2 cups extra-virgin olive oil,
   divided
Salt and freshly ground black
   pepper, to taste
2-3 bulbs of garlic, peeled, cloves
   finely chopped, to taste
½ teaspoon crushed red pepper
   flakes
1 bunch of fresh parsley, finely
   chopped, divided
2 (6-ounce) cans of clams, drained
1½ pounds of angel hair pasta

In a large skillet, over low heat, sauté the shrimp shells in 1 tablespoon of butter and 4 tablespoons of the olive oil for 1 to 2 minutes. Remove and discard shells. Add the shrimp to skillet; season with salt and pepper. Sauté just until shrimp are pinkish-red; transfer to a bowl and set aside. Add the remaining olive oil and garlic to skillet; sauté until garlic begins to change color. (Do not allow garlic to brown.) Add pepper flakes and ¾ of the parsley to skillet; stir to combine. Add the remaining 2 tablespoons of butter. Add clams to skillet and sauté for 1 minute or until warmed through. Cook pasta according to package directions; drain and transfer to a large serving platter. Top pasta with the skillet mixture and shrimp. Sprinkle with the remaining parsley.

Yield: 10 servings

Anne McCafferty

Three Pepper Pasta

3 tablespoons olive oil
1 large red bell pepper, seeded,
    cut into ½-inch strips
1 large green bell pepper, seeded,
    cut into ½-inch strips
1 large yellow bell pepper, seeded,
    cut into ½-inch strips
1 large onion, cut into ½-inch
    strips
1½ teaspoons salt
1 tablespoon sugar
3 tablespoons balsamic vinegar
¾ teaspoon dried basil
½ teaspoon ground black pepper
8 ounces penne or mostaccioli
    pasta
Freshly grated Parmesan or
    Romano cheese

Over medium heat, heat an 18-inch skillet. Add the olive oil. Sauté bell peppers and onions with the salt until tender and slightly browned, approximately 15 minutes. Stir in sugar, vinegar, basil and black pepper. Heat thoroughly. Prepare pasta according to package directions; drain. Toss pepper mixture with the pasta. Serve warm, topped with the Parmesan cheese.

Yield: 4 entrée servings; 6 side dish servings

Amy Kissell

Spaghetti Aglio e Olio

Spaghetti in Garlic and Oil

8 tablespoons butter
¼ cup extra-virgin olive oil
2-3 anchovies, optional
¼ cup minced garlic
1 cup sliced white mushrooms
¼ cup golden raisins
Salt, to taste
1 pound of spaghetti, prepared
    according to package
    directions, drained
½ cup chopped fresh parsley
½ cup toasted pine nuts
Freshly grated Parmesan cheese

In a large saucepan, melt the butter over low to medium heat. Add the olive oil and anchovies. Using a wooden spoon, stir and crush the anchovies against side of pan until no longer visible. Add the garlic; sauté until tender. Add the mushrooms, raisins and salt. Cook over low heat for 10 minutes. Toss spaghetti with the garlic-oil mixture. Serve topped with the parsley, pine nuts and Parmesan cheese.

Variation: Substitute linguini or angel hair pasta for the spaghetti.

Yield: 4 to 6 servings

Cindy McKenna

Gourmet Macaroni and Beef

2 tablespoons butter
2 tablespoons olive oil
1½ cups diced yellow onion
4-5 cloves garlic, minced
1½ pounds ground beef
1 (28-ounce) can crushed tomatoes
1 (6-ounce) can tomato paste
8 ounces mushrooms, sliced
½ cup diced red bell pepper
½ cup diced yellow bell pepper
4 tablespoons dry French
   vermouth
½ teaspoon dried oregano
½ teaspoon dried thyme
½ teaspoon garlic salt
¼-½ cup grated Romano cheese,
   to taste
Large dash of Tabasco sauce,
   optional
Kosher salt and freshly ground
   black pepper, to taste
1½ pounds elbow macaroni

In an extra-large skillet, over medium heat, melt the butter. Add the olive oil and onion; sauté until lightly browned. Add the garlic; sauté for 2 minutes. Add the beef; cook, stirring, until browned. Add the tomatoes and tomato paste; cook for 5 minutes. Add the mushrooms and bell peppers; cook until peppers are soft. Add the vermouth; turn heat to high. Cook, stirring, for approximately 2 minutes. Reduce heat. Add the oregano, thyme, garlic salt, Romano cheese, Tabasco sauce, kosher salt and pepper. Cover and simmer beef mixture for 10 to 15 minutes. Cook the macaroni according to package directions; drain and combine with beef mixture. Serve with additional Romano cheese, if desired. *The best mac and cheese you'll ever eat.*

Yield: 8 to 10 servings

Mark Flaherty

Pasta Angelico

¾ **ounce dried porcini mushrooms**
⅔ **cup warm water**
¼ **cup olive oil**
⅔ **cup chopped shallots**
1 **pound fresh mushrooms,**
  coarsely chopped
1⅓ **cups heavy whipping cream**
3 **tablespoons salt**
1 **pound angel hair pasta**
⅓ **cup freshly grated Parmigiano-**
  Reggiano cheese
Coarse or sea salt, to taste
Freshly ground black pepper,
  to taste

Place the porcini mushrooms in a bowl; cover with the warm water. Let mushrooms soak for 45 minutes. Drain; reserve liquid. Chop the porcini mushrooms and return to reserved liquid; set aside. Heat a large skillet. Add the olive oil and shallots; sauté for 2 to 3 minutes (do not allow shallots to brown). Add the fresh mushrooms; sauté until tender. Add the porcini mushrooms and reserved liquid. Simmer, uncovered, until most of the liquid has evaporated but mixture is not over-dry; set aside. In a clean chilled bowl, whip the cream until it holds soft peaks; set aside in the refrigerator. In a large pot, bring 4 to 6 quarts of water to a boil. Add the 3 tablespoons of salt and pasta. Stir with a wooden spoon to separate the pasta as it cooks. Cover and bring to a second boil. Cook to al dente; drain immediately. Add the mushroom mixture and grated cheese to the pasta; mix well. Season with the coarse salt and black pepper. Using a large, flat rubber spatula, quickly and gently fold in the chilled cream. Serve immediately.

Yield: 4 to 6 servings

Brian Contic

Pasta with Chicken and Vegetables

4 tablespoons olive oil, divided
3 skinless, boneless chicken breast halves, cut into 1-inch cubes
2 carrots, sliced diagonally into ¼-inch pieces
1 (10-ounce) package of frozen broccoli florets, thawed, drained
2 cloves of garlic, minced
16 ounces spaghettini or 12 ounces angel hair pasta
2 cups chicken broth
½ teaspoon dried basil
¼ cup freshly grated Parmesan cheese

In a large skillet, over medium heat, heat 2 tablespoons of the olive oil. Add the chicken; cook, stirring, until cooked through, approximately 5 to 10 minutes. Remove chicken and drain on paper towels. Using the same skillet, heat the remaining 2 tablespoons of olive oil. Add the carrots; sauté for 4 minutes. Add the broccoli florets and garlic; sauté for an additional 2 minutes. Prepare spaghettini according to package directions. While pasta is cooking, add the chicken broth and basil to skillet; stir to combine. Return chicken to skillet. Gradually add the Parmesan cheese, stirring continuously. Reduce heat to low and simmer for an additional 5 minutes. Drain pasta and transfer to a large serving platter or bowl. Top with the chicken and vegetable mixture. Serve immediately, sprinkled with additional Parmesan cheese, if desired.

Yield: 4 to 6 servings

Joseph Parente

Zucchini à la Napolitano

4 tablespoons olive oil
3 cloves of garlic, chopped
1 pound chicken pieces
1 onion, chopped
1 large red bell pepper, seeded, sliced into strips
Salt and freshly ground black pepper, to taste
¼-1 teaspoon dried oregano, to taste
2 (8-ounce) cans tomato sauce
2 cups water
1-2 chicken bouillon cubes, to taste
3 small zucchini, peeled, cubed
1 pound spaghetti or penne pasta
½ cup freshly grated Pecorino Romano or Parmesan cheese

In a Dutch oven or large pot, over medium to low heat, heat the olive oil. Add the garlic, chicken, onion, and bell pepper to pot. Cook, stirring and turning chicken to evenly brown. Season with salt, pepper and oregano. Add the tomato sauce, water and bouillon. Simmer, covered, for 50 minutes. Skim fat from top of sauce. Add the zucchini and simmer for an additional 10 minutes. Cook the pasta according to package directions; drain and transfer to a serving platter. Ladle sauce and chicken over hot pasta; sprinkle with the cheese. *Good eating!*

Variation: Substitute sliced (skinless, boneless) chicken or hot or sweet Italian sausage for the chicken pieces.

Yield: 4 to 6 servings

Dom Mondelli

Traditional Lasagna

2 cloves of garlic, minced
1 medium onion, chopped
2 tablespoons olive oil
1 pound ground beef
2½ teaspoons salt
¼ teaspoon ground black pepper
½ teaspoon dried basil
1 tablespoon chopped fresh
    parsley
1 (12-ounce) can tomato paste
1½ cups hot water
2 eggs, lightly beaten
1 pound ricotta cheese
½ pound shredded mozzarella
    cheese
¼ cup grated Parmesan cheese
½ pound lasagna noodles,
    prepared according to package
    directions, drained

Preheat oven to 350 degrees. Grease a 13x9-inch baking dish; set aside. In a large skillet, over medium heat, sauté the garlic and onion in olive oil until soft. Add the beef, salt, pepper, basil and parsley. Cook, stirring, until beef is evenly browned. Add the tomato paste and water; mix well. Cover and simmer for 25 minutes. In a medium bowl, mix the eggs with the ricotta cheese; set aside. Ladle a thin layer of meat mixture over bottom of prepared baking dish. Layer ½ of the noodles over top. Spread entire ricotta mixture over noodles. Sprinkle ½ of the mozzarella over ricotta layer. Ladle ½ of the remaining meat mixture over cheeses. Top with remaining noodles. Ladle on the remaining meat mixture. Top with the remaining mozzarella and Parmesan cheeses. Bake, uncovered, for 30 minutes. Let sit for 10 minutes prior to serving. *Children love this traditional lasagna.*

Yield: 6 to 8 servings

Marilyn Radcliffe

Pasta with Ricotta

1 pound penne or ziti pasta
1 (15-ounce) container of ricotta
    cheese
8 tablespoons butter
1 cup milk
¼ cup freshly grated Parmesan
    cheese
¼ cup snipped fresh basil or
    parsley

Prepare the pasta according to package directions. Drain; return pasta to pot. Add the ricotta cheese, butter and milk. Cook over low heat, stirring, until butter melts. Remove from heat; stir in the Parmesan cheese. Garnish with the basil. Serve immediately.

Yield: 4 to 6 servings

Rita Pompeo

The Lazy Woman's Lasagna

1 pound small shell pasta
1 pound ground meat or sausage,
  cooked, drained
2 cups tomato sauce, divided
1 pound ricotta cheese
1 cup grated Parmesan cheese,
  divided
2 eggs, lightly beaten
Dried parsley, to taste
Ground black pepper, to taste
1 pound sliced mozzarella cheese

Preheat oven to 375 degrees. Cook pasta according to package directions; drain and return to pot. Add the meat and 1 cup of the tomato sauce to pasta; mix well. In a medium bowl, mix together the ricotta cheese, ½ cup of the Parmesan cheese, eggs, parsley, and pepper; set aside. Pour ½ cup of tomato sauce evenly over the bottom of a 13x9-inch baking dish. Place ½ of the pasta mixture in dish. Spread the ricotta mixture evenly over top. Arrange mozzarella slices over ricotta mixture to cover evenly. Layer the remaining pasta mixture over the mozzarella. Ladle the remaining ½ cup of tomato sauce evenly over top. Sprinkle with the remaining Parmesan cheese. Cover and bake for 35 to 40 minutes or until hot and bubbling. Let stand for 10 minutes before serving.

Yield: 4 to 6 servings

Pauline DeSimone

Dom's Spaghetti Agilio

1 pound of spaghetti
¾ cup olive oil
¼ cup vegetable oil
7-8 whole cloves of garlic
20 pimento-stuffed olives
2 (2-ounce) cans anchovy fillets,
  undrained
½-1 teaspoon crushed red pepper
  flakes, optional
1 cup freshly grated Pecorino
  Romano cheese, optional

Cook spaghetti according to package directions. In a large skillet, heat the olive and vegetable oils over low heat. Add the garlic cloves, stirring continuously until golden brown. Add the olives. When olives begin to wrinkle, add the anchovies. Drain the spaghetti; add to skillet. Toss well and transfer to serving platter. Sprinkle with red pepper flakes and cheese. *A classic Italian dinner.*

Yield: 4 to 6 servings

Dom Mondelli

Conchiglie with Vodka Sauce Marinara

3 tablespoons extra-virgin olive oil
1 small yellow onion, thinly sliced
2 cloves of garlic, minced
1 rib of celery, thinly sliced
1 carrot, peeled, thinly sliced
½ teaspoon crushed red pepper
    flakes
1 (28-ounce) can peeled, chopped
    plum tomatoes, with juice
½ teaspoon salt
½ cup vodka
1 cup heavy cream
1 pound conchiglie pasta
6 tablespoons freshly grated
    Parmesan cheese

In a large, heavy saucepan, over low heat, heat the olive oil. Sauté the onion, garlic, celery, carrot and red pepper flakes until onion is soft. Add the tomatoes with juice. Cook, stirring occasionally, until liquid evaporates, approximately 25 to 30 minutes. Add the salt. Add the vodka and cream. Continue cooking, stirring continuously, until thickened, approximately 5 to 6 minutes. While sauce is cooking, boil conchiglie in a large pot of salted water until al dente. Drain well; immediately add pasta to sauce. Toss well. Transfer to a warm serving bowl. Sprinkle with the Parmesan cheese.

Note: Conchiglie are medium-sized shell shaped pasta. In the summer, substitute 1½ pounds ripe plum tomatoes, peeled and chopped, for the canned tomatoes.

Yield: 6 to 8 servings

Joanne Redondo

Penne with Baby Peas and Gorgonzola Cheese Sauce

1 cup frozen baby peas
1 cup heavy cream
1 large clove of garlic, unpeeled, smashed
8 tablespoons unsalted butter
6 ounces gorgonzola cheese, crumbled
½ cup grated Pecorino Romano cheese
½ teaspoon freshly ground white pepper
1 pound penne pasta
2 tablespoons chopped fresh parsley or basil

Rinse peas quickly in cold water to thaw; set aside to drain. In a heavy, medium saucepan, over low heat, combine the cream, garlic and butter. Cook slowly until butter melts. Remove garlic clove and skin; discard. Stir in the gorgonzola and Pecorino Romano cheeses. Cook over medium heat until cheeses are incorporated and smooth. Add the white pepper. Cook the penne according to package directions until al dente; drain and return to pot. Add the sauce and peas to penne; mix well. Serve immediately, garnished with parsley.

Yield: 4 to 6 servings

Mark Flaherty

Baked Spaghetti

1 pound thin spaghetti or angel hair pasta
½ pound butter, softened
8 eggs, lightly beaten
¼ cup milk
1¼ cups grated Parmesan cheese
1-2 teaspoons salt, to taste
½ teaspoon ground black pepper

Preheat oven to 350 degrees. Lightly grease a 13x9-inch baking dish; set aside. Cook the spaghetti according to package directions; drain and return to pot. Add the butter; stir over low heat until melted. Add the eggs, milk, Parmesan cheese, salt and pepper to the spaghetti; mix well. Place spaghetti mixture into prepared dish. Bake for 30 minutes. Cut into squares. Serve warm or cold. *An easy make-ahead meal.*

Note: Recipe freezes well. Bring to room temperature before reheating.

Yield: 10 to 12 servings

Ellen McCormick

Pasta Primavera with Fresh Asparagus and English Peas

1 pound gemelli pasta
1½ pounds thin fresh asparagus, ends trimmed, cut into 1-inch diagonal pieces
1½ pounds fresh English green peas, shelled
Nonstick vegetable or olive oil cooking spray
2 teaspoons olive oil
1 large yellow or orange bell pepper, seeded, cut into thin strips
½ large red onion, thinly sliced
4 cloves of garlic, minced
1 cup halved cherry tomatoes
¾ cup fat-free chicken broth
⅔ cup whipping cream
1 teaspoon salt
1 teaspoon crushed red pepper flakes
½ cup freshly grated Parmesan cheese
⅓ cup thinly sliced fresh basil

Prepare the pasta according to package directions. Add the asparagus and peas during the last minute of cooking. Drain well; transfer to a serving bowl. While the pasta is cooking, coat a large skillet with the cooking spray. Over medium heat, heat the olive oil. Add the bell pepper, onion, and garlic; sauté for 5 minutes. Add the tomatoes; sauté for 1 additional minute. Stir in the broth, cream, salt and red pepper flakes; cook for 3 to 5 minutes or until sauce is heated through. Add the cream sauce to the drained pasta; toss well. Sprinkle with the Parmesan cheese and basil. *This pasta with fresh spring vegetables is a delicious, easy-to-prepare meal.*

Yield: 6 to 8 servings

Joanne Redondo

Spinach Noodles

1 (12-ounce) bag flat, broad egg
  noodles
3 tablespoons butter
1 small onion, chopped
2 cloves of garlic, minced
1 pound fresh spinach, stems
  removed
15 ounces ricotta cheese
4 ounces shredded mozzarella
  cheese
¼ cup freshly grated Parmesan
  cheese
Salt and ground black pepper,
  to taste
2 tablespoons dry breadcrumbs

Preheat oven to 400 degrees. Lightly butter a 3½-quart casserole; set aside. Prepare the egg noodles, according to package directions, until firm. (Do not overcook.) Drain and place in a large bowl. In a large skillet, over low to medium heat, melt the butter. Sauté the onion, garlic and spinach until onion is soft and spinach wilts, approximately 5 minutes. Add spinach mixture to the noodles. Stir in the ricotta, mozzarella and Parmesan cheeses. Season with salt and pepper. Transfer to the prepared casserole. Sprinkle the breadcrumbs over top. Bake, uncovered, for 15 minutes. Cover; bake for an additional 15 to 20 minutes or until hot and bubbly.

Variation: Substitute feta or goat cheese for the Parmesan.

Yield: 6 to 8 servings

Dorianne DiGregorio

Halushki

Slovakian Cabbage and Noodles

Noodles
2 cups flour
1 egg, beaten
⅛ teaspoon salt
4 tablespoons milk

2 tablespoons vegetable oil
1 medium onion, finely chopped
3 cloves of garlic, minced
1 small head of cabbage, thinly
    sliced
4 tablespoons cold butter, cut in
    small pieces
Salt and freshly ground black
    pepper, to taste

To prepare the noodles, in a medium mixing bowl, combine the flour, egg, and salt. Add the milk, one tablespoon at a time, until a stiff dough forms. Bring a large pot of water, over high heat, to a boil. On a lightly floured surface, roll out dough to a ¼-inch thickness. Using a sharp knife, cut the dough into 2x1-inch noodles. Drop noodles into the boiling water; cook for 3 minutes. Drain noodles; rinse and let dry on waxed paper. In a large skillet, over low heat, heat the vegetable oil. Add the onion; sauté until translucent. Add the garlic and cabbage. Lay butter over cabbage; season with salt and pepper. Cover skillet; cook, stirring occasionally, for 1 hour or until cabbage is tender and golden in color. Add the noodles to skillet; mix well. Season with additional salt and pepper.

Variation: Crisp-fried, crumbled bacon may be added for flavor.

Yield: 6 to 8 servings

Juanita McCormick

Orzo with Roasted Vegetables

Dressing

⅓ cup freshly squeezed lemon
   juice
⅓ cup olive oil
1 teaspoon salt
½ teaspoon ground black pepper

1 small eggplant, peeled, diced,
   ¾-inch pieces
1 red bell pepper, seeded, sliced
1 yellow bell pepper, seeded, sliced
1 red onion, sliced
2 cloves of garlic, minced
⅓ cup olive oil
1½ teaspoons kosher salt
½ teaspoon ground black pepper
6 cups water with 1 teaspoon salt
   added
½ pound orzo
4 scallions (white part and small
   amount of green), minced
¼ cup pignolia nuts, toasted
¾ pound feta cheese, crumbled
15 sprigs fresh basil, leaves
   chopped

Preheat oven to 425 degrees. In a small bowl, whisk together all dressing ingredients; set aside. In a large bowl, toss the eggplant, bell peppers, onion and garlic with the olive oil, salt and pepper. Transfer vegetable mixture to a large baking sheet with sides. Roast for 20 minutes. Using a spatula, turn vegetables; roast for an additional 20 minutes. In a 4-quart pot, bring the salted water to a boil. Add the orzo and cook for 7 to 9 minutes, stirring occasionally. Drain; transfer to a large serving bowl. Add vegetable mixture to the orzo; toss. Pour dressing over top; toss to coat. Let cool to room temperature. Just prior to serving, add the scallions, pignolia nuts, feta cheese and basil.

Yield: 6 servings

Donna McCormick

Quinoa with Leeks and Sun-Dried Tomatoes

1 cup quinoa
2 cups water
½ teaspoon salt
2 tablespoons olive oil
3 cups finely chopped leeks (white and pale green parts)
Salt and freshly ground black pepper, to taste
2 cups sun-dried tomatoes, softened in hot water, quartered or chopped
2 tablespoons freshly squeezed lemon juice
3 tablespoons chopped fresh basil
2 tablespoons toasted pine nuts, optional
Lemon wedges
Basil leaves

Place quinoa in a strainer; rinse under cold running water for 1 minute. Place quinoa, water and salt in a medium, heavy saucepan. Bring to a boil. Reduce heat to medium-low; simmer, covered, until quinoa is just tender, approximately 20 minutes. Drain well; transfer to a serving bowl. In a large non-reactive skillet, over medium heat, heat the olive oil. Add the leeks; sauté until tender, approximately 5 to 10 minutes. Season with salt and pepper. Add the sun-dried tomatoes, lemon juice and basil; stir to combine. Toss leek mixture with the quinoa. Sprinkle on the pine nuts. Serve warm or cold garnished with lemon wedges and basil leaves.

Note: Quinoa, a protein-rich grain, is found at natural food stores and in large grocery stores.

Yield: 5 cups

Diane DeNardo

Rice Pilaf with Peas

8 slices of bacon, diced
1 medium onion, finely chopped
2 cups long-grain rice
1 (10-ounce) package frozen peas
2 cups water
1 (13¾-ounce) can chicken broth
1½ teaspoons salt
¼ teaspoon ground black pepper

In a large skillet, fry the bacon until crisp. Remove bacon from skillet; set aside on paper towels to drain. Sauté the onions in the bacon drippings until tender, approximately 5 minutes, stirring occasionally. Add the rice, peas, water, chicken broth, salt and pepper to skillet; bring to a boil. Reduce heat to low; simmer, covered, approximately 20 minutes or until the rice is tender. Add the bacon; toss. Serve immediately.

Yield: 8 servings

Sylvia Stehlik

Wild Rice and Cranberry Salad

1 (6-ounce) package long-grain
   and wild rice, herbs omitted,
   prepared according to package
   directions
½ cup diced celery
½ cup diced red bell pepper
½ cup diced yellow bell pepper
½ cup chopped pecans
¾ cup craisins (dried cranberries)

Dressing
3 tablespoons balsamic vinegar
¼ teaspoon salt
1 tablespoon brown sugar
½ teaspoon Dijon mustard
¼ cup olive oil
¼ cup vegetable oil

In a large serving bowl, combine the rice, celery, bell peppers, pecans and craisins. In a separate bowl, whisk together all of the dressing ingredients. Pour dressing over the rice mixture. Toss well to thoroughly coat. *A delicious side dish any time of the year.*

Note: Recipe may be made 1 day ahead. Cover and refrigerate.

Yield: 6 to 8 servings

Marcella Karvellis McGuire

Saffron Risotto

4-5 cups low-sodium chicken
   broth, to taste
3 tablespoons butter
1 small yellow onion, finely diced
2 cups Arborio or long-grain rice
½ cup freshly grated Parmigiano-
   Reggiano cheese
¼ teaspoon saffron threads
Salt and freshly ground black
   pepper, to taste

In a small saucepan, over low to medium heat, warm the chicken broth. Remove from heat; cover to keep warm. In a large, heavy saucepan, over medium heat, melt the butter. Add the onion; sauté until softened and translucent. Add the rice; stir well to coat. Ladle ½ cup of chicken broth over the rice. Decrease heat to simmer. Cook, stirring, until liquid has been absorbed. Continue adding broth, ½ cup at a time, stirring frequently, until rice is al dente and risotto is creamy. Stir in the cheese and saffron. Season with salt and pepper; continue cooking for an additional 2 to 3 minutes. Serve immediately.

Yield: 4 servings

Christina DeNardo

Observatory Hill

*O*bservatory Hill, one of Pittsburgh's northern-most neighborhoods, sits on a high plateau. Settlement in the remote area began in the eighteenth century. Its most well-known thoroughfare, Perrysville Avenue, originated as a Native American Indian path called the Venango Trail. The trail later served as a convenient roadway for Commodore Perry in moving military supplies northward to defeat the British in the Battle of Lake Erie during the War of 1812.

Until the 1890's, most of today's Observatory Hill was farmland which was controlled by two prominent landowners, Samuel Watson and John Dunlap. They owned large land tracts on both sides of Perrysville Avenue. A lack of convenient and reliable transportation through this hilly terrain delayed housing development until the mid-1890's at which time a trolley line opened. This allowed for transportation to the city of Pittsburgh, five miles away. Landowners began to break up their large tracts into housing parcels and home-building began in earnest. In 1894, Dunlap sold to the then city of Allegheny a large parcel of land, which became Riverview Park.

In 1858, several Pittsburgh businessmen had formed the Allegheny Telescope Association and began to lay the groundwork for what became Observatory Hill's namesake, the Allegheny Observatory in Riverview Park. Architect Thorsten Billquest designed the Observatory, whose cornerstone was laid in 1900. Classical aesthetic elements include a pedimented portico, Ionic columns, and decorative stonework. The names of famous astronomers are carved into the cornice stone. At the Observatory, scientists devised a system of measuring time based on the movement of the stars known as "Allegheny Time." It became the official clock of the Pennsylvania Railroad. The ashes of Pittsburgh's beloved astronomer John Brashear and his wife are buried under one of the Observatory's famous telescopes.

By the 1920's, Observatory Hill was filled with spacious and gracious homes in a full complement of architectural styles. With large porches and landscaped lawns, they continue to attract families and restoration enthusiasts today. In addition to tours of the Observatory, Riverview Park offers horseback riding, tennis, summer films, hiking, biking, and swimming. Observatory Hill's annual spring House Tour showcases homes and churches that have been lovingly restored, and which reflect the community spirit that has preserved this neighborhood as one of Pittsburgh's crown jewels. ♥♥

Stuffed Artichokes Italiano

1¼ cups homemade or packaged
    plain breadcrumbs
3 tablespoons freshly grated
    Pecorino Romano cheese
½ cup freshly grated Parmigiano-
    Reggiano cheese
2 cloves of garlic, minced
3 tablespoons chopped fresh
    flat-leaf parsley
Salt and ground black pepper,
    to taste
½ cup extra-virgin olive oil
4 large artichokes

In a medium bowl, combine the breadcrumbs, cheeses, garlic, parsley, salt and pepper; mix well. Slowly add the olive oil, stirring to thoroughly mix. Cut ¾-inch off the tops of each artichoke. Cut stems off the bottoms so that artichokes sit flat. Gently pull open the leaves. Place equal amounts of breadcrumb mixture between leaves. Place stuffed artichokes in a heavy pot that holds them snugly; add 1-inch of water to pot. Bring to a boil; cover and reduce heat to medium-low. Simmer 30 to 45 minutes or until leaves are tender. Serve hot or at room temperature.

Note: To make breadcrumbs, remove the crust from 1 loaf of day-old Italian bread. Process in a food processor to fine crumbs.

Yield: 4 servings

Terry Pegnato

Spinach Artichoke Casserole

4 ounces feta cheese, crumbled
¼ cup seasoned Italian
    breadcrumbs
½ cup butter, softened
1 (8-ounce) package cream cheese,
    softened
2 tablespoons Worcestershire
    sauce
1 teaspoon salt
½ teaspoon garlic powder
⅛ teaspoon cayenne pepper
⅛ teaspoon Tabasco sauce
1 tablespoon lemon juice
3 (10-ounce) packages frozen
    chopped spinach, thawed,
    well-drained
3 (14-ounce) cans artichoke
    hearts, drained, cut in half

Preheat oven to 350 degrees. Grease a 2-quart casserole; set aside. In a small bowl, mix together the feta cheese and breadcrumbs; set aside. In a medium saucepan, over low heat, melt the butter and cream cheese. Add the Worcestershire sauce, salt, garlic powder, cayenne pepper, Tabasco sauce and lemon juice; mix well. Add the spinach; mix well to thoroughly combine. Place a layer of artichoke hearts in the bottom of prepared casserole. Spoon on a layer of the spinach mixture. Repeat artichoke and spinach mixture layers. Top casserole with cheese and breadcrumb mixture. Bake, uncovered, for 30 minutes.

Variation: Substitute your favorite cheese for the feta.

Yield: 8 to 10 servings

Linda Hillenburg

113

Stuffed Artichokes

2 artichokes

Stuffing
2 tablespoons olive oil, divided
1 onion, chopped
1 small green bell pepper, seeded,
  finely chopped
2-3 ribs of celery, finely chopped
1 cup seasoned Italian
  breadcrumbs
1 egg, beaten
½ cup finely diced cooked ham,
  optional
¼ cup chicken broth

To prepare the artichokes, trim stems off so that they sit flat. Cut 1 to 2 inches off of the tops. Place artichokes in a large saucepan. Cover with water and boil for 45 minutes or until the base is easily pierced with a fork; drain and let cool. Using a small knife, carefully remove the center choke of artichokes and discard. Loosen leaves and spread apart. Place artichokes in a small glass baking dish. Preheat oven to 350 degrees. To prepare the stuffing, in a large skillet heat 1 tablespoon of olive oil. Add the onion, bell pepper and celery; sauté over medium heat until soft, approximately 5 minutes. Add breadcrumbs to skillet; stir to thoroughly combine. Stir in the egg, ham and as much broth as needed to make a moist mixture. Fill center of artichokes with stuffing. Place the remaining stuffing between leaves. Drizzle the remaining olive oil over tops. Pour boiling water into the baking dish to fill to a 1-inch level. Bake for 30 minutes. Allow stuffed artichokes to sit for 2 to 3 minutes before serving.

Variation: Substitute ½ pound of bulk sausage, browned and well-drained, for the ham.

Yield: 2 servings

Georgia Moncada

Grand Mère's Creamed Cauliflower

1 head of cauliflower, cleaned, left
  whole
4 tablespoons margarine
2 tablespoons flour
2 cups milk
Salt and ground black pepper,
  to taste
Paprika, to taste

Place head of cauliflower in a large saucepan or pot. Add 2 inches of water. Cover and steam over medium to high heat until fork-tender, approximately 20 minutes. (Add additional water as needed.) To prepare the sauce, melt the margarine in a small saucepan over medium heat. Add the flour; stirring until smooth. Add the milk; stirring continuously over medium to high heat, until thickened, approximately 12 to 15 minutes. Season with salt and pepper. Using 2 large forks, carefully transfer cauliflower to a serving bowl. Pour sauce over top; sprinkle with paprika. Serve immediately. *Grandma's Sunday dinner crowd pleaser.*

Yield: 4 to 6 servings

Mathilda Roberge

Sesame Green Beans

1½ pounds green beans, washed,
  ends trimmed
2 cloves of garlic, finely chopped
¼ cup soy sauce
1 tablespoon sesame oil
2 teaspoons oyster sauce
2 teaspoons lemon juice
1 teaspoon sugar
¼ teaspoon freshly ground black
  pepper
¼ cup sesame seeds, toasted

Fill a large saucepan with 2 inches of water. Add the green beans; cover and bring to a boil. Cook for 3 minutes, or just until crisp-tender. Rinse beans with cold water and drain; place in a serving bowl. In a small saucepan, combine the garlic, soy sauce, sesame oil, oyster sauce, lemon juice, sugar and pepper. Cook, over medium to high heat, until bubbles appear at the edge of pan. Watch carefully. When bubbles extend to the middle of pan, immediately remove pan from heat. Pour sauce over the beans; toss to coat. Sprinkle with the sesame seeds; re-toss. Serve beans warm or at room temperature. *A family favorite.*

Yield: 6 to 8 servings

Martino Parente

Sauterne Stuffed Mushrooms

1 pound medium-large fresh
   mushrooms, approximately
   15 to 20, cleaned
½ cup butter or margarine,
   melted, divided
¼ cup finely chopped green onions
   (white part and small amount
   of green)
¼ cup Sauterne wine, or to taste
1 cup herb-seasoned croutons,
   crushed

Preheat oven to 350 degrees. Remove stems from mushrooms; finely chop and set aside. Dip mushroom caps into the melted butter; place cap side down in a shallow baking pan. In a small skillet, over medium heat, sauté chopped mushroom stems and onions in the remaining butter until soft, approximately 5 to 7 minutes. Remove skillet from heat. Add the wine and croutons; toss lightly. Spoon mixture into mushroom caps. Bake for 10 to 15 minutes or until heated through. *An easy but elegant side dish for pasta and meat dishes.*

Yield: 6 servings

Donna Linnelli

Roasted Asparagus with Balsamic Browned Butter

2 pounds asparagus,
   approximately 40 spears,
   cleaned, ends trimmed
2-3 tablespoons olive oil
¼ teaspoon Kosher salt
⅛ teaspoon ground black pepper
2 tablespoons butter
2 teaspoons soy sauce
1 teaspoon balsamic vinegar

Preheat oven to 400 degrees. Arrange the asparagus in a single layer on a baking sheet with sides. Coat asparagus with the olive oil; season with salt and pepper. Roast for 12 minutes or until tender. In a small skillet, melt the butter over medium heat for 3 minutes until lightly browned. Remove skillet from heat; stir in the soy sauce and vinegar. Drizzle over hot roasted asparagus; serve immediately. *Our recipe testers loved this dish.*

Note: In place of the olive oil, asparagus may be coated with vegetable oil cooking spray.

Yield: 8 servings

Janice Burgett and Joanne Redondo

Asparagus with Lemon-Thyme Sauce

3 cups chicken broth
1½ pounds asparagus spears, ends
   trimmed

Lemon-Thyme Sauce
2 tablespoons olive oil, divided
1 cup chopped green onion
   (white part and small amount
   of green)
⅓ cup minced shallots
1 tablespoon minced garlic
1½ tablespoons Dijon mustard
1 tablespoon freshly squeezed
   lemon juice
2 teaspoons minced fresh thyme
½ teaspoon grated lemon peel
Salt and freshly ground black
   pepper, to taste

½ cup diced red bell peppers,
   optional

In a large pot, over medium to high heat, bring the chicken broth to a boil. Add the asparagus; cook until just tender, approximately 4 minutes. Transfer asparagus to a bowl of ice water; let cool. Reserve 1 cup of the chicken broth. Drain asparagus; pat dry and set aside. To prepare the sauce, in a nonstick skillet, over medium heat, heat 1 tablespoon of the olive oil. Add the green onion and shallot; sauté until tender, approximately 5 minutes. Add the garlic to skillet; sauté an additional 2 minutes. Stir in the reserved chicken broth, remaining 1 tablespoon of olive oil, mustard, lemon juice, thyme and lemon peel. Simmer until slightly thickened and liquid is reduced to 1¼ cups, approximately 5 minutes. Season with salt and pepper. Remove from heat; let cool to room temperature. Spoon sauce over asparagus; sprinkle with the red bell peppers.

*Note: Asparagus spears may be prepared
1 day ahead. Wrap the spears in paper
towels; seal in a plastic bag and refrigerate.
Cover and refrigerate the reserved broth.*

Yield: 8 servings

Toni Black

Roasted Asparagus

4 pounds asparagus, ends
   trimmed
¼ cup olive oil
½ teaspoon salt
¼ teaspoon freshly ground black
   pepper

Preheat oven to 400 degrees. Line a baking sheet with aluminum foil. Arrange asparagus on baking sheet in a single layer. Drizzle olive oil over asparagus; season with the salt and pepper. Bake, uncovered, for 12 to 15 minutes or until just crisp-tender, turning once. *A quick and easy side dish.*

Yield: 10 to 12 servings

Betty Gaston

Asparagus Parmesan

2 tablespoons olive oil
1 tablespoon dry white wine
1 teaspoon white vinegar
3 garlic cloves, crushed
Salt and ground black pepper,
    to taste
1¼ pounds asparagus, cleaned,
    ends trimmed
¾-1 cup grated Parmesan cheese

In a large baking dish, combine the olive oil, wine, vinegar, garlic, salt and pepper. Add the asparagus; toss to coat. Cover baking dish; let sit for 15 minutes. Preheat oven to 400 degrees. Sprinkle Parmesan cheese on a plate. Roll asparagus spears in the cheese to coat. Return asparagus to baking dish, arranging spears in a single layer. Roast for 15 to 20 minutes until lightly browned and sizzling hot; serve immediately.

Yield: 4 to 6 servings

Janice Burgett

Green Beans Italiano

1 tablespoon olive oil
1 rib of celery, diced
½ medium red bell pepper, sliced
¼-½ teaspoon dried oregano,
    to taste
1 (14½-ounce) can cut or whole
    green beans, drained
1 (15-ounce) can garbanzo beans,
    drained
Salt and ground black pepper,
    to taste

Heat a 10-inch skillet. Add the olive oil. Sauté the celery and bell pepper over medium to high heat until tender. Sprinkle with the oregano. Reduce heat to medium. Add the beans to skillet; toss well. Season with salt and pepper. Cook until beans are heated through.

Yield: 4 to 6 servings

Lauren McKenna

Broccoli with Red Peppers

1 head of broccoli, flowerettes left
    whole, stems sliced on the
    diagonal
½ red bell pepper, seeded, thinly
    sliced
1 clove of garlic, minced
1 tablespoon olive oil
Salt and ground black pepper,
    to taste
1 teaspoon lemon zest
⅓ cup chicken broth

In a large skillet, over medium to high heat, sauté the broccoli, red bell pepper and garlic in the olive oil for 2 minutes. Season with salt and pepper. Sprinkle on the lemon zest. Reduce heat to medium; add the chicken broth in small amounts, stirring frequently, until broccoli is cooked to desired tenderness, approximately 5 to 6 minutes. Serve immediately.

Yield: 4 to 6 servings

Marty Parente

Broccoli Casserole

2 tablespoons butter, divided
2 (10-ounce) packages frozen
chopped broccoli
1 cup grated mild Cheddar cheese
1 (10¾-ounce) can cream of
mushroom soup, undiluted
1 cup mayonnaise
1 small onion, finely chopped
3 eggs, beaten
¼ teaspoon ground black pepper
⅛ teaspoon nutmeg, optional

Preheat oven to 350 degrees. Grease a 2-quart casserole dish with 1 tablespoon of the butter or spray with a nonstick vegetable oil cooking spray; set aside. Cook broccoli, according to package directions, for 5 minutes; drain thoroughly. In a large mixing bowl, combine the Cheddar cheese, mushroom soup, mayonnaise, onion, eggs, pepper and nutmeg. Add the broccoli; stir gently to combine. Spread the broccoli mixture evenly into prepared casserole; dot with the remaining 1 tablespoon of butter. Bake, uncovered, for 50 to 60 minutes.

Yield: 10 servings

Rebecca Lando

Broccoli Bake

½ cup butter, divided
2 cups packaged stuffing mix
⅔ cup hot water
2 (10-ounce) packages frozen
chopped broccoli or 2 heads
fresh broccoli florets, cooked,
drained
4 tablespoons flour
1 (14½-ounce) can chicken broth
1 cup milk
Salt and freshly ground black
pepper, to taste

Preheat oven to 350 degrees. Grease a 2-quart casserole; set aside. In a medium saucepan, over low to medium heat, melt 4 tablespoons of the butter. Add the stuffing mix and hot water; stir well with a fork and set aside. Place the broccoli in prepared casserole. In a small saucepan, over medium heat, melt the remaining 4 tablespoons of butter. Whisk in the flour until smooth. Add the broth and milk; continue whisking until thoroughly combined. Season with salt and pepper. Pour sauce over top of broccoli. Spread stuffing evenly over top. Bake, uncovered, for 30 to 40 minutes.

Yield: 8 to 10 servings

Anne Krupa

Stir-Fried Spinach with Ginger and Garlic

2 teaspoons olive oil
1 teaspoon finely minced fresh
   gingerroot
1-2 teaspoons finely minced garlic,
   to taste
2 pounds fresh spinach, washed,
   drained, stems removed
Salt and ground black pepper,
   to taste

In a wok or large heavy skillet, heat the oil over medium to high heat. Stir in the gingerroot and garlic; stir-fry until fragrant and garlic is soft, approximately 1 minute. Add the spinach; stir-fry until wilted, approximately 4 to 5 minutes. Season with salt and pepper.

Yield: 6 servings

Patty Just

Zesty Spinach

2 tablespoons butter
2 tablespoons olive oil
2 pounds spinach, washed,
   drained, stems removed
2-3 teaspoons lemon zest, to taste
2-3 teaspoons lime zest, to taste
Salt and freshly ground black
   pepper, to taste

In a large skillet, over medium heat, heat the butter and olive oil. Add the spinach. Cover skillet; cook for 3 minutes. Uncover skillet; continue cooking until spinach has wilted. Remove skillet from heat. Stir in the lemon and lime zest. Season with salt and pepper. Serve immediately.

Variation: Substitute grapefruit zest for the lemon and lime zest.

Yield: 6 to 8 servings

Diane DeNardo

Spinach Squares

¼ cup butter, melted
3 eggs, beaten
1 cup flour
1 cup milk
1½ teaspoons salt
2 (10-ounce) packages chopped
   spinach, thawed, well-drained
1 pound Monterey Jack cheese,
   shredded

Preheat oven to 350 degrees. Pour the melted butter into a 13x9-inch glass baking dish. In a large bowl, combine all other ingredients. Spread spinach mixture into baking dish; stir to combine with the melted butter. Bake, uncovered, for 30 to 40 minutes until lightly browned on top. Let sit for 10 minutes. Cut into squares. *Delicious hot from the oven or served at room temperature.*

Yield: 8 to 12 servings

Susan Parente

Company Carrot Casserole

16 carrots, quartered or cut in
   strips
1 small onion, finely chopped
1 tablespoon horseradish
¾ cup mayonnaise
½ (6-ounce) package dried bread
   cubes
1-2 tablespoons butter

Preheat oven to 350 degrees. Place a steamer rack in a large pot; add 2 inches of water. Place carrots on rack. Cover pot and steam over high heat for 10 minutes or until just crisp-tender. Drain, reserving ½ cup of the liquid. In a small bowl, combine the reserved liquid, onion, horseradish and mayonnaise; mix well. In a 3-quart casserole, toss carrots with the onion mixture. Top with bread cubes; dot with butter. Bake, uncovered, for 30 minutes. *A colorful, easy and delicious side dish.*

Note: Recipe may be made ahead and refrigerated. Bring to room temperature before reheating.

Yield: 12 to 16 servings

Deborah McCarthy

Carrot Soufflé

2 pounds carrots, steamed or
   boiled until tender
6 eggs
1 cup sugar
2 tablespoons flour
2 teaspoons baking powder
2 teaspoons vanilla extract
¾ cup butter or margarine,
   melted

Topping
½ cup cornflake crumbs
4 tablespoons butter or
   margarine, melted
5 tablespoons brown sugar
Dash of cinnamon

Preheat oven to 350 degrees. Grease a 3-quart casserole; set aside. Using a food processor, purée the carrots. Add the eggs, sugar, flour, baking powder, vanilla extract and butter; process until well combined. Spread the carrot mixture into prepared casserole. In a small bowl, mix together all topping ingredients; sprinkle over carrot mixture. Bake, uncovered, for 45 to 60 minutes. *Adds sweetness and color to the meal.*

Note: An electric mixer may be used in place of the food processor.

Yield: 8 to 10 servings

Barb Dunn

Zucchini Breadcrumb Bake

3 medium zucchini, cleaned,
   quartered lengthwise
½ cup butter or margarine
1½ cups regular or Italian
   breadcrumbs

Preheat oven to 350 degrees. Line a baking sheet with foil. Place zucchini quarters, skin side down, on the foil. In a small saucepan, over low heat, melt the butter. Gradually add the breadcrumbs, stirring until smooth and spreadable. Generously spread the breadcrumb mixture over top of the zucchini. Bake, uncovered, for 20 minutes or until zucchini are soft when pierced with a fork and topping is lightly browned.

Yield: 12 servings

Tookie Wozniak

Anne's Zucchini Cakes

1½ cups seasoned breadcrumbs,
   divided, and to taste
2 cups peeled, grated zucchini,
   approximately 1 medium
   zucchini
1 teaspoon Old Bay seasoning
1 egg, beaten
1 tablespoon mayonnaise
Chopped onion, to taste, optional
Canola or vegetable oil for frying

In a medium bowl, mix together 1 cup of the breadcrumbs, zucchini, Old Bay, egg, mayonnaise and onion. If mixture is too soft, add additional breadcrumbs. Divide mixture and form into 6 (3-inch) cakes. Dip cakes in the remaining breadcrumbs to lightly coat. Heat 1-inch of canola oil in a large skillet. Fry cakes over medium heat until browned, approximately 3 to 4 minutes per side; drain well. Serve with your favorite tartar, cocktail or tomato sauce.

Yield: 6 cakes

Anne Krupa

Grandma Jenny's Eggplant Patties

1 large eggplant
4 eggs, lightly beaten
8 tablespoons grated Romano
 cheese, divided
1 cup Italian breadcrumbs
4 cloves garlic, minced
¼ cup chopped fresh parsley
2 teaspoons salt
Freshly ground black pepper,
 to taste
2-3 tablespoons olive oil
2 cups of your favorite tomato or
 marinara sauce

Preheat oven to 350 degrees. Grease a baking sheet; set aside. Quarter the eggplant lengthwise. Remove skin in 1½-inch wide sections the length of the eggplant quarters. Cut each skin section into 3-inch pieces; place on prepared baking sheet and set aside. (Skins will serve as the base of the patties.) Shred eggplant with a hand-held grater or chop very finely with a knife. Place in a colander; allow to drain, pressing out excess liquid. In a large bowl, combine the shredded eggplant, eggs, 6 tablespoons of the Romano cheese, breadcrumbs, garlic, parsley, salt and pepper. Spoon 2 tablespoons of the eggplant mixture onto center of each skin. Drizzle a small amount of the olive oil over each patty. Bake for 40 minutes. Remove from oven. Heat oven to broil. Spread 1 tablespoon of tomato sauce over each patty; sprinkle with the remaining 2 tablespoons of Romano cheese. Broil for 1 to 2 minutes until hot and bubbly. *Serve as a side dish with your favorite pasta, poultry or fish dinner.*

Note: Recipe may be made ahead and frozen in freezer bags. Bake as directed; do not broil. To serve, heat frozen patties on a greased baking sheet at 350 degrees for 10 to 15 minutes until hot. Broil as directed.

Yield: 8 to 12 patties

Pat and John Rodella

Cheese Tomatoes

3 large tomatoes, sliced ¾ to
   1-inch thick
¼-½ cup butter or margarine,
   to taste
Freshly grated Parmesan cheese,
   to taste
Salt and ground black pepper,
   to taste

Turn on oven broiler. Cover a baking sheet with foil. Place the tomato slices on baking sheet. In a small saucepan, over low heat, melt the butter. Add the cheese gradually, stirring continuously until smooth and spreadable. Spoon a generous amount of cheese mixture onto each tomato. Season with salt and pepper. Broil for 3 to 5 minutes until cheese is lightly browned.

Yield: 8 servings

Tookie Wozniak

Turnip, Carrot and Broccoli Medley

2-3 tablespoons olive oil
4 turnips, peeled, cut into
   2x¼-inch strips
4 carrots, peeled, cut into
   2x¼-inch strips
½ pound broccoli florets
Salt and freshly ground black
   pepper, to taste

In a heavy skillet, over medium heat, heat the olive oil. Add the turnips and carrots. Sauté for 2 minutes or until soft. Add the broccoli to skillet; cook, covered, for an additional 5 minutes, stirring occasionally. Season with salt and pepper. Serve immediately.

Yield: 6 to 8 servings

Toni Black

Morningside

*M*orningside, a charming well-maintained neighborhood in the East End of Pittsburgh, is said by many to be one of the city's best-kept secrets. The residential neighborhood has a flat to gently sloping topography and sits on the edge of a steep drop-off above the Allegheny River. It was so named for Morningside Valley, a deep crevice of open land that physically separates Morningside from neighboring Highland Park. This unique geography positions Morningside to catch the earliest rays of morning sunlight, henceforth its name.

The City of Pittsburgh annexed Morningside in 1868. Settled later than many city neighborhoods, Morningside was sparsely populated even in the early 1900's. It was originally part of Collins Township. Most of the area was farmland that included dairy farms belonging to the Cook, Weber, and Dieffenbacher families and a vegetable farm owned by the Reichenbeckers.

Until 1906, when the Pittsburgh Railroad built a streetcar line along Chislett Street, Morningside consisted of only 80 houses. The new public transportation to this relatively remote section of the city spurred housing construction and population growth. Many of the new residents came from Millvale and Lawrenceville to escape the industrial pollution and overcrowding of those nearby mill communities. Skilled craftsmen and laborers of German, Irish, English and Scottish descent moved into Morningside and worked as machinists, pattern makers, carpenters, and brick layers.

By 1930, 600 homes had been built and small family-owned businesses developed to support the growing community. A brickyard on Standish Street provided employment and, not coincidentally, most of Morningside's houses were constructed of brick.

In the 1950's, Italian families settled in Morningside, broadening the ethnic mix of the neighborhood. St. Raphael's Parish laid the cornerstone for its new church on March 16, 1959. Each year, the parish celebrates the Feast of St. Rocco by holding a mass in Italian that is followed by a procession through the streets.

As Morningside grew, playgrounds were built, beautifully landscaped gardens became commonplace, and well-maintained athletic fields, one with lighting for nighttime baseball, testified to Morningside's political clout. Many city firefighters, police, and other city employees had become a significant segment of the population.

Today, Morningside enjoys the distinction of being the "best dressed" Pittsburgh neighborhood during Halloween and Christmas. People drive to Morningside from all over the city to see astounding outdoor decorations and seasonal scenarios that range from the outrageous to the sublime. ♥♥

Italian Potato Balls

1½ pounds potatoes, peeled, cubed
2 egg yolks
½ cup freshly grated Parmesan
   cheese, optional
4 tablespoons finely chopped
   onion
2 tablespoons butter
¼ cup freshly chopped parsley
1 teaspoon salt
Ground white pepper, to taste
Flour for dredging
2 eggs, lightly beaten, mixed with
   2 tablespoons water
2 cups fine breadcrumbs
   (seasoning optional)
Vegetable oil for frying

In a large pot of salted water, boil potatoes until soft. Drain potatoes; place in a large mixing bowl. Using a hand held masher or electric mixer, mash the potatoes with the egg yolks and cheese. In a small skillet over low heat, sauté the onion in the butter until golden (do not brown). Add the onion, parsley, salt and pepper to potato mixture. Using a wooden spoon or spatula, mix to form a smooth paste. Roll mixture into walnut-sized balls. Roll balls in flour to lightly coat. Dip in beaten egg to moisten. Coat with breadcrumbs; set aside on waxed paper. Preheat oven to 270 degrees. Place enough oil for frying in a large skillet, approximately ½ full. Place skillet over medium heat. Oil is hot enough for frying when crackling occurs when a water drop is placed in oil. Fry potato balls in batches, turning frequently until golden and crisp. Drain on paper towels. Keep warm in oven until ready to serve.

Note: Potato balls may be prepared 1 day ahead (do not fry). Cover and refrigerate. Bring to room temperature before frying.

Yield: 6 servings; approximately 30 potato balls

Frances Reichl

Curried Potatoes

2 pounds unpeeled small yellow
   potatoes (approximately 24),
   halved or quartered
3 cups coarsely chopped cabbage
⅓ cup olive oil
1 tablespoon curry powder, or
   to taste
3 tablespoons balsamic vinegar
1 tablespoon coarse-grain mustard
1 teaspoon salt
½ teaspoon ground black pepper
¾ cup chopped celery
Fresh parsley sprigs, optional

In a large pot, bring 8 to 10 cups of water to a boil. Add potatoes; cook, uncovered, until just fork-tender, approximately 12 to 15 minutes. Using a slotted spoon, remove potatoes and place in a large bowl to cool. Add cabbage to pot; cook, covered, for 1 to 2 minutes. Drain cabbage and place in bowl with potatoes. In a small saucepan, over medium heat, heat the olive oil. Stir in curry powder; cook for 1 minute. Stir in vinegar, mustard, salt and pepper. Remove saucepan from heat. Add olive oil mixture and celery to potatoes and cabbage; toss well to coat. Cover and chill. Serve cold, garnished with fresh parsley.

Yield: 8 to 10 servings

Lila Decker

Potato Pancakes

An Austrian Dish

2½ cups shredded uncooked,
   peeled potatoes
½ cup flour
1 small onion, grated
1 egg
1 teaspoon salt
¼ teaspoon ground black pepper
Vegetable oil for frying

In a large bowl, combine the first 6 ingredients; mix well. In a large skillet, over medium heat, heat ¼ cup of oil. In batches, place ¼ cupfuls of potato mixture in skillet. Using a spatula, flatten into 4-inch pancakes. Fry pancakes until browned and crisp on underside, approximately 5 minutes. Turn; continue frying until browned and crisp on other side. Add additional oil as needed between batches (allow oil to reheat before frying). Drain pancakes on paper towels. Serve warm with sour cream or applesauce.

Yield: 12 potato pancakes

Maura Petrone

Mom's Potato Stuffing

5 pounds potatoes, peeled and
cubed
5 ribs of celery, chopped
2 onions, chopped
1 (16-ounce) loaf of white bread,
cubed
½ pound butter, melted
3 eggs, lightly beaten
1 tablespoon dried parsley
Salt, to taste
Poultry seasoning, to taste

In a large pot of salted, boiling water, cook potatoes, celery and onion until potatoes are fork-tender; drain well. Place bread in a large bowl. Pour butter over top. Add eggs and parsley; mix together with hands until all bread cubes are moistened. Add potatoes, celery and onion to bowl; mix well. Season with the salt and poultry seasoning. Fill chicken or turkey cavity with cooled stuffing prior to roasting. Leftover stuffing may be placed in a greased casserole; cover and bake at 350 degrees for 45 to 60 minutes.

Note: Mom's Potato Stuffing is also a delicious side dish for a lamb, pork or beef roast.

Yield: Approximately 16 cups

Till Kennon

Holiday Sweet Potatoes

5 large sweet potatoes, cooked,
peeled, sliced ¼-inch thick
3 tablespoons butter, chilled

Topping
⅔ cup packed brown sugar
1 tablespoon heavy cream
½ cup chopped pecans
3 tablespoons butter
½ teaspoon ground cinnamon
¼ teaspoon ground nutmeg
¼ teaspoon ground ginger
⅛ teaspoon ground cloves
⅛ teaspoon salt

Preheat oven to 350 degrees. Grease a 2-quart casserole. Layer potato slices in casserole. Dot with the butter; set aside. To prepare topping, combine all topping ingredients in a small sauce pan. Cook over medium heat, stirring, until butter is melted and topping is smooth. Spread topping evenly over potatoes. Bake for 15 to 20 minutes, or until heated through. *A wonderful addition to a holiday buffet.*

Note: Recipe may be made up to 2 days ahead. Cover tightly and refrigerate. Bring to room temperature before baking.

Yield: 6 to 8 servings

Karen Raffensperger

Twice Baked Potatoes

6 medium Idaho potatoes, washed,
   dried, skins rubbed with butter
Salt, to taste
1 (8-ounce) package cream cheese,
   softened
2 tablespoons butter, softened
½ cup hot milk
½-1 teaspoon onion salt, to taste
Freshly ground black pepper,
   to taste
Paprika, to taste
½ cup finely chopped fresh
   parsley

Preheat oven to 350 degrees. Line a baking sheet with parchment paper or foil; set aside. Salt potato skins. Using a sharp fork, prick potatoes 4 to 6 times across top. Place potatoes on prepared baking sheet; bake for 1 hour. Remove from oven and allow to cool for approximately 15 minutes. Cut potatoes in half lengthwise. Scoop out cooked potato from skins and place in a large bowl. Place potato skins back on baking sheet; set aside. Add cream cheese, butter, milk, onion salt, pepper and additional salt to bowl with potatoes; mash together well. In equal amounts, mound potato mixture into potato skins. Top with paprika and parsley. Return to oven; bake for 20 minutes.

Note: Potatoes may be prepared ahead and frozen. (Do not bake the second time.) Place prepared potatoes in zip-top plastic bags and freeze. Thaw on a baking sheet for 1 hour. Bake as directed.

Yield: 12 servings

Pat Knavish

Tarragon Roasted Potatoes

4 large Idaho potatoes, peeling
   optional
3 tablespoons olive oil
4 cloves garlic, minced
1½ tablespoons freshly chopped
   tarragon
Salt and freshly ground black
   pepper, to taste

Preheat oven to 400 degrees. Cut potatoes lengthwise into 2-inch wide wedges. Cut wedges in half. Place potatoes, olive oil, garlic and tarragon in a large bowl. Season with salt and pepper; toss to coat. Arrange potatoes in a single layer on a baking sheet with sides. Bake for 20 to 40 minutes, stirring with a metal spatula every 10 minutes, until tender and browned.

Yield: 4 to 6 servings

Julia Anna Raffensperger

Goat Cheese and Garlic Potato Gratin

1 cup half & half, divided
1 tablespoon flour
4 ounces goat cheese, crumbled
1 cup skim milk
1 teaspoon salt
¾ teaspoon freshly ground black pepper
2 cloves garlic, minced
2½ pounds Yukon Gold potatoes, peeled, thinly sliced (approximately 5 cups)

Preheat oven to 400 degrees. Coat an 11x7-inch baking dish with nonstick vegetable oil cooking spray; set aside. In a large bowl, whisk together 2 tablespoons of the half & half with the flour until smooth. Add the remaining half & half, goat cheese, milk, salt, pepper and garlic; whisk together well. Arrange ½ of the potato slices in a single layer in baking dish. Re-whisk goat cheese mixture; pour ½ of mixture over top of potato layer. Repeat with the remaining potato slices and goat cheese mixture. Bake, uncovered, until potatoes are tender and golden brown on top, approximately 1 hour.

Yield: 6 to 8 servings

Donna Caligiuri

Potatoes Williamsburg

5 large potatoes, unpeeled
1 small onion, chopped
1 cup shredded Cheddar cheese
1 (10½-ounce) can cream of chicken soup
½ cup butter, melted
1 cup sour cream
4 tablespoons chilled butter, cut into pieces
½ cup plain breadcrumbs

In a large pot of boiling, salted water, cook potatoes until fork-tender, approximately 15 to 20 minutes. Cool potatoes under cold running water; drain well. Set aside to completely cool. Preheat oven to 350 degrees. Grease a 3-quart baking dish; set aside. In a large bowl, mix together the onion, Cheddar cheese, soup, melted butter and sour cream; set aside. Peel and dice potatoes; add to bowl, stirring gently to combine. Place mixture in prepared baking dish. Top with chilled butter and breadcrumbs. Bake for 45 minutes, until bubbly and golden.

Yield: 10 servings

Karen Mitchell

Stuffed Spinach Rolls

Mashed Potato Layer
3 pounds potatoes, peeled, quartered
3 egg yolks
6 tablespoons butter, softened
¼ cup milk
Dash of nutmeg
Salt, to taste

Spinach Layer
4 tablespoons butter
⅓ cup minced white onion
3 (10-ounce) packages frozen chopped spinach, cooked according to package directions, drained thoroughly
¼ cup heavy cream
Salt and freshly ground black pepper, to taste
5 eggs, separated

Melted butter, to taste
¼ cup freshly grated Parmesan cheese
Fresh parsley sprigs

To prepare mashed potato layer, place potatoes in a large pot. Cover with water; bring to a boil and cook just until fork-tender. Drain. Using an electric mixer, mash the potatoes with the egg yolks, softened butter, milk, nutmeg and salt until smooth and creamy; cover and set aside. Preheat oven to 350 degrees. Line a 15x10-inch sided baking sheet, with waxed paper. Butter paper generously including sides; set aside. To prepare spinach layer, in a large skillet, over medium heat, melt the 4 tablespoons butter. Add onions; sauté until soft, approximately 2 minutes. Add spinach; sauté for 2 to 3 minutes. Add cream to the skillet, stirring until absorbed, approximately 3 to 4 minutes. Season with salt and pepper. Transfer spinach mixture to a large mixing bowl. Using an electric mixer, beat the 5 egg yolks, one at a time, into the spinach mixture. In a separate bowl, beat the 5 egg whites until stiff. Fold ¼ of the egg whites into the spinach mixture. Gently fold in the remaining egg whites. Spread mixture evenly onto prepared baking sheet. Bake for 20 to 25 minutes or until firm. Cover baking sheet with a dish towel. Place a second baking sheet over towel; invert baking sheets. Starting in one corner, carefully remove waxed paper. Using the dish towel, roll up spinach mixture jelly-roll fashion around the towel. Set spinach roll aside to cool. On a flat surface, un-roll cooled spinach roll. Spread evenly with the mashed potatoes. Re-roll without the towel; cover with plastic wrap and refrigerate for 1 hour or overnight. Preheat oven to 375 degrees. Generously grease a large baking sheet with butter. Slice stuffed spinach roll into ¾-inch thick slices. Arrange in a single layer on prepared baking sheet. Brush with melted butter; sprinkle on Parmesan cheese. Cover with foil; bake for 20 minutes. Remove from oven. Turn oven to broil. Uncover

Stuffed Spinach Rolls (continued)

and broil for 2 to 3 minutes or until lightly browned. Garnish with parsley sprigs and serve immediately. *Stuffed spinach rolls make an elegant presentation for dinner parties and holiday celebrations.*

Note: Recipe requires advance preparation.

Yield: 10 to 12 servings

Diane DeNardo

Elegant Stuffed Tomatoes

8 large ripe tomatoes
6 medium potatoes, peeled, cubed
½ cup heavy cream
4 tablespoons butter, softened
2 eggs, lightly beaten
¼ cup chopped scallions
Salt and ground white pepper,
    to taste
2 tablespoons butter, melted
Freshly grated Parmesan cheese
Fresh basil leaves, snipped,
    optional

Preheat oven to 400 degrees. Cut small slices off bottoms of tomatoes so they will sit flat. Cut off tops of tomatoes and scoop out the liquid and seeds. Discard bottoms, tops and insides of tomatoes. Set tomatoes in a baking dish, upside-down, to drain. In a large pot of salted water, boil potatoes until tender; drain well. Using an electric mixer, mash the potatoes with the cream and softened butter. Add the eggs slowly (to prevent curdling), mixing until smooth. Add the scallions. Season with salt and pepper. Remove tomatoes from baking dish; discard drainage. Place tomatoes back in baking dish, bottoms down. Spoon potato mixture into tomatoes to fill to heaping. Brush tops with the melted butter and sprinkle with Parmesan cheese. Bake for 10 to 15 minutes until tops are golden. Serve warm, garnished with basil.

Note: Recipe may be prepared ahead prior to topping with butter and cheese. Refrigerate in a tightly sealed container. Allow to come to room temperature. Top with the melted butter and cheese. Bake for 15 to 20 minutes, until warmed through.

Variation: For a different flavor, use crumbled feta cheese in place of the Parmesan cheese.

Yield: 8 servings

Meghan Storb

133

Potato and Leek Tart

2 large Idaho potatoes, peeled
1 (17.3-ounce) box frozen puff
   pastry, thawed
4 tablespoons butter
4 large leeks, trimmed, cleaned,
   thinly sliced
4 tablespoons heavy cream
¼ teaspoon ground nutmeg
¼ teaspoon salt, or to taste
¼ teaspoon ground black pepper,
   or to taste

In a medium pot of salted water, boil potatoes until just fork-tender. Drain and set aside to cool. Preheat oven to 350 degrees. On a lightly floured surface, roll out puff pastry sheets to a ⅛-inch thickness, pinching edges together to form a large rectangle. Transfer pastry to an 11½x17-inch ungreased baking sheet; set aside. In a large skillet, over medium heat, melt the butter. Add the leeks; sauté until tender, approximately 7 to 10 minutes. Add cream, nutmeg, salt and pepper to skillet; stir well to combine. Cook until slightly thickened, approximately 2 minutes. Spread mixture evenly over pastry. Thinly slice potatoes. Arrange potato slices over top of pastry. Bake for 30 to 40 minutes, or until heated through and lightly browned. Allow tart to cool slightly before slicing.

Yield: 10 to 12 servings

Karen Storb

Gratin Dauphinois

2 garlic cloves, halved
6 medium red potatoes, peeled,
   approximately 2 pounds
3 tablespoons butter, melted,
   divided
¾ teaspoon salt, or to taste,
   divided
¼ teaspoon ground black pepper,
   or to taste, divided
¾ cup shredded sharp Cheddar
   cheese, divided
1 cup skim milk

Preheat oven to 425 degrees. Rub an 11x7-inch baking dish with cut sides of garlic cloves and coat with nonstick vegetable oil cooking spray; set aside. Slice potatoes to ⅛-inch thickness. Arrange ½ of the potato slices over bottom of prepared baking dish. Drizzle ½ of the butter over potato slices. Sprinkle with ½ of the salt and ½ of the pepper. Top with ½ of the cheese. Repeat layering one more time. In a small saucepan over low to medium heat, bring the milk to a boil. Pour hot milk over potatoes. Bake, uncovered, for 40 minutes until top is golden and potatoes are tender.

Yield: 6 to 8 servings

Joanne Redondo

Pierogies

Polish Filled Dumplings

Dough
2 cups flour
½ teaspoon salt
1 egg, lightly beaten
1 tablespoon vegetable oil
½ cup very hot water

Potato Filling
2 cups mashed potatoes
½ medium onion, finely chopped, sautéed in butter until soft

Sauerkraut Filling
1 pound sauerkraut, rinsed, drained
1 medium onion, finely chopped, sautéed in butter until soft

Cheese Filling
2 cups crumbled farmer's cheese
1 egg, lightly beaten

Salt and ground black pepper, to taste

To prepare the dough, in a medium bowl, mix together the flour and salt. Beat together the egg and oil. Make a well in the flour. Pour egg and oil into center and, using a fork, begin to mix the dough. Add the hot water; continue mixing until a soft dough forms. On a floured surface, lightly knead dough until no longer sticky. Cover dough with plastic wrap; set aside to rest for 30 minutes. Select a filling to prepare. In a large bowl, combine desired filling ingredients; mix well. Season with salt and pepper. On a lightly floured surface, roll out dough to ⅛-inch thickness. Using a knife, biscuit cutter or an inverted glass, cut dough into 3 or 4-inch circles. Spoon a small amount of filling into center of each circle. Fold dough in half over top of filling to form a semi-circle. Using wet fingers, dampen the edges and press together to seal. Crimp edges with a fork. Working in batches, place pierogies in a large pot of boiling, salted water. Boil for 4 to 5 minutes. Pierogies will float to the top when done. (Avoid crowding the pierogies to prevent sticking.) Using a slotted spoon, remove cooked pierogies. Serve hot coated with melted butter.

Variation: In a large skillet, sauté additional onion in butter until soft. Add cooked pierogies to skillet and pan-fry until lightly browned, turning once. Serve warm.

Yield: 16 to 20 pierogies

Maura Petrone

135

Vegetable and Pinto Bean Medley

2 tablespoons olive oil
1 small onion, chopped
½ large green bell pepper, seeded,
　chopped
1 teaspoon minced garlic
1 (15-ounce) can pinto beans, with
　liquid
1 (15-ounce) can diced tomatoes
1 small zucchini, thinly sliced
　(peeling optional)
6 ounces mushrooms, thinly sliced
½ teaspoon salt
¼ teaspoon ground black pepper

In a medium skillet, over low to medium heat, heat the olive oil. Add the onion, bell pepper and garlic; sauté for 2 to 3 minutes, until onion and bell pepper soften. Place skillet mixture and all remaining ingredients in a 3-quart saucepan. Bring to a boil over medium to high heat. Decrease heat. Simmer, uncovered, stirring occasionally, until vegetables and beans are tender, approximately 30 to 40 minutes. Serve over rice, lentils or barley for a tasty vegetarian dish.

Variation: For a zestier flavor, add chopped fresh parsley, basil, oregano or cilantro.

Yield: 4 servings

Dorianne DiGregorio

Katie's Black Bean Stew

2 tablespoons olive oil
1 onion, chopped
4-6 cloves garlic, minced, to taste
1 green bell pepper, seeded,
　chopped
4 (15½-ounce) cans black beans,
　rinsed, drained
1½ tablespoons chili powder
1 teaspoon cumin
⅛ teaspoon ground cloves, or to
　taste, optional
2 cups chicken broth
1 (8-ounce) can tomato sauce
2 tablespoons chili sauce
1½ cups grated Monterey Jack
　cheese, to taste
Chopped fresh cilantro

In a large saucepan, over medium heat, heat the olive oil. Add the onion and garlic; sauté until onion is translucent. Add the green pepper; sauté until soft. Add the beans, chili powder, cumin, cloves, broth, tomato and chili sauces to pan. Simmer, stirring occasionally, over medium heat for 20 to 30 minutes. Serve topped with grated cheese and cilantro. *An easy, quick and tasty entrée.*

Yield: 6 servings

Belle Moldovan

Three Bean Vegetarian Cassoulet

1 (15-ounce) can butter beans,
   rinsed, drained
1 (15-ounce) can great Northern
   beans, rinsed, drained
1 (15-ounce) can garbanzo beans,
   rinsed, drained
1 (16-ounce) can stewed tomatoes,
   drained (juice reserved),
   chopped,
1 cup finely chopped carrots
1 cup finely chopped onions
2 cloves garlic, minced
2 teaspoons dried parsley
1 teaspoon dried basil
½ teaspoon salt
¼ teaspoon freshly ground
   black pepper
1 bay leaf

Heat a 2-quart slow cooker or crock pot to high. Add all ingredients, including reserved juice; mix together well. Cover and cook for 30 minutes. Decrease heat setting to low. Continue cooking for 5 to 6 hours, or until vegetables are tender. Remove bay leaf before serving. *Serve with white rice for a delicious meatless meal.*

Note: Cassoulet may be prepared in the oven. Place all ingredients in an ungreased 2-quart casserole. Bake, covered, for 35 to 45 minutes at 350 degrees, stirring occasionally.

Yield: 6 servings

Joanne Redondo

Four Bean Salad

Salad
1 (15-ounce) can wax beans,
   drained
1 (15-ounce) can green beans,
   drained
1 (15-ounce) can dark red kidney
   beans, rinsed, drained
1 (15-ounce) can garbanzo beans,
   rinsed, drained
2 small onions, sliced
1 red or orange bell pepper,
   seeded, diced

Dressing
½ cup canola oil
½ cup apple cider vinegar
⅔ cup sugar
½ teaspoon salt
½ teaspoon ground black pepper

Combine all salad ingredients in a large serving bowl. In a separate bowl, whisk together all dressing ingredients. Pour dressing over salad; toss to combine. Cover and refrigerate until ready to serve. *Perfect for a summer picnic.*

Yield: 10 to 12 servings

Amy Spence

Falafel

An Israeli Sandwich

2 (1-pound) cans chick peas,
    rinsed, drained
1 clove garlic, minced
1 tablespoon cumin
2 teaspoons salt
1 teaspoon cayenne pepper
1 teaspoon dried oregano
1 teaspoon coriander
½ cup flour
2 eggs, lightly beaten
Vegetable oil for frying
6 pita bread halves

Salad Ingredients
Shredded lettuce, cabbage and
    carrots
Thinly sliced radishes
Diced tomatoes

Tahini Dressing, to taste

In a medium bowl, grind, mash or chop the chick peas until very fine. Add the garlic, cumin, salt, cayenne pepper, oregano, coriander, flour and eggs. Mix well to thoroughly combine. Roll chick pea mixture into 18 (1-inch) balls. In a large skillet, heat 1 inch of oil to 390 degrees. Fry balls, in batches, until evenly browned. Drain on paper towels; cover to keep warm. To assemble Falafel, place 3 warm chick pea balls in each pita pocket half. Add desired salad ingredients. Spoon Tahini dressing over top.

Yield: 6 servings

Maura Petrone

Garfield

$\mathcal{G}$arfield lies on a steep slope of land about three and a half miles east of downtown Pittsburgh. From atop Hillcrest Street, there is a breathtaking view looking out over the East End of the city.

Garfield's history goes back to pre-Revolutionary War days when it was an Indian Territory that was claimed by English settlers as their own. The first European owners of the neighborhood were Caspar Taub and George Croghan. They acquired Garfield as part of a large land holding that also included what is today Lawrenceville, Bloomfield, East Liberty, Squirrel Hill, Oakland, and Hazelwood. Unfortunately, Croghan was heavily involved in land speculation and this proved to be financially disastrous for him—he died penniless and despised.

Joseph Conrad Winebiddle, Taub's son-in-law, inherited the land during the Revolutionary War. He built a large estate on the highest point of the area. For the next 100 years, the Winebiddle estate was one of two residences in what was then called Collins Township. Winbiddle Street is a reminder of this early history.

In 1867, Collins Township was annexed to the City of Pittsburgh and, by 1881, the estates began to be divided into smaller parcels for housing construction. The first buyer of a lot was given the privilege of naming the area. President James Garfield was being buried on the same day as the land sale. The buyer chose the name to honor the recently inaugurated president who had been shot on July 2, 1881 by a disappointed office-seeker.

Irish immigrants were the first to settle in Garfield, followed later by Slavic and German immigrants. In the twentieth century, Italian and African-American families began settling there. Most of the residents were workers in the foundries and factories along the Allegheny River in Lawrenceville and in nearby stores and warehouses.

As the Catholic population of Garfield grew, St. Lawrence O'Toole parish was founded. The first church, located on Kincaid Street, was dedicated on June 27, 1897. The modern church on Penn Avenue was built in 1965.

Today, Garfield's business district, located along Penn Avenue, is transforming into an arts and cultural district lined with a diverse blend of cafes, ethnic restaurants, galleries, and a theatre company. There are also non-profit service organizations with world-view perspectives including the Thomas Merton Center and Global Links. Murals painted by both local students and professional artists add a colorful palette to the neighborhood. ♥♥

Winston's Cornish Hens

4 Cornish hens
Salt, to taste

Stuffing
6 slices of bacon
1 cup finely chopped carrots
¼ cup minced fresh parsley
¼ teaspoon dried savory
Dash of ground black pepper,
  or to taste
3 cups bread cubes
½ teaspoon chicken bouillon
  granules
¼ cup hot water

Canola oil

Basting Sauce
½ cup dry red wine
2 tablespoons butter, melted
3 tablespoons orange juice

Serving Sauce
2 tablespoons light brown sugar
2 tablespoons cornstarch
1 teaspoon chicken bouillon
  granules
¼ teaspoon salt

Preheat oven to 375 degrees. Clean cavities of Cornish hens and pat dry with paper towels. Season cavities with salt. Set hens aside. To prepare the stuffing, in a large skillet, cook bacon until crisp. Remove bacon; drain on paper towels. Crumble; set aside. Drain skillet, reserving 2 tablespoons of the bacon fat. Sauté the carrots in reserved fat until tender; remove skillet from heat. Stir the bacon, parsley, savory and pepper into carrots. Stir in the bread cubes. Dissolve the ½ teaspoon chicken bouillon in hot water; drizzle over bread cubes and toss well. Allow stuffing to cool to room temperature. Fill hen cavities with bread stuffing. Pull neck skin, if present, to back of each hen. Twist wing tips under backs to hold neck skin in place. Place hens, breast side up, on a rack in a shallow roasting pan. Brush with a small amount of canola oil. Cover hens loosely with foil. Roast for 30 minutes. To prepare the basting sauce, in a small bowl, mix together the wine, butter and orange juice. Uncover hens and brush with basting sauce. Roast, uncovered, for 1 additional hour or until drumsticks twist easily in socket. Brush hens with basting sauce 3 to 4 additional times during the last hour of roasting. Remove hens to a serving platter; keep warm. To prepare serving sauce, pour drippings from roasting pan into a large measuring cup. Skim fat from surface. Stir in the remaining basting sauce. Add water, if necessary, to make 1½ cups of liquid. Transfer mixture to a small saucepan. Add the brown sugar, cornstarch, 1 teaspoon chicken bouillon and salt. Cook until slightly thickened, stirring, approximately 2 to 4 minutes. Strain sauce into a serving bowl. Serve sauce on the side with hens.

Yield: 4 servings

Winston McKenna

Alfredo Chicken with Prosciutto and Italian Greens

6 large skinless, boneless chicken breast halves

Breading
1 cup flour
Salt and freshly ground black pepper, to taste
4 eggs
¼ cup milk
2 cups Italian seasoned breadcrumbs
½ cup freshly grated Parmesan cheese

1 cup canola or olive oil, and as needed

Italian Greens
3 tablespoons olive oil
2 heads of escarole, washed, drained and torn into small pieces
4 cloves garlic, minced
Salt and freshly ground black pepper, to taste

Alfredo Sauce
¼ cup butter
¾ cup freshly grated Parmesan cheese
½ cup heavy whipping cream
½ teaspoon freshly ground black pepper

½ pound prosciutto, thinly sliced
12 (1-ounce) slices Muenster cheese

To prepare the chicken, place each chicken breast half between 2 sheets of wax paper. Using a meat mallet or rolling pin, pound to ¼-inch thickness. Cut each breast half in half; set the 12 pieces aside. To prepare the breading, in a small bowl, combine the flour, salt and pepper. In a separate bowl, whisk the eggs and milk together. In a third bowl, combine the breadcrumbs and Parmesan cheese. In a large skillet or electric frying pan, heat the oil to 375 degrees or until oil bubbles vigorously when a bread cube is placed in pan. While pan is heating, dredge each chicken piece in the flour mixture. Dip in the egg mixture and then coat with breadcrumb mixture. Place coated chicken in skillet; fry until golden brown, approximately 2 to 3 minutes. Transfer to paper towels; drain. If needed, discard used oil, wipe skillet clean, add new oil and reheat skillet. To prepare the Italian greens, in a large skillet, heat olive oil for 2 minutes over low heat. Place the escarole in skillet; cover with lid; cook on medium to low heat for a ½ hour. Drain excess water from skillet. Add the garlic, salt and pepper. On low heat, cook until liquid completely evaporates and escarole cooks to a ¼ of its starting amount. Remove from heat and let cool. Preheat oven to 350 degrees. To prepare the Alfredo Sauce, in a medium saucepan, melt the butter. Add the Parmesan cheese. Stir in the whipping cream and pepper; heat until boiling, stirring continuously. To assemble, spray a 13x9-inch jelly-roll pan with nonstick vegetable oil cooking spray. Pour Alfredo Sauce evenly over the pan. Place chicken breasts on top of sauce. Spread greens evenly over top of each chicken breast. Top each chicken piece with 1½ to 2 pieces of prosciutto. Top each with 1 slice of cheese. Cover

Alfredo Chicken with Prosciutto and Italian Greens (continued)

pan with foil; bake for 35 minutes. Remove foil; bake an additional 10 minutes. Serve with your favorite pasta. *A beautiful presentation.*

Yield: 6 to 8 servings

Joanne Redondo

Marinated Fried Chicken with Green Onion Dressing

A Japanese Entrée

Green Onion Dressing
3 tablespoons soy sauce
3 tablespoons sugar
3 tablespoons white vinegar
1 red bell pepper, seeded, diced
½ Asian green onion, diced
1 teaspoon chopped fresh ginger

1¼ pounds skinless, boneless chicken thighs
1 tablespoon Japanese sake
1 tablespoon soy sauce
3-5 tablespoons potato or corn starch
Vegetable oil for frying
½ head of lettuce, cleaned, dried, and chopped
2 Japanese or seedless cucumbers, peeled, cut into very thin slices

To prepare the dressing, in a small bowl combine all dressing ingredients. Mix well; set aside. Using a fork, prick holes all over the chicken thighs; cut into 1½-inch pieces. In a medium bowl, stir together the sake and soy sauce. Add the chicken pieces to bowl and rub with the sake-soy marinade. Let sit for 15 minutes. Remove chicken from marinade. Pat dry with paper towels and place in a bowl. Discard any remaining marinade. Lightly dust chicken pieces with the potato starch. Using a deep fryer or large skillet, heat the oil to 330 to 340 degrees. In batches, fry the chicken slowly until completely cooked through, approximately 10 to 12 minutes. To serve, place lettuce and cucumbers on a serving platter. Top with chicken pieces and the *Green Onion Dressing.*

Note: Japanese cooking ingredients are found at Asian food markets or in the specialty food section of your grocery store.

Variation: The Green Onion Dressing is also delicious served over chilled tofu.

Yield: 4 servings

Hiroko Nemoto

143

Roast Chicken with Apples and Cranberries

1 (5-pound) roasting chicken
4 tablespoons butter, softened
Salt and freshly ground black
  pepper, to taste
4 Granny Smith apples, peeled,
  cored, cut into large chunks
2 red onions, thinly sliced
4 cloves garlic, chopped
1 cup cranberries
2 tablespoons chopped fresh
  ginger
1 tablespoon chopped fresh
  rosemary
Juice of 1 lemon
1 cup chicken broth
1 cup apple cider
¼ cup balsamic vinegar
¼ cup honey
¼ cup assorted chopped fresh
  herbs (parsley, sage, thyme)

Preheat oven to 425 degrees. Rub the chicken all over with butter; season inside and out with salt and pepper. Tie the chicken legs together. In a 7-quart roasting pan or Dutch oven, mix together the apples, onions, garlic, cranberries, ginger, rosemary and lemon juice. Place chicken in center of pan surrounded by the apple mixture. Add the chicken stock. Cover and roast for 1 hour. Remove pan from oven; baste with the juices. Add the apple cider. Reduce oven temperature to 375 degrees; roast, uncovered, for 45 to 60 additional minutes. Remove chicken from pan; cover with foil and allow to rest. Add the balsamic vinegar, honey and the assorted fresh herbs to pan. Place pan on stove top over medium to high heat. Boil until liquid is reduced by half. Skim off any fat; season with salt and pepper. Slice chicken and place on a serving platter. Serve with fruit and sauce on the side. *A wonderful centerpiece for a delicious home-cooked meal.*

Variation: Stir 1 cup of toasted chopped walnuts or pecans into the sauce just before serving.

Yield: 4 to 6 servings

Anne McCafferty

Kotopoulo Riganato

Chicken Oregano

3 pounds chicken parts or breast
   halves
Juice of 2 lemons
½ cup olive oil
1 tablespoon salt
2 teaspoons ground black pepper
1 tablespoon dried oregano
1 tablespoon minced garlic
¼ cup water
4 tablespoons chilled butter, sliced
Oregano sprigs, optional

Place chicken in a 3-quart casserole or 13x9-inch baking dish. In a small bowl, whisk together the lemon juice, olive oil, salt, pepper, oregano and garlic. Pour lemon mixture over the chicken; cover and refrigerate overnight. Preheat oven to 350 degrees. Add the water to casserole. Lay the butter slices over top of chicken. Bake, uncovered, for approximately 30 minutes or until the skin begins to brown. Cover casserole; return to oven for 15 minutes or until chicken is cooked through. Uncover casserole; bake until chicken is golden brown. Garnish with oregano sprigs. Serve with Pilafi, found in the *Uniquely Pittsburgh* section of this book.

Note: Chicken may also be broiled or grilled. Baste occasionally with the marinade. Discard leftover marinade before serving.

Yield: 4 servings

St. Nicholas Cathedral
Greek Food Festival, Oakland
neighborhood of Pittsburgh, PA

Chicken with Grapes and Blue Cheese

4 (6 to 7-ounce) boneless, skinless
  chicken breast halves
1 (3-ounce) package cream cheese,
  softened
2 tablespoons crumbled blue
  cheese
⅓ cup flour
1 teaspoon salt, and to taste
1 teaspoon black pepper, and
  to taste
¼ cup olive oil
16 pearl onions
2 tablespoons minced garlic
2 cups white wine
2 tablespoons honey
1 tablespoon chopped fresh
  rosemary
32 seedless red or green grapes
2 tablespoons unsalted butter

Preheat oven to 425 degrees. Place each chicken breast half between 2 sheets of plastic wrap. Pound with a meat mallet or rolling pin until ¼-inch thick. In a small bowl, using a fork, mix together the cream cheese and blue cheese until smooth. Place equal amounts of the cheese mixture over top of each chicken breast half. Fold each chicken breast half in half; place between plastic wrap and pound edges of chicken to seal. Remove plastic wrap. In a small bowl, mix together the flour, 1 teaspoon of salt and 1 teaspoon of pepper. Dredge chicken breast halves in flour mixture. In a large ovenproof skillet, over medium heat, heat the olive oil. Add the chicken; sauté until lightly browned on each side. Transfer chicken to a plate. In the same skillet, sauté the onions and garlic for 1 to 2 minutes. Do not let garlic burn. Deglaze pan with the wine, over high heat, until liquid is reduced by half. Stir in the honey; return chicken to skillet. Sprinkle with rosemary. Place skillet in oven; bake for 10 minutes. Add the grapes; bake for 5 additional minutes. Remove skillet from oven; transfer chicken to a serving platter. Add the butter to skillet; season with additional salt and pepper. Spoon hot sauce over the chicken.

Yield: 4 servings

Barb Dunn

Chicken Marbella

1 bulb of garlic, peeled
½ cup balsamic or red wine
    vinegar
½ cup olive oil
2½-3 pounds boneless, skinless
    chicken breast, cut into 2-inch
    pieces
1 cup pitted prunes
½ cup pitted Spanish green olives
½ cup capers with 2 tablespoons
    of the jar liquid
¼ cup dried oregano
6 bay leaves
1 cup dry white wine
½-1 cup brown sugar, to taste
¼ cup finely chopped Italian flat
    leaf parsley
Salt and freshly ground black
    pepper, to taste

Using a blender, purée the garlic with the vinegar and olive oil. In a large bowl or zip-top plastic bag, combine the chicken, garlic mixture, prunes, olives, capers and juice, oregano, and bay leaves. Cover bowl; marinate in refrigerator overnight. Preheat oven to 350 degrees. Arrange the chicken in a single layer in a shallow baking dish. Pour the marinade over chicken. Add the wine; sprinkle brown sugar over top. Bake for 45 to 60 minutes until chicken is cooked through. Using a slotted spoon, transfer chicken and prunes to a serving platter; sprinkle with the parsley. Season with salt and pepper. Remove bay leaves and serve pan juice in a gravy boat. *A great make-ahead dish for entertaining.*

Note: Requires advance preparation.

Variation: Substitute cilantro for the Italian flat leaf parsley.

Yield: 6 servings

Susan Limoncelli and Mary Pitcher

Zucchini-Chicken Casserole

Nonstick butter flavored cooking spray

1½ pounds skinless, boneless chicken breast, cut into 1-inch pieces

¼-½ cup flour

4-5 medium zucchinis, sliced or cut into 1-inch pieces, peeling optional

1 large onion, thinly sliced

1 (28-ounce) can diced seasoned tomatoes

1-2 tablespoons dried oregano, to taste

Salt and freshly ground black pepper, to taste

1 (14½-ounce) can chicken broth, to taste (see note)

1½ cups white or brown instant rice

Freshly grated Parmesan cheese, to taste

Coat a very large skillet with nonstick butter-flavored cooking spray. Place the chicken in a medium mixing bowl; lightly sprinkle with flour; toss to coat. Heat the skillet. Add the chicken; brown over medium to high heat. Remove chicken pieces and set aside. In the same skillet, add the zucchini, onion and tomatoes. Stirring occasionally, cook over medium heat until soft, approximately 10 to 12 minutes. Season with the oregano, salt and pepper; mix well. Add the broth. Return the chicken to skillet; mix well. Cook for an additional 3 to 5 minutes. Add the rice, stirring to completely combine. Remove skillet from heat; cover tightly. Allow rice to absorb the liquid, approximately 5 to 7 minutes. To serve, sprinkle with the Parmesan cheese. *Serve with salad and an iced beverage for a tasty light summer meal.*

Note: If there is a lot of liquid in the skillet after cooking the vegetables, add broth sparingly.

Yield: 4 to 6 servings

Patricia Faub

Classic Chicken Divan

2 (10-ounce) packages frozen
   broccoli spears
½ cup butter
¾ cup flour
½ teaspoon salt
Ground black pepper, to taste
4 cups chicken broth
1 cup half & half or whipping
   cream
½ cup dry white wine
6-8 skinless, boneless chicken
   breast halves, broiled or
   pan-fried
6 tablespoons freshly grated
   Parmesan cheese, divided

Preheat oven to 350 degrees. Cook the broccoli according to package directions; drain well. Arrange cooked broccoli in a 10x15-inch baking dish. In a medium saucepan, over low to medium heat, melt the butter. Blend in the flour, salt and pepper. Add the chicken broth. Cook, stirring, until mixture thickens and bubbles. Stir in the half & half and wine; remove from heat. Pour half of the sauce over the broccoli. Layer the cooked chicken over top. Stir 4 tablespoons of Parmesan cheese into the remaining sauce; pour over chicken. Sprinkle the remaining 2 tablespoons of Parmesan cheese over top. Bake for 20 minutes or until heated through. Increase oven temperature to broil. Broil for 5 minutes or until sauce is golden. Serve over your favorite pasta.

Yield: 6 to 8 servings

Francine Marthens

149

Grilled Chicken with Pesto and Marinated Tomatoes

6 boneless, skinless chicken breast
  halves
⅔ cup homemade or prepared
  basil pesto
3 tablespoons lemon juice, divided
3 tablespoons extra-virgin olive oil
1½ teaspoons red wine vinegar
1 clove garlic, minced
1 generous teaspoon Dijon
  mustard
2 tablespoons chopped fresh basil
Salt and freshly ground black
  pepper, to taste
4 ripe plum tomatoes, seeded,
  coarsely chopped

Place each chicken breast half between 2 sheets of plastic wrap. Using a smooth meat mallet or rolling pin, pound to an even thickness. In a small bowl, combine pesto and 2 tablespoons of the lemon juice. Arrange the chicken in a single layer in a shallow dish. Rub pesto mixture over chicken; set aside and allow to marinate for 30 minutes. In small bowl, combine the olive oil, vinegar, garlic, mustard, basil, salt, pepper and remaining 1 tablespoon of lemon juice; mix well. Add tomatoes to bowl; toss to coat and set aside. Prepare outdoor grill. Remove chicken from pesto marinade. Shake gently to allow excess marinade to drip off. Season with additional salt. Grill the chicken, turning once, until golden on both sides and cooked through. Transfer to a serving platter. Spoon tomato mixture over top. Serve hot.

Variation: The marinated tomatoes are also delicious served on fresh Italian or French bread.

Yield: 6 servings

Martino Parente

Chicken with Blue Bird Sauce

2 tablespoons butter
4 boneless, skinless chicken breast halves, lightly pounded, dusted with flour

Blue Bird Sauce
3 tablespoons butter
3 tablespoons flour
1½ cups milk
4 ounces blue cheese, crumbled
1 tablespoon herb peppercorns

In a large skillet, over medium heat, melt the 2 tablespoons of butter. Add the chicken breasts; cook, turning once, until golden brown on both sides and cooked through. Remove chicken from heat; cover and keep warm. To prepare the sauce, in a small saucepan over medium heat, melt the 3 tablespoons of butter. Add the flour and milk; stir continuously until thickened, approximately 4 to 5 minutes. Add the blue cheese and herb peppercorns; stir until cheese melts and sauce is smooth. Immediately pour sauce over warm chicken. Serve over pasta.

Note: If desired, strain sauce before serving to remove peppercorns.

Yield: 4 servings

Marc Storb

Chicken Saltimbocca

6 large boneless, skinless chicken breast halves
6 (1-ounce) slices baked ham
3 (1-ounce) slices mozzarella cheese, halved
1 medium ripe tomato, seeded, chopped
½-1 cup dry fine breadcrumbs
2 tablespoons freshly grated Parmesan cheese
2 tablespoons snipped fresh parsley
½ teaspoon crushed dried sage
2 tablespoons butter or margarine, melted

Preheat oven to 350 degrees. Spray a shallow baking dish with nonstick vegetable oil cooking spray; set aside. Using a sharp knife, slice through one edge of each chicken breast half to create a deep pocket ¾-way through. Top each slice of ham with a slice of cheese and 1 teaspoon of tomato. Fold in half; place inside chicken pockets. In a small bowl, combine the breadcrumbs, Parmesan cheese, parsley and sage. Dip chicken breasts in the butter; roll in breadcrumb mixture. Arrange chicken in prepared baking dish; bake for 40 to 50 minutes until cooked through. *Delicious served with Charred Tomato Sauce found in the Beverages, Sauces & Marinades section of this cookbook.*

Yield: 6 servings

Donna Linnelli

Our Favorite Vegetable Chicken Pot Pie

Crust

2½ cups flour
2 tablespoons chopped fresh
    parsley
1 tablespoon chopped fresh thyme
1 teaspoon salt
1 teaspoon sugar
½ cup chilled butter, cut into
    ½-inch pieces
½ cup chilled shortening, cut into
    ½-inch pieces
5-7 tablespoons cold water

Filling

4 pounds chicken, with bones,
    with or without skin
6 cups low-salt chicken broth
1 pound small red potatoes,
    halved or quartered
3 carrots, peeled, cut into ½-inch
    pieces
2 ribs of celery, cut into ½-inch
    pieces
9 ounces baby spinach
1 (4 or 5-ounce) can peas, drained

Sauce

¼ cup butter
3 medium leeks (white and 1-inch
    of greens), rinsed and cut into
    ½-inch pieces
2 large shallots, finely chopped
2 tablespoons chopped fresh
    thyme
½ cup flour
½ cup dry white wine, optional
½ cup heavy cream
Salt and ground black pepper,
    to taste

Butter a 4-quart casserole or baking dish; set aside. To prepare the crust, using a food processor, pulse together the flour, parsley, thyme, salt and sugar. Add the butter and shortening; process until mixture resembles coarse meal. Place mixture in a large mixing bowl. Add the cold water, one tablespoon at a time, mixing with a fork until dough starts to form a ball. Shape dough into a flat rectangle; cover with plastic wrap and refrigerate for at least 30 minutes. To prepare the filling, place chicken and broth in a large heavy pot over medium heat. If needed, add just enough water to cover chicken. Bring to a boil. Reduce heat and simmer, covered, for 20 minutes or until chicken is just cooked through. Using tongs, remove chicken to a plate; set aside to cool. Add the potatoes, carrots and celery to pot. Simmer, uncovered, for 10 minutes or until potatoes are tender but firm when pierced with a fork. Using a slotted spoon, transfer potatoes and vegetables to prepared casserole. Add the spinach and peas to pot; cook for 1 minute or until spinach wilts. Using a slotted spoon, transfer the spinach and peas to a colander; drain well and add to casserole. Remove the bones and skin from chicken; discard. Cut chicken into ½-inch pieces. Transfer to casserole; mix with the potatoes and vegetables. To prepare the sauce, strain liquid from pot and reserve 4 cups. Skim fat from top of reserved liquid; set aside. Using the same pot, over medium heat, melt the butter. Add the leeks, shallots and thyme; sauté over medium heat for 8 minutes, or until leeks are tender. Add the flour gradually, whisking for 2 minutes. Add the 4 cups of reserved liquid and the wine.

Our Favorite Vegetable Chicken Pot Pie (continued)

Bring to a boil, whisking continuously. Add the cream; boil for 5 minutes, whisking frequently, until the sauce thickens and coats a spoon. Season with salt and pepper. Pour ½ of the sauce into casserole; mix well. Add additional sauce to just reach top of chicken and vegetables. (Do not overfill.) Let casserole mixture cool for 30 to 45 minutes. Preheat oven to 400 degrees. Allow the chilled dough to soften slightly. On a floured surface, roll dough to ½-inch larger than the casserole. Place dough over casserole. Tuck dough edges inside of casserole. Use any leftover dough to cut out cookie cutter shapes; wet bottoms with water or milk and place on top of pot pie. Cut slits in dough to allow steam to escape. Place casserole on a baking sheet. Bake in top ⅓ of the oven for 50 minutes or until sauce is bubbling and top is lightly browned. *Worth the time and effort!*

Note: Dough may be made up to 2 days ahead; wrap tightly and refrigerate. Filling and sauce may be made 1 day ahead; mix together as instructed. Cover tightly and refrigerate. Do not assemble pot pie until ready to bake.

Yield: 8 servings

Antonia DeNardo Piccoli

Orange and Ginger Glazed Chicken

½ cup hoisin sauce
2 tablespoons soy sauce
2 tablespoons minced fresh ginger
2 cloves garlic, minced
Juice of 2 oranges
Zest of 2 oranges
4 pounds skinless chicken
    drumsticks or thighs
4 tablespoons finely chopped
    scallions, optional

Preheat oven to 400 degrees. Line a shallow 15x10-inch baking dish with aluminum foil; set aside. Line broiler pan with aluminum foil; set aside. In a medium bowl, whisk together the Hoisin and soy sauces, ginger, garlic, orange juice and zest. Dip each piece of chicken into the sauce. Place in the prepared baking dish. Pour the remaining sauce evenly over chicken. Bake on the highest oven rack for 30 to 40 minutes or until the chicken is cooked through. Transfer chicken to prepared broiling pan. Baste with the sauce. Heat oven to broil. Broil for approximately 5 minutes, turning once. The chicken is done when browned and the sauce has formed a glaze. Transfer to a serving platter; garnish with the scallions.

Note: Organic low-sodium Hoisin sauce provides the best flavor. The orange and ginger sauce may also be used to prepare country style ribs.

Yield: 6 servings

Denise O'Connor

Dae's Chicken in Phyllo

Marinade
1 cup dry white wine
½ cup olive oil
3 cloves garlic, minced
1 bay leaf
2 teaspoons dried oregano
Salt and freshly ground black
  pepper, to taste

12 boneless, skinless chicken
  breast halves

Filling
⅓ cup finely chopped scallions
  (white part and small amount
  of green)
¼ cup dry white wine
¾ pound feta cheese, crumbled
3 tablespoons freshly grated
  Romano cheese

1 (1-pound) package phyllo
1½ cups butter (no substitutions)

To prepare the marinade, combine all marinade ingredients in a large bowl; mix well. Pierce chicken breasts with a fork; add to bowl. Cover; marinate overnight in the refrigerator. Preheat oven to 350 degrees. To prepare the filling, in a small skillet, over low heat, sauté scallions in wine until soft. In a medium bowl, combine the feta and Romano cheeses. Add the scallions; mix to combine and set aside. In a small saucepan, melt the butter. Open phyllo package. Unfold phyllo sheets and lay flat on a clean surface; cover with a damp towel to prevent phyllo from drying out. Place 1 sheet of phyllo on a work surface. Generously brush with melted butter. Place a second sheet on top; brush with melted butter. Place 1 chicken breast half on top of the 2 phyllo sheets. Spread 2 tablespoons of filling on top of chicken. Roll 1 end of phyllo over top of chicken; fold in sides. Continue rolling phyllo to close packet. Place seam side down on an ungreased baking sheet with sides. Brush top of roll with additional melted butter. Repeat for remaining chicken breast halves. Discard marinade. Bake for 1 hour or until phyllo is a deep golden brown. *Serve with a salad of mixed field greens, toasted walnuts and raspberry vinaigrette for a special luncheon.*

Note: Recipe requires advance preparation. The Chicken in Phyllo packets may be individually frozen before baking. Wrap in plastic wrap and then in aluminum foil. Defrost in refrigerator prior to baking.

Yield: 12 servings

Dae Machin

Easy Turkey Pot Pie

Crust
3 cups sifted flour
1½ cups shortening
1 teaspoon salt
1 large egg, beaten
1 tablespoon white vinegar
6-7 tablespoons ice water

Filling
4 tablespoons butter
¼ cup flour
2 tablespoons chicken bouillon granules dissolved in 2 cups boiling water
1 cup milk
3 cups cooked turkey, shredded or cut into 1-inch pieces
5 medium baking potatoes, microwaved with skins on, cooled, peeled, cut into 1-inch cubes
1 cup frozen peas and carrots, thawed, drained
½ teaspoon ground black pepper
½ teaspoon salt

To prepare crust, in a large mixing bowl, combine the flour, shortening and salt with a pastry blender or 2 knives until crumbly. In a small bowl, beat together the egg, vinegar and ice water with a fork. Add egg mixture to flour mixture. Use a dough mixer or fork to combine. Roll ⅓ of the dough between 2 pieces of lightly floured waxed paper to form a 13x9-inch crust; set aside. Freeze remaining dough. Preheat oven to 425 degrees. Spray a 13x9-inch baking dish with nonstick vegetable oil cooking spray; set aside. To prepare filling, in a Dutch oven, over medium heat, melt the butter. Add the flour, whisking continuously for 3 minutes until smooth and bubbly. Gradually add the chicken bouillon and milk, stirring, until mixture thickens and boils. Remove from heat; add remaining filling ingredients. Pour filling into prepared baking dish. Top with crust. Using a fork, prick top of crust all over to vent and allow steam to escape. Bake for 20 minutes or until crust is golden brown and filling is bubbly. Let rest for 10 minutes before serving.

Yield: 8 servings; dough for 3 pot pies
Cathryn Yackovich

Turkey Chili

1½ pounds lean ground turkey
2 medium onions, chopped
½ red bell pepper, seeded, chopped
½ orange bell pepper, seeded, chopped
1 (1.25-ounce) package hot or mild chili seasoning mix
3 bay leaves
2 teaspoons salt
1 teaspoon cayenne pepper
2 teaspoons chili powder
1 teaspoon paprika
1 (28-ounce) can crushed tomatoes
1 (15½-ounce) can black beans, rinsed, drained
1 (15½-ounce) can navy beans, rinsed, drained
Tortilla chips
Grated sharp Cheddar cheese

Spray a large pot with nonstick vegetable oil cooking spray. Add the turkey, onion, and bell peppers. Cook, stirring, over medium heat until turkey browns. Drain pot if necessary. Add the chili seasoning mix, bay leaves, salt, cayenne pepper, chili powder, paprika and tomatoes. Cook, covered, over low heat for 30 minutes. Add the beans; cook, covered, for an additional 1 hour, stirring occasionally. Remove bay leaves. To serve, place tortilla chips in bottoms of individual serving bowls. Add chili and top with Cheddar cheese.

Yield: 6 to 8 servings

Cindy McKenna

Hungarian Paprikas Cirke

Paprika Chicken

2 tablespoons vegetable oil
1 onion, chopped
½ green bell pepper, seeded, diced
1 medium tomato, diced
3 tablespoons sweet Hungarian paprika
1 cup chicken broth or water
2-3 pounds chicken parts
1 cup sour cream

In a large skillet, over medium heat, heat the oil. Add the onions; sauté until golden brown. Add the bell pepper, tomato, paprika and chicken broth; stir to combine. Add the chicken. Cook, covered, for 45 minutes or until chicken is tender. In a small bowl, combine the sour cream and 4 tablespoons of hot liquid from the skillet. Pour mixture over the chicken. Cook 1 additional minute; transfer to a serving platter. *Serve with spatzle or halushki for a traditional Hungarian dinner.*

Yield: 4 to 6 servings

Maura Petrone

Chicken Kiev

Ukrainian Stuffed Chicken

**4 skinless, boneless chicken breast
  halves**
4 tablespoons cold butter
½ teaspoon salt
¼ teaspoon ground black pepper
**1 tablespoon chopped fresh
  parsley**
¼ cup flour
1 egg, beaten
¼ cup breadcrumbs
¼ cup vegetable or canola oil

To prepare the chicken, place each chicken breast half between 2 sheets of plastic wrap. Using a smooth meat mallet or rolling pin, pound chicken halves to ¼-inch thickness. Divide butter into 4 pieces and roll each piece into an oval shape. In a small bowl, combine the salt, pepper and parsley. Roll each butter oval in the parsley mixture. Add flour to remaining parsley mixture; set aside. Place 1 butter oval in center of each chicken breast half. Fold 3 edges of chicken breast half over butter oval and carefully roll up toward 4th edge; secure with pick. Roll chicken breast halves in parsley-flour mixture. Dip in the egg, coating all sides. Roll in breadcrumbs to lightly coat. Preheat oven to 350 degrees. In a large skillet, heat the oil. Cook the chicken for 10 minutes. Turn and cook an additional 5 minutes, or until browned. Transfer chicken to a baking dish; bake for 15 minutes. *Serve with potato pancakes, pierogies or cabbage and noodles for a traditional Ukrainian dinner.*

Yield: 4 servings

Maura Petrone

Balsamic Chicken with Almonds and Peppers

6 skinless, boneless chicken breast halves
2½ tablespoons olive oil, divided
2 large red bell peppers, seeded, cut into 2-inch strips
1 large yellow bell pepper, seeded, cut into 2-inch strips
1 large orange bell pepper, seeded, cut into 2-inch strips
⅔ cup raisins, optional
½ cup plus 2 tablespoons premium balsamic vinegar, or to taste, divided
3 teaspoons sugar
½ teaspoon salt
¼ teaspoon freshly ground black pepper
¼ cup slivered almonds, toasted
½ cup dry breadcrumbs
½ cup freshly grated Parmesan cheese
½ cup flour
3 egg whites
2 tablespoons water

Place each chicken breast half between 2 sheets of plastic wrap. Pound with a smooth meat mallet or rolling pin to ¼-inch thickness; set aside. In a large nonstick skillet, over medium to high heat, heat 2 teaspoons of the olive oil. Add the bell peppers; sauté for 8 minutes. Add the raisins; sauté for 1 additional minute. Add ½ cup of the balsamic vinegar, sugar, salt and black pepper; sauté for 1 additional minute. Remove skillet from heat; stir in the almonds. Set bell pepper mixture aside; keep warm. In a medium bowl, combine the breadcrumbs and cheese. Dredge each chicken breast half in the flour. Dip in the egg whites and coat with breadcrumb mixture. In a large nonstick skillet, over medium heat, heat the remaining 2 tablespoons of the olive oil. Add the chicken; cook for approximately 8 minutes on each side until cooked through. Remove skillet from heat. Transfer chicken to a serving platter; top with the bell pepper mixture and keep warm. Add the remaining 2 tablespoons of balsamic vinegar and the water to skillet; stir with a wooden spoon to loosen browned bits. Spoon drippings over chicken. Serve with couscous or rice.

Yield: 6 servings

JoAnne Redondo

159

Highland Garden Club Jambalaya

2 tablespoons olive oil
2 onions, chopped
1 green bell pepper, seeded, chopped
6-8 ribs of celery with leaves, chopped
1 whole chicken, skinned, cut up
½ pound cooked ham, cubed
1 pound kielbasa or Cajun-style sausage, cut into ¼-inch slices
1-2 quarts boiling water
2 tablespoons instant chicken bouillon granules
1 (12-ounce) jar of spaghetti sauce
Cajun-style seasoning, to taste
3-4 cups instant rice

In a large stockpot, heat the oil. Add the onions, bell pepper, and celery; sauté until soft. Add the chicken; cook, turning, until lightly browned. Add the ham and kielbasa to stockpot. Add the boiling water, bouillon and spaghetti sauce. Season with the Cajun-style seasoning. Lower heat and simmer until chicken falls off the bone. Remove bones from pot. Skim fat from surface. Add the rice 10 minutes prior to serving. *The Highland Garden Club serves this perennial favorite each spring at the "May Market" in Pittsburgh's Mellon Park.*

Note: Rice will soak up most of the liquid, but Jambalaya should not be dry.

Yield: 4 to 6 generous servings

Georgia Moncada

Wine Braised Stuffed Chicken Breasts

Stuffing

**4 ounces bulk sweet Italian
    sausage**
½ cup breadcrumbs
**½ cup freshly grated Parmesan or
    Romano cheese**
1 large shallot, minced
1 large egg
**1 tablespoon chopped fresh
    parsley**
2 teaspoons chopped fresh thyme
½ teaspoon salt
¼ teaspoon ground black pepper

**8 large boneless, skinless chicken
    breast halves, pounded to
    ¼-inch thickness**
**Salt and ground black pepper,
    to taste**
2 tablespoons olive oil
¼ cup chopped pancetta or bacon
¾ cup finely chopped onion
6 large cloves garlic, minced
**1 (750-milliliter) bottle Chianti or
    dry red wine**
3 cups chicken broth
1 bay leaf
1 teaspoon dried basil
2 cups crushed tomatoes in purée
**1 pound of your favorite pasta or
    egg noodles**

In a large mixing bowl, combine all of the stuffing ingredients; mix well. Place 1 to 2 tablespoons of stuffing atop each chicken breast half. Roll breasts; tie with string. Season with salt and pepper; set aside. In a large skillet, over medium heat, heat the olive oil. Add the pancetta; cook until browned and fat has rendered. Remove pancetta to paper towels to drain. Add chicken to skillet, Cook, turning, until evenly browned, approximately 10 minutes. Transfer to a plate; set aside. In the same skillet, sauté the onion and garlic. Return pancetta to skillet. Add the Chianti; bring to a boil and simmer until liquid is reduced to 2 cups, approximately 10 minutes. Add the broth, bay leaf, basil and tomatoes. Return chicken breasts to skillet; bring to a boil and simmer until sauce reduces again to 2 cups and thickens, approximately 10 to 12 minutes. Remove bay leaf; season with additional salt and pepper. Cook pasta according to package directions. Serve chicken over the pasta. Ladle on the sauce.

Yield: 8 servings

Barb Dunn

Summer Seafood Stew

Broth
¼ cup olive oil
5 cups chopped onions
3 tablespoons minced garlic
2 (28-ounce) cans diced tomato
    in juice
3 cups Chardonnay wine
3 (8-ounce) bottles clam juice
¾ cup tomato paste, approximately
    1½ (6-ounce) cans
3 bay leaves
2 tablespoons chopped fresh thyme
2½ teaspoons grated orange peel
2½ teaspoons crushed fennel seeds
¾ teaspoon dried crushed red
    pepper flakes

Seafood
24 littleneck clams, scrubbed
2¾ pounds cod fillets, cut into
    2-inch pieces
1½ pounds large shrimp, peeled
    and deveined
1 pound bay scallops
Salt and freshly ground black
    pepper, to taste

Chopped fresh basil

In a heavy 8 to 10-quart pot, heat the olive oil over medium heat. Add the onion and garlic; sauté until onions are tender, approximately 10 minutes. Add remaining broth ingredients; bring to a boil. Reduce heat and simmer, uncovered, for 45 minutes or until flavors blend and liquid is slightly reduced. Remove bay leaves. Add the clams; cover pot and cook until clams open, approximately 10 minutes. (Discard any clams that do not open.) Add the cod, shrimp and scallops; simmer until seafood is cooked through, approximately 5 minutes. Season with salt and pepper. Serve in individual bowls garnished with the basil.

Note: Stew broth may be prepared one day ahead. Let cool; cover and refrigerate. Bring to a simmer before adding seafood.

Yield: 12 servings

Beth Bergman

Seafood Newburg

3 tablespoons flour
½ teaspoon salt
⅛ teaspoon nutmeg
Dash of cayenne pepper
¼ teaspoon seasoned salt
4 tablespoons butter
2 cups assorted fresh seafood
    (shrimp, crab, lobster, scallops)
1 (12-ounce) can evaporated milk
2-3 tablespoons dry sherry,
    to taste

In a small bowl, mix together the flour, salt, nutmeg, cayenne pepper and seasoned salt; set aside. In a large skillet, over low to medium heat, melt the butter. Add the seafood; sauté for approximately 2 to 3 minutes until seafood loses its opacity. Sprinkle the seasonings over seafood. Add the evaporated milk, stir continuously until thickened, approximately 5 to 8 minutes. Slowly add the sherry, stirring continuously. Serve immediately over toast or pastry shells. *This quick and elegant meal is prepared in under 20 minutes.*

Yield: 4 servings

Suzanne Chybrzynski

Lew's Favorite Pecan-Crusted Salmon

½ cup pecan halves
¼ cup plain dry breadcrumbs
1 teaspoon grated orange zest
½ teaspoon salt
¼ teaspoon ground black pepper
4 (6-ounce) salmon fillets,
    1½-inches thick
1 tablespoon olive oil

Sauce
2 tablespoons mayonnaise
2 tablespoons sour cream
2 tablespoons capers, drained,
    chopped
¼ teaspoon grated orange zest

Orange slices

Preheat oven to 400 degrees. Using a food processor, combine the pecans, breadcrumbs, the 1 teaspoon orange zest, salt and pepper. Process until fine crumbs form. Transfer mixture to a shallow bowl. Coat both sides of salmon fillets with the pecan mixture. In a large skillet, heat the olive oil over medium to high heat. Cook the salmon until browned, approximately 2 minutes on each side. Transfer salmon to an ovenproof baking dish; bake for 6 to 8 minutes, or until salmon is cooked through and coating is crispy. To prepare sauce, in a small bowl, mix together the mayonnaise, sour cream, capers and the ¼ teaspoon orange zest. Serve salmon with the sauce and garnish with orange slices.

Yield: 4 servings

Lewis Storb

Salmon with Pineapple Glaze

3 cups pineapple juice
6 teaspoons soy sauce
6 (6½-ounce) salmon steaks or
    fillets
Fresh pineapple slices

In a small non-reactive saucepan, over low to medium heat, bring the pineapple juice to a boil. Continue cooking until juice reduces to 1½ cups. Remove saucepan from heat; let cool. Whisk soy sauce into the pineapple juice. Place salmon in a single layer in a shallow baking dish. Pour pineapple-soy sauce mixture over salmon. Cover dish and refrigerate for 1 hour, turning once. Heat a large nonstick skillet. Place salmon in skillet; sear for 3 minutes on each side or until cooked through. To prepare pineapple glaze, pour the remaining pineapple-soy mixture into a small saucepan. Cook over medium to low heat until reduced by half, approximately 5 minutes. Place salmon on a serving platter. Brush with a small amount of glaze. Layer pineapple slices over top. Serve any remaining glaze on the side.

Yield: 6 servings

Betty Gaston

Poached Salmon Fillets with Bermuda Onions and Tomato

1 medium onion, finely chopped
1 carrot, finely chopped
1 rib of celery, finely chopped
2 bay leaves
6 (5-ounce) salmon fillets
Salt and freshly ground black
    pepper, to taste
2 cups white wine
1 cup water
1 tablespoon olive oil
1 tablespoon butter
3 Bermuda or sweet yellow
    onions, sliced
3 ripe tomatoes, diced

Sauce
1 pound mascarpone cheese,
    cubed
1 (6-ounce) can tomato paste,
    to taste
1-2 teaspoons sugar, to taste

Preheat oven to 350 degrees. Spread the onions, carrots, celery and bay leaves over bottom of a large baking dish. Place the salmon fillets over top of vegetables. Season with salt and pepper. Add the wine and water to baking dish; cover tightly with foil. Bake for 15 minutes or until the fish is tender. Discard bay leaves. In a large skillet, heat the olive oil and butter. Sauté the Bermuda onions; season with salt and pepper. When onions are soft, toss in the tomato. Sauté for 1 to 2 additional minutes; remove from heat; set aside. To prepare the sauce, in a heavy saucepan, heat the mascarpone cheese over medium low heat, stirring, until softened. Stir in the tomato paste. Season with the sugar. To serve, ladle sauce on individual plates. Place 1 salmon fillet and a small amount of vegetables over the sauce; top with the Bermuda onion and tomatoes. Discard baking dish liquid.

Variation: For a summertime treat, grill the sliced Bermuda onions and sliced tomatoes.

Yield: 6 servings

*Rania Harris, owner,
Rania's To Go Catering*

Lavender Hill's Salmon and Red Pepper Wrap

4 (10-inch) flour tortillas
2 (6-ounce) salmon fillets, broiled
   or seared for approximately
   4 minutes per side
1 red bell pepper (cut into thin
   strips), sautéed, parboiled,
   or roasted
½ carrot, grated or thinly sliced
1 (6-ounce) bag baby spinach
Vinaigrette or Italian dressing,
   to taste

Preheat oven to 220 degrees. Warm tortillas on a baking sheet for approximately 5 minutes. Place ½ of each salmon fillet in the center of each tortilla. Spread bell peppers and carrots evenly over the salmon. Mix spinach with the Italian dressing. Top each tortilla with equal amounts of spinach. To roll wraps, fold the lower end up over the salmon and spinach. Fold sides in to the middle. Finish by rolling the wrap completely. Serve with any left over spinach on the side. Add fresh fruit for a delicious healthy lunch or dinner. *Take one with you to work, school or on a summer picnic.*

Note: Try substituting chicken or pork for the fish. Black or pinto beans add protein. Monterey Jack, Cheddar, provolone or crumbled blue cheese add a nice flavor. Choose herbs or a dressing that complement the wrap ingredients.

Yield: 4 servings

Flowers in the Attic, formerly
Lavender Hill Tea House
Ken Milko, owner
Martha Burkholder, former owner

Seared Cod with Habanero Lime Aïoli

**2 pounds fresh cod fillets,
  1-1½ inches thick, cut on bias
  into 8 serving pieces
2 tablespoons Cajun seasoning**

Habanero Lime Aïoli
**1 clove garlic, minced
1 teaspoon kosher salt
1 large egg
1 egg yolk
1 cup canola or vegetable oil
Zest of 1 lime
2 tablespoons lime juice
1 orange habanero pepper,
  seeded, minced, to taste**

**3 tablespoons unsalted butter,
  divided
3 tablespoons olive oil, divided
2 tablespoons chopped fresh
  tarragon**

Rub both sides of fish with the Cajun seasoning. Cover fish and refrigerate. To prepare aïoli, using a food processor fitted with metal blade, pulse together the garlic and salt. Add egg and egg yolk; pulse until smooth. With processor running, slowly add the oil, a few drops at a time, then in a slow stream until the aïoli emulsifies. Pulse in lime zest and lime juice to combine. Transfer aïoli to a bowl. Stir habanero pepper into aïoli a little at a time, to desired level of hotness; cover and refrigerate until ready to serve. To prepare cod, heat a dry nonstick frying pan over very high heat until nearly smoking. Test by placing a drop of water on the surface. If it really dances, you're hot enough! Add ½ of the butter and ½ of the oil to pan. Place 4 cod pieces in pan. Brown for 4 minutes; turn and cook for 1 additional minute. Remove fish to a warmed plate; wipe off pan. Cook remaining cod pieces with the remaining butter and oil. Cod will be crisp on one side and moist throughout. Serve cod garnished with tarragon and topped with the aïoli. *Our recipe testers loved this dish.*

Note: This recipe contains uncooked egg whites.

Yield: 6 to 8 servings

Mark Flaherty

Poached Cod with Lemon Butter Sauce

1¾ pounds cod fillets
1 cup milk
1½ cups water
1 bay leaf
4 sprigs fresh parsley
4 whole peppercorns
2 whole cloves
Salt to taste, optional

Lemon Butter Sauce
4 tablespoons chilled butter,
**   divided**
½ teaspoon finely minced garlic
3 tablespoons finely chopped
**   shallots**
Juice of ½-1 lemon, to taste
2 tablespoons finely minced fresh
**   parsley**
Salt and freshly ground black
**   pepper, to taste**

Cut the cod fillets crosswise into 4 equal pieces. In a large skillet, arrange fillets in a single layer. Pour the milk into skillet; add enough of the water to just cover fillets. Add the bay leaf, parsley sprigs, peppercorns and cloves to skillet. Season with salt. Bring to a simmer; cover and cook gently, approximately 3 to 4 minutes, until fish flakes easily with a fork. Remove skillet from heat; set aside. To prepare the Lemon Butter Sauce, in a small saucepan, heat 1 tablespoon of the butter. Add the garlic and shallots; sauté just until softened. Remove ¼ cup of the cooking liquid from skillet; add to saucepan and stir. Bring sauce to a boil; cook until reduced by ½. Add the lemon juice. Remove sauce from heat. Whisk in the remaining butter until melted. Season with the minced parsley, salt and pepper. Drain the cod. Serve with the sauce.

Yield: 4 servings

Susan Parente

Bacalao

4½ pounds skinless, boneless bacalao
4½ cups olive oil, divided
7 whole cloves garlic
7 cloves garlic, minced
2 large onions, finely chopped
2 large fresh red pimentos, cut into thin strips
1 bunch fresh parsley, finely chopped
14 almonds, peeled, finely chopped
4½ pounds tomatoes, peeled, chopped
1 (13-ounce) can tomato purée
1 (8-ounce) jar pimentos, drained
25 olives
2 tablespoons capers
Salt, to taste

One day ahead, fill a roasting pan with hot water. Soak the bacalao for 24 hours, changing water 3 to 4 times, to desalt. In a pot of fresh water, cook the bacalao, over low heat, for one hour or until tender; drain well. Finely shred the bacalao removing any remaining bones or skin; set aside. In a medium saucepan, heat 3 cups of the olive oil. Add the 7 whole garlic cloves; sauté over low heat until soft. Remove from heat; set aside. In a large pot or Dutch oven, heat the remaining 1½ cups of olive oil. Sauté the minced garlic and onion until onion is soft. Add the fresh pimentos, parsley, almonds, and chopped tomatoes. Cook for 10 minutes, stirring occasionally. Add the tomato purée, jarred pimentos, reserved olive oil and 7 garlic cloves. Simmer for 20 minutes, stirring continuously. Add the bacalao, olives and capers; simmer for 10 additional minutes. Season with salt, if desired.

Note: Bacalao is a dried fish purchased at Spanish and Italian groceries or specialty food stores. To make the peeling of the almonds and tomatoes easier, place them in boiling water until skins begin to pull away, approximately 5 minutes.

Yield: 12 servings

Rebecca Dosal de Carballido

Grilled Stuffed Swordfish Steaks

2 tablespoons butter

3 tablespoons olive oil

1 tablespoon plus 1 teaspoon
  chopped fresh tarragon,
  divided

2 ounces Jarlsberg cheese, cut into
  thin strips

1 cup finely chopped fresh spinach
  leaves

4 strips of bacon, cooked crisp,
  crumbled

4 (6 to 8-ounce) swordfish steaks,
  approximately 1-inch thick

1 teaspoon salt

¼ teaspoon freshly ground black
  pepper

To prepare outdoor grill, oil the grill rack and place 6 inches from coals. Preheat grill to medium heat. In a small saucepan, over low heat, stir butter, olive oil and 1 tablespoon of the tarragon together until butter melts; set aside. In a small bowl, combine the remaining 1 teaspoon of tarragon, cheese, spinach and bacon. Using a small, sharp knife, cut into fleshy side of each steak to create a deep pocket. Stuff each steak with equal amounts of the spinach mixture. Brush outside of each steak with the butter mixture. Season with salt and pepper. Grill for 4 to 6 minutes; turn and re-brush with butter mixture. Continue grilling until steaks are just cooked through and cheese is melted, approximately 4 to 6 additional minutes. Serve immediately, drizzled with any remaining butter mixture.

Yield: 4 servings

Barbara Dickson

Baked Flounder with Tomato Sauce

1¼ pounds flounder fillets
½ cup fresh basil leaves
1 (4-ounce) can pitted black olives,
  optional
1 tablespoon canola oil
1 cup chopped onion
1 cup thinly sliced zucchini
½ cup chopped green bell pepper
2 cloves garlic, minced
1 (16-ounce) can tomatoes in juice,
  chopped, juice reserved
2 tablespoons tomato paste
1 tablespoon chopped fresh
  parsley
½ teaspoon salt
1 bay leaf
⅛ teaspoon dried oregano
⅛ teaspoon dried basil
⅛ teaspoon freshly ground black
  pepper
2 tablespoons dry white wine

Divide fillets into 8 equal portions. Using a food processor, purée the basil and black olives. Spread purée evenly over fillets. Roll each portion up; secure with a toothpick. Cover flounder rolls; refrigerate until needed. In a large stockpot, over medium heat, heat the canola oil. Sauté the onion, zucchini, bell pepper and garlic, stirring occasionally, for 5 minutes or until soft. Add the tomatoes, reserved juice, tomato paste, parsley, salt, bay leaf, oregano, basil, and black pepper. Simmer, uncovered, stirring occasionally, for 10 minutes. Preheat oven to 375 degrees. Pour ⅔ of the tomato sauce into an 11x7-inch baking dish. Arrange the flounder rolls over sauce, seam-side down. Pour the remaining sauce over fish. Sprinkle with the wine. Cover dish with aluminum foil; bake for 25 to 30 minutes or until fish flakes easily with a fork. Remove bay leaf. Serve over rice.

Note: If omitting black olives, chop the basil and sprinkle over fillets before rolling. To increase the amount of sauce, use additional canned tomatoes and adjust spices to taste.

Variation: Sole fillets may be substituted for the flounder.

Yield: 4 servings

Diane Charles

Calamari

2 pounds squid, cleaned (see note)
1 teaspoon coarsely ground fresh
  black pepper
8 cloves garlic, minced
2 teaspoons paprika
1 teaspoon dried oregano
½ teaspoon dried thyme
¼ cup extra-virgin olive oil
2 lemons, halved
¼ cup dry white wine
2 teaspoons kosher salt
¼ cup chopped fresh parsley

Cut squid bodies into ½-inch diagonal slices. Leave squid tentacles whole. Set squid aside in a colander to drain. In a small bowl, mix together the pepper, garlic, paprika, oregano, thyme and olive oil; set aside. Cut 1 lemon half into 4 wedges; set aside. In a small bowl, squeeze the juice from the remaining lemon halves. Add wine to the lemon juice; set aside. Heat a large, heavy skillet over high heat. Add the olive oil mixture; sauté, stirring, for 1 minute, until garlic is lightly cooked. Quickly add the squid and lemon-wine mixture. Sprinkle on salt. Cook, stirring continuously for 1 minute, until squid is cooked through. Add the parsley; cook, stirring, for 10 to 20 additional seconds. (Do not overcook or squid will toughen.) Remove squid and skillet liquid to serving bowl. Garnish with lemon wedges. Serve with crusty French bread.

Note: To clean squid, place on a drainable cutting surface and, using a sharp knife, cut body of squid away from tentacles just below the eye, being careful not to cut into the eye or ink sac which lies close by. Gently remove the tooth from the circular area at top portion of tentacles and discard. Keep tentacles whole unless excessively large; set aside. Insert fingers into squid body and gently remove and discard spine. The spine will usually come out intact. If spine breaks, simply feel for and remove any remaining pieces left inside squid body. Under running water gently rinse inside of squid body, removing ink sac and any insides that remain. Using a small paring knife, gently scrape the pink skin off of squid body. Proceed with cutting squid body into ½-inch diagonal slices.

Yield: 6 to 8 entrées; 15 to 20 appetizer servings

Karen Raffensperger

Maryland Crab Cakes

1 pound lump crabmeat, picked
    through
3 cups fresh breadcrumbs,
    divided, and to taste
⅓ cup minced green onion
⅓ cup chopped fresh parsley
2 tablespoons lemon juice
1 tablespoon 2 percent milk
1 teaspoon hot sauce
½ teaspoon salt
¼ teaspoon ground black pepper
4 egg whites
2 tablespoons vegetable oil,
    divided
Lemon wedges

In a medium bowl, combine the crabmeat, 1½ cups of the breadcrumbs, onion, parsley, lemon juice, milk, hot sauce, salt, pepper and egg whites; mix well. Divide crabmeat mixture into 8 equal portions. Shape each portion into an approximately 3½-inch round and ½-inch thick cake. Place the remaining breadcrumbs in a shallow dish. Dredge each crab cake in the breadcrumbs continuing to shape cakes as you coat. In a large nonstick skillet, heat 1 tablespoon of the oil over medium heat. Place 4 crab cakes in skillet; cook for 3 minutes. Turn and cook an additional 3 minutes until golden. Wipe skillet and add the remaining 1 tablespoon of oil; continue cooking additional crab cakes. Serve with lemon wedges.

Yield: 8 appetizers; 4 entrées

Lila Decker

Crab Cakes

4 tablespoons butter, divided
¼ cup finely chopped red bell
    pepper
¼ cup finely chopped red onion
¼ cup finely chopped celery
8 ounces crabmeat, drained,
    picked through
¼-½ cup crushed salted butter
    crackers
1 egg
1 tablespoon Worcestershire sauce
2 tablespoons mayonnaise
1 teaspoon spicy brown mustard
Seasoned breadcrumbs
Old Bay Seasoning, to taste
Freshly ground black pepper,
    to taste

In a large skillet, over medium heat, melt 2 tablespoons of the butter. Add vegetables; sauté until soft (do not brown). Remove skillet from heat. Transfer vegetables to a mixing bowl. Add the crabmeat, crackers, egg, Worcestershire sauce, mayonnaise, and mustard; mix well. Divide the crabmeat mixture into 4 equal portions. Form each portion into a 3 to 4-inch round cake. Coat each cake with breadcrumbs. Melt the remaining 2 tablespoons of butter in skillet. Sauté crab cakes over medium-low heat until golden on both sides. Season with Old Bay and black pepper.

Yield: 2 servings; 4 crab cakes

Francine Marthens

Lobster Tails in Champagne Sauce

2 (10 to 12-ounce) frozen lobster
   tails
⅔ cup Champagne
2 scallions, minced (white part
   and small amount of green)
¼ teaspoon salt
¼ cup heavy cream
4 tablespoons unsalted chilled
   butter

2 scallions, cut into very thin
   strips, optional

Rinse lobster tails; set aside. (Do not thaw.) In a medium skillet, combine the Champagne, minced scallions and salt. Place lobster tails in the skillet shell-side up and laying side by side, fin to tail. Heat to boiling. Reduce heat and simmer, covered, for 10 minutes. Remove lobster tails, reserving liquid in skillet. To prepare the sauce, add heavy cream to skillet. Boil quickly to reduce to ⅓ cup of liquid. Whisk in the butter, one tablespoon at a time, until smooth. Keep sauce warm. Remove lobster meat from shells; slice into ½-inch medallions. Spoon sauce over lobster meat. Garnish with scallion strips. *Enjoy this elegant dish with the rest of the Champagne!*

Yield: 2 servings

Chris McCormick

Sweet Mustard Shrimp

Marinade
½ cup Dijon mustard
2 teaspoons dry mustard
1 teaspoon dry ginger or
   1 tablespoon grated fresh ginger
2 tablespoons lemon juice
6 tablespoons sugar
½ cup cider vinegar
½ cup olive oil
1 tablespoon cinnamon
1-2 tablespoons dried dill
3 tablespoons chopped red onion

2 pounds medium or large
   shrimp, cleaned, steamed

To prepare the marinade, in a large bowl, combine the Dijon mustard, dry mustard, ginger, lemon juice, sugar and vinegar. Whisk in the olive oil. Stir in the cinnamon, dill and red onion. Add the shrimp to marinade. Cover and refrigerate for 2 hours or overnight. *Serve on greens as a first course or alone as an appetizer. For a special luncheon, serve as a salad with fresh fruit and crusty bread.*

Note: Marinade may be prepared in advance. Cover and refrigerate for up to 1 week. Marinade is also delicious with broiled chicken.

Yield: 8 to 10 servings

Sally Werner

Stuffed Shrimp with Crabmeat

5 tablespoons butter, melted,
  divided
12 jumbo shrimp, peeled,
  deveined, tails left on
1 tablespoon extra-virgin olive oil
1 rib of celery, finely chopped
1 small onion, finely chopped
¼ red bell pepper, finely chopped,
  optional
1 (6-ounce) can lump crabmeat,
  drained, picked through
¼ teaspoon thyme or poultry
  seasoning
¼ teaspoon paprika
1 tablespoon chopped fresh
  parsley, optional
Salt and pepper, to taste
Breadcrumbs

Preheat oven to 400 degrees. Brush a 13x9-inch baking dish with 1 tablespoon of the melted butter. Using a sharp knife, cut into back of shrimp, along the deveining line, into and almost through the shrimp meat. Place shrimp in baking dish, butterflied side down and tail up. Brush shrimp with 2 tablespoons of the melted butter; set aside. Add the remaining 2 tablespoons of melted butter and the olive oil to a medium skillet. Sauté the celery, onion and red bell pepper for 5 minutes or until tender. Add the crabmeat, thyme, paprika and parsley; cook for an additional 5 minutes, stirring occasionally. Season with salt and pepper. Remove skillet from heat. Place equal amounts of crab mixture atop each shrimp. Sprinkle lightly with the breadcrumbs. Bake for 8 to 10 minutes, or just until shrimp are pink and firm.

Yield: 4 servings

Sylvia Stehlik

Duquesne Heights

The picturesque neighborhood of Duquesne Heights is perched on a rocky plateau just 1.2 miles from downtown Pittsburgh. Its steep elevation, however, creates an optical illusion that suggests a much longer distance. The neighborhood was named after Fort Duquesne, a military outpost built by the French in 1754 at the fork of the Ohio River. The short-lived fort, soon replaced by the much larger British Fort Pitt, is a reminder of the importance western Pennsylvania played in the French and Indian War. From Duquesne Heights, one can look down on the point of land formed by the three rivers and imagine the struggles that took place there over 250 years ago; struggles which decided the future of our nation.

Duquesne Heights and its sister neighborhood, Mt. Washington, share a picturesque skyline. A steep hillside covered with lush greenery, a cut-out silhouette of buildings and church spires, and two historic inclines create a romantic vista that is a defining visual for Pittsburgh residents. The view from Duquesne Heights offers a panoramic vista of the downtown skyline. One sees tugboats, barges, kayaks and sculls sharing the rivers, an array of architecturally significant bridges and the meandering plateaus, dotted with other city neighborhoods, that form the region's topography and character.

Prior to the mid-1800's, Duquesne Heights was a largely unsettled area. The steep terrain made it inaccessible while nearby neighborhoods offered plenty of decent and convenient housing close to work in the city's mills and factories. However, as the South Side flats along the Monongahela River began to swell with industry and job opportunities, Duquesne Heights became more attractive for development. On May 20, 1877, the Duquesne Incline opened to the public, playing a significant role in making the neighborhood accessible to prospective residents. German immigrants, followed by Italians, were among the first and largest groups to settle in the neighborhood. Duquesne Heights quickly became home to ethnic organizations and clubs including the "Maennerchor," a German men's singing group which formed in 1893 at the home of George Klinze.

Today, hillside homes and restaurants with spectacular views share the neighborhood. Tourists and residents alike use the Duquesne Incline to traverse the steep pathway to Duquesne Heights to enjoy panoramic vistas of the city and to commute to downtown. The neighborhood has succeeded in balancing its nostalgic history and its impressive urban environment in an attractive manner. ♥♥

Fillet of Beef with Roasted Garlic, Shallots and Red Wine Sauce

18 large cloves of garlic, peeled
18 shallot cloves, peeled
3 tablespoons vegetable oil,
    divided
Salt and freshly ground black
    pepper, to taste

Sauce
1½ cups dry red wine
¾ cup chopped shallots
3 cloves garlic, chopped
4 sprigs fresh thyme
1 bay leaf
1½ cups chicken broth
1½ cups beef broth
6 tablespoons unsalted butter,
    chilled

6 (6-ounce) beef tenderloin fillets,
    cut 1-inch thick

Preheat oven to 375 degrees. Line a baking sheet with heavy-duty aluminum foil. Place garlic and shallot cloves on prepared baking sheet. Drizzle with ½ tablespoon of the oil. Season with salt and pepper. Bring corners of foil together and twist to seal, forming a package. Roast for 30 minutes. Open foil package and roast for an additional 30 minutes until garlic and shallots are tender and golden. Remove from oven; re-cover with foil to keep warm and set aside. To prepare the sauce, place the red wine, chopped shallots, chopped garlic, thyme and bay leaf in a heavy, medium saucepan. Bring to a boil over medium to high heat. Boil until liquid is reduced by half, approximately 6 minutes. Add chicken and beef broths. Boil until liquid reduces to ¾ cup, approximately 30 to 40 minutes. Remove sauce from heat; cover and set aside. In a large skillet, over medium to high heat, heat the remaining 2½ tablespoons of oil. Season fillets with salt and pepper. Place fillets in skillet. Cook to desired doneness, turning once, approximately 4 minutes per side for rare. Transfer fillets and roasted garlic and shallots to a serving platter; cover with foil to keep warm. Re-warm sauce over low heat. Add the butter, 1 to 2 tablespoons at a time, whisking until smooth. Using a cheesecloth, strain the sauce. Season with additional salt and pepper, if desired. Ladle warm sauce over fillets, garlic and shallots.

Yield: 6 servings

Rania Harris, owner,
Rania's To Go Catering

Korean Barbecue Beef I and II

Version I Marinade
1 tablespoon water
1½ tablespoons red cooking wine
⅓ cup sesame oil
⅓ cup soy sauce
⅓ cup lemon-lime flavored soft drink
⅓ cup brown sugar
½ teaspoon ground black pepper

Version II Marinade
3 tablespoons red cooking wine
⅓ cup sesame oil
⅓ cup soy sauce
2½ tablespoons brown sugar
½ teaspoon ground black pepper
½ medium white onion, minced
1 tablespoon minced garlic

2½ pounds spencer or eye of round roast, cut into ⅛ to ¼-inch slices

In a large bowl, combine all marinade ingredients for version I or II. Add beef slices. Mix gently to coat. Cover and marinate in refrigerator for 1 to 2 hours. Turn on oven broiler or prepare outdoor grill. Place beef slices on skewers. Broil or grill to desired doneness. Discard marinade after use. Serve hot with white rice.

Note: Meat may also be stir-fried in a very hot, ungreased heavy skillet.

Variation: Pork may be substituted for the beef.

Yield: 6 to 8 main course servings; 15 appetizer portions

Seung Jin Choi

Steak with Wine and Mushrooms

1 (2-pound) beef sirloin steak
Old Bay Seasoning, to taste
2 tablespoons butter
1 tablespoon olive oil
2 large cloves garlic, minced
½ pound fresh mushrooms, sliced
½-¾ cup Marsala wine, to taste

Preheat oven to 200 degrees. Season steak with Old Bay; set aside. In a large, heavy skillet, over high heat, heat the butter and oil. Add garlic; cook, stirring, for 1 minute (do not brown). Place steak in skillet. Cook for 8 minutes, turning once to sear both sides. Decrease heat to medium. Add mushrooms to skillet. Continue cooking steak to desired internal temperature. Remove steak to an ovenproof platter; place in oven to keep warm. Add wine to skillet with the mushrooms. Increase heat to high; cook, stirring, until mixture becomes slightly thickened. Remove steak from oven. Slice meat thinly across the grain; place on a serving platter. Spoon mushrooms and a small amount of sauce over meat slices. Serve additional sauce on the side.

Yield: 4 to 6 servings

Patty Just

Baked Country Short Ribs

¼ cup flour
2 teaspoons salt, divided
½ teaspoon ground black pepper,
　divided
4 pounds beef short ribs, cut into
　serving-size pieces
2 tablespoons vegetable oil
1 cup chopped onion
1 cup chopped green bell pepper
1 (10½-ounce) can beef consommé
3 tablespoons white or red wine
　vinegar
1 (8-ounce) can tomato sauce
2 teaspoons Worcestershire sauce
1½ cups water
¼ cup chopped fresh parsley
½ teaspoon dry mustard
12 white pearl onions, peeled
4 carrots, peeled, cut into
　1½-inch pieces

Preheat oven to 350 degrees. Place flour, 1 teaspoon of the salt and ¼ teaspoon of the black pepper in a large plastic bag. Shake well to combine. Add ribs; shake to coat. In a large skillet, over medium heat, heat the vegetable oil. Place ribs in skillet; brown on all sides. Transfer ribs to a 3-quart casserole; set aside. Using the same skillet, sauté the onions and bell peppers until soft, approximately 5 minutes. Add the consommé, vinegar, tomato sauce, Worcestershire sauce, water, parsley, dry mustard, the remaining 1 teaspoon of salt and ¼ teaspoon black pepper; mix well. Cook, stirring, until heated through. Pour skillet mixture over ribs. Cover and bake for 1½ hours, stirring once. Add pearl onions and carrots to casserole. Re-cover and bake for an additional 30 minutes or until carrots and onions are tender. Skim fat from top of casserole. Place ribs in a large serving dish. Sauce may be thickened, if desired. Transfer to a medium saucepan; over medium heat, stir in additional flour to obtain desired consistency. Pour sauce over ribs.

Yield: 6 servings

Betty Gaston

Pork Loin with Fall Stuffing

1 (2 to 3-pound) boneless, center-
 cut pork loin roast
1 (8-ounce) bottle teriyaki sauce,
 to taste

Stuffing
⅓ cup chopped dried apricots
⅓ cup dried currants
⅓ cup golden raisins
⅓ cup dried cranberries
4 tablespoons chopped fresh sage
½ cup water

Place pork loin in a zip-lock plastic bag or glass baking dish. Coat with desired amount of teriyaki sauce. Seal bag or cover baking dish with plastic wrap; marinate in refrigerator for 2 to 3 hours or overnight. To prepare the stuffing, place all stuffing ingredients in a medium saucepan. Cook, stirring, over medium heat until water is absorbed. Set stuffing aside to cool. Remove pork loin from refrigerator; bring to room temperature. Discard leftover marinade. Preheat oven to 350 degrees. Cut a large X into each end of pork loin. Using a wooden spoon or knife, push through X cuts to create a tunnel the entire length of pork loin. Fill opening with cooled stuffing. Place pork loin in a shallow roasting pan. Roast until internal temperature reaches 160 to 170 degrees, approximately 50 to 75 minutes. Allow pork loin to rest for 10 to 15 minutes before slicing.

Yield: 4 to 6 servings

Barb Dunn

Pork Roast with Sweet Apple Sauerkraut

1 (5 to 6-pound) boneless pork
 roast
Salt and ground black pepper,
 to taste
1 (2-pound) bag fresh sauerkraut,
 rinsed, drained
2 apples, peeled, cored and diced
1 cup raisins
1 cup dark brown sugar

Preheat oven to 350 degrees. Place roast fat side up in a large roasting pan. Season with salt and pepper. Roast, uncovered, to internal temperature of 140 degrees, approximately 1½ to 2 hours. In a large bowl, mix together the sauerkraut, apples, raisins and brown sugar. Place mixture in roasting pan around the pork. Continue roasting to an internal temperature of 160 to 170 degrees, approximately 45 additional minutes. If roast begins to look dry, baste with juices and cover to continue roasting.

Note: Bagged fresh sauerkraut is found in the meat department of most grocery stores.

Yield: 8 to 10 servings

Georgia Moncada

Pork Chops with Creamy Tomato-Porcini Sauce

2 ounces dried porcini mushrooms
4 tablespoons vegetable oil,
  divided, and to taste
8 (¾-inch thick) center-cut loin
  pork chops
1 cup dry white wine
1 cup chopped plum tomatoes
1 cup heavy whipping cream
Salt and freshly ground black
  pepper, to taste
1 pound white button mushrooms

Preheat oven to 400 degrees. Place porcini mushrooms in a small saucepan. Cover with water and boil until softened. Drain, chop and set aside. In a large skillet, over medium heat, heat 2 tablespoons of the oil. Place 4 pork chops in skillet; brown on both sides. Remove and set aside to drain. Repeat for the remaining 4 pork chops, adding additional oil as needed. Transfer to 2 (9x13-inch) shallow baking pans, placing chops in a single layer; set aside. Drain oil from skillet and discard. To prepare the sauce, add wine to the same skillet; simmer for 20 seconds using a wooden spoon to loosen any bits of meat from bottom. Add the chopped porcini mushrooms, tomatoes and cream. Season with salt and pepper. Cover skillet; simmer for 3 minutes. Spoon sauce evenly over the pork chops; turning chops once to coat both sides. Cover baking pans tightly with aluminum foil. Bake for 20 to 35 minutes until meat is tender. In a large separate skillet, over high heat, heat the remaining 2 tablespoons of oil. Add the button mushrooms. Cook, stirring, until liquid released from cooked mushrooms evaporates. Season with additional salt and pepper. When pork chops are tender, add the cooked button mushrooms to baking pan. Turn pork chops. Re-cover pan and continue cooking for 5 to 8 additional minutes. Transfer pork chops to a serving platter. Spoon sauce and mushrooms over top; serve immediately.

Yield: 8 servings

Greg Welsh

Sweet Cherry Pork Chops

4 (1-inch thick) boneless pork
  chops
1 tablespoon vegetable oil
1 cup orange juice
¾ cup pitted sweet cherries,
  halved
2 green onions (white part and
  small amount of green), sliced
¼ cup cherry preserves
4 teaspoons cornstarch mixed
  with 3 tablespoons cold water
4-6 cups hot cooked rice

In a large skillet, over medium to high heat, sauté the pork chops in the oil until browned on both sides; drain. Add the orange juice, cherries and onions to skillet; bring to a boil. Decrease heat; simmer, uncovered, turning chops twice, for 15 minutes until cooked through. Remove pork chops from skillet; keep warm. Stir the cherry preserves into pan juices. Add the cornstarch. Bring to a boil; cook, stirring continuously, for 1 to 2 minutes or until sauce thickens. Ladle sauce over the pork chops and rice.

Yield: 4 servings

Betty Gaston

Sausage and Bell Pepper Medley

12 (hot, sweet or a combination)
  Italian sausages
½ cup extra-virgin olive oil
2 green bell peppers, seeded,
  sliced lengthwise into 1-inch
  thick strips
2 yellow bell peppers, seeded,
  sliced lengthwise into 1-inch
  thick strips
2 red bell peppers, seeded, sliced
  lengthwise into 1-inch thick
  strips
2 large onions, sliced
6 cloves garlic, thinly sliced
Salt and freshly ground black
  pepper, to taste
Freshly grated Parmesan cheese

Pierce sausage casings 4 to 6 times with a fork. In a large skillet or Dutch oven, over medium to high heat, brown the sausages in the olive oil, turning frequently. Continue cooking, turning, until cooked through, approximately 10 to 15 minutes. Add the green, yellow and red bell peppers, onion and garlic to skillet. Season with salt and pepper. Cook, stirring, over medium heat until peppers are soft, approximately 5 additional minutes. Drain off any remaining oil and fat before serving. Serve with Parmesan cheese and a side of crusty Italian bread.

Yield: 6 to 8 servings

Lisa Emily Raffensperger

Veal Rolls with Prosciutto

10-12 boneless veal cutlets,
   ½ to ¾-inch thick
8 tablespoons minced garlic
¼ cup extra-virgin olive oil
Salt and freshly ground black or
   white pepper, to taste
2 tablespoons dried sage
1 pound prosciutto, thinly sliced
¼ cup butter
2 cups dry white wine
6 fresh sage leaves, chopped
2 tablespoons flour
2 tablespoons butter, melted
Freshly grated Parmesan cheese,
   to taste

Place each cutlet between waxed paper or oiled parchment paper. Using a smooth meat mallet, pound each cutlet to a ¼ to ⅛-inch thickness. In a small bowl, combine the garlic and olive oil. Brush each cutlet with olive oil mixture. Season with salt and pepper. Sprinkle dried sage evenly over cutlets. Top with equal layers of prosciutto. Roll up cutlets lengthwise; secure with toothpicks. In a large skillet, over low heat, melt the ¼ cup butter. Sauté veal rolls until evenly browned, approximately 4 to 6 minutes. Add the wine and sage leaves to skillet. Season with additional salt and pepper. Cover and simmer over low heat until tender, approximately 8 to 10 minutes. Remove veal rolls to a warming tray. Dissolve flour in the 2 tablespoons melted butter; add to skillet. Stir, scraping bottom of skillet, until liquid thickens to a sauce consistency. Remove toothpicks from veal rolls; place on a serving platter. Ladle sauce over veal rolls and top with Parmesan cheese. *Delicious served over white rice or egg noodles.*

Yield: 8 to 10 servings

Cynthia Francescon

Veal with Mustard Cream Sauce

4 tablespoons sweet butter
2 tablespoons olive oil
3 scallions, (white part and small amount of green) chopped
2 pounds veal cutlets, pounded to a ¼ to ⅛-inch thickness
Salt and freshly ground black pepper, to taste
⅓ cup dry white wine
1-2 tablespoons Dijon mustard, to taste
⅓ cup half & half
1 large firm ripe tomato, seeded, chopped

In a large skillet, over medium heat, melt the butter. Add olive oil and scallions; sauté until tender, approximately 4 minutes. Add veal; season with salt and pepper. Sauté until veal is cooked through, approximately 2 to 3 minutes per side. Remove veal from skillet; keep warm. Add wine to skillet; boil until reduced to several syrupy spoonfuls. Whisk in the mustard and half & half; boil for 2 to 3 additional minutes. Season sauce with salt and pepper. Arrange warm veal on individual plates. Spoon sauce over veal and top with tomato. *Serve with rice and steamed vegetables for an easy and elegant dinner.*

Variation: Chicken breast halves may be substituted for the veal cutlets.

Yield: 4 to 6 servings

Susan Limoncelli

Veal Marengo

1 pound stewing veal, cut into 2-inch pieces
¾ cup flour
3 tablespoons olive oil
2 tablespoons butter
Salt and freshly ground black pepper, to taste
18 pearl onions
1 carrot, coarsely chopped
¼ cup diced green bell pepper
⅛ teaspoon dried thyme
1 (14½-ounce) can diced tomatoes, drained
½ cup chicken or beef broth
¼ cup dry white wine
2 tablespoons orange liqueur
½ teaspoon finely minced lemon zest
12 ounces mushrooms, chopped or sliced
½ teaspoon dried tarragon
1 cup croutons, optional

Dredge the veal pieces in the flour. In a large skillet, over medium heat, heat the olive oil and butter until butter melts. Add veal, in batches, cooking until lightly browned on all sides. Transfer veal to a plate; season with salt and pepper. Cover to keep warm; set aside. Add onions, carrot, bell pepper and thyme to skillet. Cook, stirring, until vegetables soften slightly and lightly brown. Remove excess fat from skillet. Return veal to skillet. Add tomatoes, broth, wine, liqueur and lemon zest. Decrease heat to low; cover and simmer for 20 minutes. Add mushrooms; simmer, covered, for an additional 10 minutes. Sprinkle with tarragon and top with croutons prior to serving. Serve with white rice.

Yield: 4 servings

Kathy Leh

Grilled Leg of Lamb

Marinade

**1 medium onion, peeled,
    quartered**
3 cloves garlic, peeled
**1 piece fresh ginger
    (approximately 1½-2 inches),
    peeled**
**½ medium jalapeño pepper,
    seeded**
¼ cup soy sauce
¼ cup honey
2 tablespoons peanut or canola oil

1 (4-5 pound) boneless leg of lamb

Place the onion, garlic, ginger and jalapeño pepper in small bowl of a food processor. Process until mixture is puréed, approximately 20 seconds. Add the soy sauce, honey and oil. Pulse until just combined. Place lamb in a zip-top plastic bag. Pour marinade over lamb, turning to coat. Marinate overnight in the refrigerator, turning bag occasionally. Prepare outdoor grill. Preheat oven to 180 degrees. Place lamb on grill rack 2 to 3 inches from coals. Discard marinade. Sear lamb on all sides, turning over coals for 8 to 10 minutes until evenly browned. Transfer lamb to a roasting pan; insert meat thermometer. Place in oven. Roast for 30 to 60 minutes until internal temperature reaches 130 to 140 degrees for rare to medium-rare. (Increase cooking time for more well-doneness.) Allow lamb to rest for 5 to 10 minutes before carving.

Note: Marinade may also be used for grilled flank steak or chicken.

Yield: 6 to 8 servings

Bernadette West

Rack of Lamb with Port-Currant Sauce

3 (8-chop) racks of lamb,
  approximately 1¾ pounds per
  rack
Salt and freshly ground black
  pepper
2 tablespoons chopped fresh
  rosemary

Sauce
1 cup plus 2 tablespoons Ruby
  Port
⅔ cup orange juice
¾ cup red currant jelly
6 tablespoons fresh lemon juice
3 tablespoons orange zest
2 tablespoons lemon zest

Fresh rosemary sprigs

Preheat oven to 425 degrees. Place 2 of the racks of lamb on a baking sheet. Place the third rack on a separate baking sheet. Season with salt, pepper and the chopped rosemary. Cover rib bone ends with heavy-duty aluminum foil. Insert meat thermometer. Roast until internal temperature reaches 130 to 140 degrees for rare to medium-rare, approximately 20 to 25 minutes. To prepare the sauce, in a medium, heavy saucepan over medium to high heat, bring the port, orange juice, currant jelly, lemon juice and zests to a boil, stirring continuously. Reduce heat and simmer until sauce thickens slightly, approximately 5 minutes. Cut lamb between the bones. Place three chops on each individual plate. Garnish with rosemary sprigs. Serve *Port Currant Sauce* on the side.

Note: Sauce may be prepared up to 3 days ahead. Cover and refrigerate; re-warm over low heat.

Yield: 8 servings

Rania Harris, owner,
Rania's To Go Catering

Rabbit Sauce over Polenta

1 pound rabbit meat, cut into
    1-inch pieces
2-4 tablespoons olive oil
3 cloves garlic, minced
½ medium onion, chopped
Salt and freshly ground black
    pepper, to taste
1 (28-ounce) can tomato purée
1 (28-ounce) can whole tomatoes,
    pulsed in blender for 5 seconds
1 tablespoon chopped fresh
    rosemary, optional
1 cup instant polenta
Chopped fresh basil
Freshly grated Parmesan cheese

In a large, heavy pot or Dutch oven, over medium heat, brown the rabbit in the olive oil. Add garlic and onion; sauté for 1 minute. Season with salt and pepper. Add the tomato purée, whole tomatoes and rosemary. Cover and simmer for 1½ hours. Prepare the polenta according to package directions. Place cooked polenta on a serving platter. Ladle the rabbit sauce over polenta. Garnish with basil and top with Parmesan cheese. *Serve with crusty Italian bread and red wine for a rustic Italian meal.*

Variation: Squirrel meat may be substituted for the rabbit meat.

Yield: 2 servings

Dom Mondelli

Enchilada Pie

1 pound ground beef
1 large onion, chopped
2 cloves garlic, minced
1 (10¾-ounce) can tomato soup
1 (8-ounce) can tomato sauce
1 cup water
3 tablespoons flour dissolved in
    3 tablespoons water
2 teaspoons chili powder, or to
    taste
¾ teaspoon crushed red pepper
    flakes, or to taste
1 tablespoon apple cider vinegar
1 teaspoon salt, optional
30-36 saltine crackers
    (approximately 1 sleeve),
    divided
1 (12-ounce) bag shredded
    Cheddar cheese, divided
Sour cream, optional
Guacamole, optional

Preheat oven to 350 degrees. Grease a 2-quart casserole; set aside. In a large skillet, over medium heat, sauté the meat, onion and garlic until meat browns; drain well. Stir in the tomato soup, tomato sauce and water. Add the flour, chili powder, red pepper flakes, vinegar and salt to skillet. Cook, stirring, over medium to high heat until thickened, approximately 5 minutes. Set aside 1 cup of the meat sauce. Layer ⅓ of the remaining meat sauce in bottom of prepared casserole. Top with ⅓ of the crackers and ⅓ of the cheese. Repeat layers. Top casserole with the reserved meat sauce. Bake for 45 minutes or until heated through. Serve with sour cream and guacamole.

Variation: For a tasty low-fat variation, substitute ground turkey for the ground beef.

Yield: 6 to 8 servings

Kathy Raffensperger

Bacon and Swiss Cheese Meatloaf

¾ **pound sliced bacon, cut into**
¼-inch pieces
4 large white mushrooms,
chopped
1 small white onion, chopped
1 pound extra-lean ground beef
1 egg, lightly beaten
¼ cup half & half
8 ounces shredded Swiss cheese,
or to taste
½ cup crushed cornflakes

Preheat oven to 350 degrees. Grease a 9x5x3-inch loaf pan; set aside. In a large skillet, fry bacon until crisp. Using a slotted spoon, remove bacon; set aside on paper towels to drain. Drain skillet, reserving 1 teaspoon of bacon fat. Sauté mushrooms and onion in the reserved fat until tender; set aside to cool. In a large bowl, mix together the ground beef, egg and half & half. Set aside 2 tablespoons of the bacon and 2 tablespoons of the cheese. Add the mushrooms, onion, bacon, cheese and corn flakes to meat mixture; thoroughly combine. Shape mixture into a loaf; place in prepared pan. Bake for 1 hour. Drain fat from loaf pan. Sprinkle the reserved bacon and cheese over top of loaf. Bake for an additional 5 minutes, or until cheese is bubbly. Let rest for 10 minutes before removing meat from pan and slicing.

Yield: 4 to 6 servings

Matthew McKenna

Mom's Chipped Ham BBQ Sandwiches

BBQ Sauce
¼ **cup butter**
½ **cup finely chopped onion**
1 (15-ounce) can tomato sauce
½ **teaspoon salt**
¼ **teaspoon ground black pepper**
2 teaspoons Worcestershire sauce
1 tablespoon brown mustard
2 tablespoons brown sugar
2 tablespoons freshly squeezed
   lemon juice
½ **cup water**

1 pound chipped ham

In a large saucepan, over medium heat, melt the butter. Add the onion; sauté until soft. Add the remaining BBQ Sauce ingredients; stir to combine. Cover pot and simmer for ½ hour. Place chipped ham in sauce. Simmer for an additional 20 minutes, or until ham is heated through. Serve ham and sauce on sandwich buns.

Note: In Pittsburgh, Isaly's is the chipped ham of choice.

Yield: 6 servings; 2½ cups BBQ Sauce

Dorothy Rauch

Steeler Sunday Lunch

Hot Shredded Roast Beef Sandwiches

1 (5-pound) boneless chuck roast
2-4 tablespoons olive oil, to taste
3 (10½-ounce) cans condensed
   French onion soup
1 tablespoon Italian seasoning,
   optional
½ **teaspoon crushed red pepper**
   flakes, optional

Preheat oven to 325 degrees. Cut roast into cubes. In a large skillet, over medium heat, cook the meat in the olive oil, stirring, until evenly browned. Transfer meat to a large baking pan or casserole. Pour condensed soup over meat and sprinkle with the Italian seasoning and red pepper flakes. Add enough water to pan to just cover meat. Bake, uncovered, for 3 to 4 hours; adding water as needed to maintain moistness. Shred cooked meat and transfer to a serving dish. Pour any remaining juice from baking pan over meat. Serve warm with sandwich rolls. *Add a green salad and potato dish for a hearty Steeler game-day luncheon.*

Note: Place cooked meat and liquid in a crockpot, set on low, for an easy buffet entrée.

Yield: Approximately 30 servings

*Elizabeth Ann DeNardo Stumpf
and Angie Sassos*

Sloppy Josephines

1 pound lean ground beef or
  turkey
½ onion, chopped
1 cup water
1 egg, beaten
1 tablespoon sugar
1 tablespoon white vinegar
⅔ cup cornflakes, crushed
1 (19-ounce) bottle ketchup

In a large skillet, over medium heat, sauté the meat and onion until the meat is cooked through and browned; drain well. Add the water, egg, sugar and vinegar; cook over low heat for 20 minutes, stirring occasionally. Add the cornflakes and ketchup; simmer for 15 minutes. Serve on hamburger buns.

Yield: 6 to 8 servings

Anne McCafferty

Vietnamese Lettuce Wraps

1 head of Boston lettuce
  (approximately 24 leaves)
3 stalks of lemon grass, peeled,
  chopped
2 serrano chiles, seeded, chopped
1 tablespoon chopped cilantro
  stems
1 tablespoon minced garlic
1 tablespoon sugar
1 pound ground pork
2 tablespoons fish sauce
1 teaspoon freshly ground black
  pepper, and to taste
4 tablespoons peanut oil, divided
8 scallions (white part and small
  amount of green), finely sliced
⅓ cup dry-roasted peanuts, finely
  chopped
Fresh cilantro
Fresh mint sprigs

Gently remove individual leaves from head of lettuce. Rinse under cold water and set aside to drain. Using a food processor, pulse together the lemon grass, serrano chiles, cilantro stems, garlic and sugar until finely ground. In a medium bowl, mix together the lemon grass mixture, ground pork, fish sauce, black pepper and 1 tablespoon of the peanut oil; set aside. In a large skillet, over high heat, heat 2 tablespoons of the peanut oil. Add scallions; stir-fry for 2 minutes. Remove scallions from skillet; set aside to drain on paper towels. Add the remaining 1 tablespoon of peanut oil to skillet. Decrease heat to medium. Add pork mixture. Cook, stirring, until pork browns completely, approximately 8 to 12 minutes. Season with additional black pepper, if desired. Place pork mixture on a serving platter; garnish with the scallions and chopped peanuts. To assemble, place approximately ¼ cup of the pork mixture on an individual lettuce leaf. Garnish with cilantro and a sprig of mint. *Roll up and enjoy.*

Yield: Approximately 24 wraps; 12 servings

Linda Hillenburg

N. Point Breeze

*C*entrally located in Pittsburgh's East End, North Point Breeze is one of Pittsburgh's smallest neighborhoods but one that is replete with history, charm and natural beauty. Its name originated in the late 1800's when residents identified their community as being north of the well-known Point Breeze Hotel. The establishment, which catered to travelers in wagons and carriages, was located on the Greensburg Pike where Fifth and Penn Avenues meet today.

After streetcars opened up the East End to development in the late 1880's, North Point Breeze was one of the first planned suburban developments in the U.S. Thomas, Meade and McPherson Boulevards were designed to resemble large French boulevards with wide divided roads, floral islands and a mix of mansions and apartment buildings. These are still present today along with many original ornate entranceways and hitching posts.

The streets of North Point Breeze echo national historical periods. Thomas Boulevard was named for General George Thomas, a decorated Civil War hero. Meade Street was named for General George Meade who served with distinction in both the Mexican and Civil Wars. Civil War history and memories were still fresh at the time the neighborhood's streets were laid out. Immense estates in the area were broken up into smaller parcels for housing development. The "smaller" lots, however, were still quite large and allowed for low-density development and the building of grand houses with expansive porches and lawns. Most of the homes are brick and nearly all have level lots, a very unusual feature in Pittsburgh.

Much of North Point Breeze history is woven into Pittsburgh's economic history. Many prominent industrialists such as H.J. Heinz and George Westinghouse called the area home. Westinghouse Park is a reminder of this influence. Adjoining North Point Breeze is Point Breeze, home of the Frick Art and Historical Center. This Victorian-era complex includes "Clayton" the restored estate of the wealthy Pittsburgh industrialist Henry Clay Frick and his family, the Frick Art Museum, the Carriage Museum, and a lovely café.

In addition to Westinghouse Park, North Point Breeze residents are close to Frick Park and Mellon Park. Within a short walking distance, the city parks offer art fairs, community festivals, concerts, tennis courts, lawn bowling, ball fields, walking paths and natural beauty. ♥♥

Gingersnaps

2 cups flour
3 teaspoons baking soda
¼ teaspoon salt
1 teaspoon ground cloves
1 teaspoon cinnamon
1 teaspoon ginger
¾ cup shortening
1½ cups sugar, divided
¼ cup molasses
1 egg, lightly beaten

In a small bowl, mix together the flour, baking soda, salt and spices; set aside. In a large mixing bowl, using an electric mixer, cream together the shortening and 1 cup of the sugar. Add the molasses and egg; mix well. Decrease mixer speed to low. Add the flour mixture slowly until thoroughly combined. Cover dough and refrigerate for a minimum of 1 hour. Preheat oven to 350 degrees. Shape dough into 1-inch balls. Roll dough balls in the remaining ½ cup of sugar. Place 2 inches apart on ungreased baking sheets. Bake for 8 to 10 minutes. Cookies will puff and develop cracks while baking. Allow cookies to cool slightly before removing to wire rack to cool completely.

Note: Dough may be prepared 1 day ahead. Cover and refrigerate. Dough freezes well.

Yield: Approximately 4 dozen

Bernadine Bonessa

Swedish Butter Cookies

1 cup butter, softened
½ cup sugar
1 teaspoon vanilla extract
2 cups flour
Colored sugar crystals

In a large bowl, cream together the butter and sugar. Add the vanilla extract. Slowly add the flour; mix well. Divide dough in half. Shape each dough half into 1 (10x2-inch) log. (If dough is sticky, chill for 5 to 10 minutes.) Spread sugar crystals on waxed paper. Roll each log in crystals to evenly coat. Wrap logs in clean waxed paper and refrigerate for 1 hour. Preheat oven to 375 degrees. Line baking sheet(s) with parchment paper. Remove logs from refrigerator; slice into ¼-inch rounds. Place cookie rounds on prepared baking sheet. Bake for 9 minutes. Allow cookies to cool on baking sheet for a few minutes to prevent crumbling.

Yield: 6 to 7 dozen

Karen Mitchell

193

Cousin Goldie's Baklava

Syrup
1 cup water
2 cups sugar
1 cinnamon stick
1 orange slice, cut ½-inch thick
½ cup light corn syrup
½ cup honey

Filling
2 pounds shelled walnuts, finely chopped
1 teaspoon ground cinnamon
½ teaspoon ground nutmeg
½ cup sugar
1 teaspoon finely grated lemon rind

Phyllo
1 (1-pound) box phyllo dough, thawed in refrigerator, brought to room temperature
1 pound butter, melted (do not substitute)

Preheat oven to 325 degrees. To prepare the syrup, in a small saucepan combine the water, sugar, cinnamon stick, and orange slice. Bring mixture to a boil over medium heat, stirring continuously. Boil, stirring, for 10 minutes. Add corn syrup and honey; boil an additional 5 minutes, stirring. Remove cinnamon stick and orange slice. Set aside to cool completely. To prepare the filling, in a medium bowl, mix together all filling ingredients; set aside. To prepare the phyllo, open package and lay phyllo sheets flat. Using a sharp knife, trim the sheets to fit a 13x9x2-inch baking pan. Immediately cover phyllo sheets with a damp towel (phyllo dries out very quickly and must be kept covered between use). Using a pastry brush, generously and evenly coat the bottom and sides of baking pan with the melted butter. Lay one sheet of phyllo on the bottom of pan; brush evenly and generously with the butter. (Do not skimp!) Repeat this step until there are 8 sheets of buttered phyllo on the bottom of pan. Sprinkle ⅓ of the filling mixture over these 8 sheets of phyllo. Place 3 more sheets of phyllo over top of filling, buttering between each sheet. Sprinkle another ⅓ of the filling over these 3 sheets of phyllo. Again, add 3 more sheets of phyllo over filling, buttering between each sheet. Sprinkle the remaining ⅓ of the filling over these sheets of phyllo. Top with the remaining 8 sheets of phyllo, buttering generously between each sheet and over the entire top of the last sheet. To form traditional diamond-shaped pieces, using a sharp knife going from top to bottom of pan, score 8 diagonal lines across baklava from left to right. Proceed by scoring 9 diagonal lines in opposite direction going from right to left. (Lines should be evenly spaced, approximately 2½x2-inches point to point.) Bake for 30 minutes to 1 hour, or until baklava is a rich

Cousin Goldie's Baklava (continued)

golden brown. Immediately after removing from oven, pour cooled syrup over the hot baklava. To serve, cut along diagonal score lines.

Note: The secret to crispy, flaky baklava is the generous use of butter throughout the recipe and the pouring of completely cooled syrup over the hot baklava.

Yield: Approximately 40 baklava

Marcella Karvellis McGuire

Nouna's Koulourakia

Greek Cookies

1 pound unsalted butter, softened (do not substitute)
1 cup sugar
2 large egg yolks
½ teaspoon baking powder dissolved in 1 tablespoon warm milk
1 teaspoon baking soda
1 teaspoon pure almond extract
2 teaspoons pure vanilla extract
⅛ teaspoon salt
5 cups flour
2 eggs, well beaten
½ cup white sesame seeds

Preheat oven to 350 degrees. In a large bowl, using an electric mixer, cream together the butter and sugar. Add egg yolks; mix well. Add the dissolved baking powder and the baking soda. Mix in the extracts and salt. Add flour, 1 to 2 cups at a time, mixing well by hand after each addition. If necessary, add a little extra flour to obtain a dough that is soft, but not sticky. To shape cookies into a traditional twist, scoop a well-rounded table-spoonful of dough; shape into a rope 6 to 6½-inches long and ½-inch thick. Fold rope in half. Fold left side of rope over right side of rope, followed by folding right side of rope over left side of rope. Place cookies on ungreased baking sheets 1½ inches apart. Brush the tops of cookies with beaten egg; sprinkle with sesame seeds. Bake for 15 to 20 minutes until light golden brown. Cool cookies on wire racks.

Note: Kept in a tightly sealed container, cookies freeze well for up to 1 month.

Yield: Approximately 46 cookies

Marcella Karvellis McGuire

Fancy Fruit Squares

1 cup butter, softened
1½ cups sugar
4 eggs, lightly beaten
1 teaspoon vanilla extract
1 teaspoon lemon extract
2 cups flour, sifted
1 (21-ounce) can cherry pie filling
Powdered sugar, to taste

Preheat oven to 350 degrees. Grease a 13x9x2-inch baking pan; set aside. In a large bowl, cream together the butter and sugar. Add the eggs; mix well. Stir in the vanilla and the lemon extracts. Gradually mix in the flour. Spread mixture into prepared pan. Using a knife, score the mixture into 12 or 16 equal sections. Place 1 heaping tablespoon of pie filling atop each section. Bake for 35 to 40 minutes. Cool in pan on wire rack. To serve, cut along score lines; sprinkle with powdered sugar.

Note: Fruit will bake into scored crevices.

Variation: Use apple pie filling in place of the cherry and sprinkle top with a mixture of powdered sugar and cinnamon.

Yield: 12 to 16 servings

Calyn Rosfeld

The Best Brownies Ever

Brownies
1 cup flour
½ cup cocoa powder
2 cups sugar
1 teaspoon salt
1 cup butter, melted
4 eggs
1 teaspoon vanilla extract

Icing
½ cup butter, softened
½ cup cocoa powder
1 teaspoon vanilla extract
1 (1-pound) box powdered sugar
4-5 tablespoons milk

Preheat oven to 350 degrees. Lightly grease a 13x9x2-inch baking pan. In a large bowl, combine the flour, cocoa powder, sugar and salt. Add the butter and eggs; thoroughly combine. Stir in the vanilla extract. Pour mixture into prepared pan. Bake for 25 minutes. (Do not overbake.) Cool in pan on wire rack. To prepare the icing, in a large bowl, mix together the butter and cocoa powder. Add vanilla; mix well. Gradually add the powdered sugar, alternating with small amounts of milk, until mixture has a smooth and spreadable consistency. Spread icing over cooled brownies. *If you have a craving for chocolate, these brownies will satisfy it.*

Note: For less sweetness, cut icing recipe in half.

Yield: 15 to 20 brownies

Eileen Solomich

Caramel Cups

Cups
6 ounces cream cheese, softened
1 cup margarine, softened
2 cups flour

Filling
60 light caramel squares from
**   1 (14-ounce) bag**
½ cup evaporated milk

Frosting
½ cup margarine, softened
½ cup evaporated milk
⅔ cup sugar
½ cup shortening
1 teaspoon vanilla extract

½ cup ground peanuts, pecans
**   or walnuts**

Preheat oven to 350 degrees. To prepare the cups, in a medium bowl, mix together all cup ingredients. Shape dough into 1-inch balls; press onto bottom and up the sides of ungreased mini-muffin tins to form dough cups. Using a fork, prick the dough of each cup 2 to 3 times. Bake for 20 minutes. Remove from oven; set aside to cool. Remove cups from pan prior to filling. To prepare the filling, using a double boiler, melt the caramel with evaporated milk, stirring until creamy. Fill cups with caramel mixture to almost level with top of cup; set aside to cool. To prepare the frosting, in a small mixing bowl, blend together all frosting ingredients; blend until smooth, approximately 10 minutes. Spread frosting over tops of cooled cups. Sprinkle with ground nuts. *These are a favorite with the Sacred Heart Elementary School teachers and staff.*

Variation: Shaved chocolate may be used in place of ground nuts.

Yield: 4 to 6 dozen, depending on amount of dough used per cup

Pam Giardina

Hot Fudge Brownies

½ cup milk
2 tablespoons butter, melted
1 teaspoon vanilla extract
1 cup flour
⅔ cup sugar
2 teaspoons baking powder
½ teaspoon salt
½ teaspoon cinnamon
½ cup cocoa powder, divided
1 cup brown sugar
1½ cups boiling water

Preheat oven to 350 degrees. Lightly grease and flour an 8x8x2-inch baking pan; set aside. In a small bowl, mix together the milk, butter and vanilla extract; set aside. In a medium bowl, mix together the flour, sugar, baking powder, salt, cinnamon and ¼ cup of the cocoa powder. Stir wet ingredients into dry until thoroughly combined and smooth. Spread mixture evenly into prepared pan. In a small bowl, mix together the remaining ¼ cup cocoa powder with the brown sugar. Sprinkle mixture over top of batter in pan. Do not mix! Pour boiling water over top of the brown sugar layer. Do not mix! Bake for 30 minutes. Cool in pan on wire rack for 10 minutes to set. *For a delicious treat, serve warm with vanilla ice cream.*

Note: Batter will separate into cake and fudge layers.

Yield: 12 servings

Mike Rosfeld

100 Second Cookies

3¾ cups flour
3 teaspoons baking powder
1½ teaspoons salt
1½ cups butter, softened
3 cups sugar
6 eggs
3 teaspoons vanilla extract

Preheat a waffle iron. In a medium bowl, sift together the flour, baking powder and salt; set aside. In a large mixing bowl, using an electric mixer, cream together the butter and sugar. Add eggs and vanilla extract; blend well. Gradually add the dry ingredients to the creamed mixture, beating until thoroughly combined. Drop 1½ to 2 teaspoonfuls of mixture onto each quarter of the waffle iron. Close lid; cook for 100 seconds.

Yield: Approximately 100 cookies

Teachers Jennifer Greenwald and Megan Shanley, in recognition of Sacred Heart Elementary School Kindergarten's 100 Day Celebration.

Sour Cream Sugar Cookies

3 cups flour
1 teaspoon baking soda
½ teaspoon baking powder
½ teaspoon salt
½ cup margarine, softened
  (do not substitute)
1½ cups sugar
2 eggs
1 teaspoon vanilla extract
1 cup sour cream

Preheat oven to 400 degrees. Grease 2 baking sheets; set aside. In a medium bowl, sift together the flour, baking soda, baking powder and salt; set aside. In a large mixing bowl, using an electric mixer, cream together the margarine and sugar. Add eggs, one at a time, beating well after each addition. Add the vanilla extract. Continue beating until mixture is light and fluffy. Add flour mixture, alternately with the sour cream, to the margarine mixture. Cream until well blended. (Batter will be thick.) Drop by teaspoonfuls onto prepared baking sheets. Bake for 8 to 10 minutes. Do not allow cookies to over-brown.

Note: These cookies are delicious plain or iced with your favorite frosting. Store cookies in a sealed container.

Yield: 6 dozen

Karen Mitchell

Peanut Butter Temptations

½ cup butter, softened
½ cup peanut butter
½ cup brown sugar
½ cup granulated sugar
1 egg
½ teaspoon vanilla extract
1¼ cups flour
¾ teaspoon baking soda
1 (13-ounce) bag miniature peanut
  butter cups

Preheat oven to 375 degrees. In a large mixing bowl, using an electric mixer, cream together the butter, peanut butter and both sugars. Add the egg and vanilla extract; beat well. In a separate bowl, sift together the flour and baking soda. Add the flour mixture to the butter mixture; mix well. Shape dough into 1-inch balls. Place dough balls in mini-muffin tins. Bake for 12 minutes. Remove from oven and immediately press a peanut butter cup into center of each cookie. Allow cookies to cool in tins.

Yield: 3 to 4 dozen

Kelly Runco

Nastar

Indonesian Filled Cookies

Filling
1 cup dried apricots, diced
1 cup water
½ cup sugar
Pinch of salt, or to taste

Dough
7 tablespoons margarine, softened
3½ tablespoons butter, softened
   (plus additional, if needed)
2 egg yolks
7 tablespoons sugar
⅛ teaspoon vanilla crystals
2¼ cups flour

To prepare the filling, place the apricots and water in a medium saucepan. Cook, stirring, over low heat, until mixture becomes a soft paste, approximately 30 minutes. Add sugar and salt, stirring until dissolved. Set filling aside to cool. Preheat oven to 375 degrees. To prepare the dough, in a large bowl, mix together the margarine, butter, egg yolks, sugar and vanilla crystals until thoroughly combined. Add the flour gradually, by hand, until dough holds together. Additional butter may be used if dough texture is too hard. Using the palm of your hands, press and shape small amounts of dough (approximately ½ tablespoon) into 2½x1½-inch ovals that are ⅛ to ¼-inch thick. Spoon approximately ¾ teaspoonfuls of filling onto center of each oval. Pinch edges of dough closed around the filling. Place cookies seam-side down on an ungreased baking sheet. Bake until lightly browned, approximately 15 to 20 minutes. *These deliciously flaky cookies always receive compliments.*

Note: Vanilla crystals are found at premium coffee shops or in Asian food stores.

Variation: Dates may be used in place of apricots.

Yield: 2½ dozen

Sonja Hissom-Braun

Apricot Almond Squares

1 cup dried apricots
½ cup unblanched almonds,
    toasted
½ cup butter, softened
¼ cup granulated sugar
1 cup flour, divided
½ teaspoon baking powder
¼ teaspoon salt
2 eggs, at room temperature
1 cup firmly packed brown sugar
½ teaspoon vanilla extract
¼ teaspoon almond extract
Powdered sugar

Preheat oven to 350 degrees. Place apricots in a small saucepan; add enough water to cover. Bring to a boil. Decrease heat; cover and simmer until tender, approximately 12 to 15 minutes. Drain well and pat dry using paper towels; set aside to cool. When able to handle, cut apricots into ⅛ to ¼-inch slivers; set aside. Using a food processor or blender, grind almonds to form coarse crumbs. In a small mixing bowl, using an electric mixer, beat together the butter and granulated sugar until fluffy. Blend in ground almonds and ½ cup of the flour. Spread mixture evenly over the bottom of an ungreased 9-inch square glass baking pan. Bake for 16 to 20 minutes, until lightly browned. Remove from oven; set aside. In a small bowl, mix together the remaining ½ cup of flour, baking powder and salt; set aside. In a large mixing bowl, using an electric mixer on high speed, beat together the eggs and brown sugar. Decrease speed to low; gradually add the flour mixture. Mix in the vanilla and almond extracts. Gently stir in the apricots. Spread mixture evenly over the baked crust. Return pan to oven; bake until top is golden, approximately 30 minutes. Remove pan to wire rack; cool for 10 minutes. Cut into squares. Sift a light layer of powdered sugar over tops of squares. Cool completely before removing from pan.

Yield: 16 to 24 squares

Dorothy Rescher

Surprise Chocolate Pudding

1 cup semi-sweet chocolate chips
1 (12-ounce) package soft tofu,
    drained
¼ cup soy or regular milk
2 tablespoons water or coffee
1-2 teaspoons vanilla extract,
    to taste
Pinch of salt

Using a microwave oven or double boiler, melt the chocolate chips. Using a blender, blend together the tofu, soy milk, water, vanilla extract and salt until smooth. On low speed, blend in the chocolate. Pour into individual serving bowls and refrigerate. Serve chilled. *No one will ever suspect that this is made with tofu.*

Yield: 4 to 6 servings

Patty Just

Pie Cookies

Crust
1 (9-ounce) box pie crust mix
    (enough for 2 (9-inch) crusts)
3-4 tablespoons water
¼ cup sugar

Filling
⅓ cup sugar
1 teaspoon cinnamon
2 tablespoons honey
1 teaspoon lemon juice
1 cup finely chopped pecans

Milk

Topping
½ cup semi-sweet chocolate chips
1 teaspoon shortening

Preheat oven to 375 degrees. Line a baking sheet with parchment paper; set aside. To prepare the crust, in a medium bowl, mix together all crust ingredients. Divide mixture in half. On a lightly floured surface, roll each crust half into a 9-inch circle. Place 1 crust half on prepared baking sheet; set second crust half aside. To prepare the filling, in a small bowl, mix together all filling ingredients. Spread filling mixture evenly over first crust to ½-inch from edge. Top with remaining crust. Using a fork, seal together the edges of both crusts. Prick top several times to allow pie to vent while baking. Brush top with a small amount of milk. Bake for 15 to 20 minutes, until slightly golden. Cool on baking sheet for 10 minutes. Cut pie into 16 to 20 wedges. To prepare the topping, in a double boiler, over low to medium heat, melt together the chocolate chips and shortening. Drizzle topping over cookie wedges.

Yield: 16 to 20 cookies

Beth Bergman

Cowboy Cookies

1 cup margarine, softened
1 cup granulated sugar
1 cup brown sugar
2 eggs, beaten
2 cups flour
1 teaspoon baking soda
½ teaspoon baking powder
½ teaspoon salt
1 teaspoon vanilla extract
1 cup flaked dried coconut
1 cup chopped nuts
2 cups unsweetened bran, oat or
   cornflakes

Preheat oven to 350 degrees. Lightly grease a baking sheet; set aside. In a large mixing bowl, using an electric mixer, cream together the margarine and sugars. Add eggs; mix well. In a medium bowl, mix together the flour, baking soda, baking powder and salt. Add flour mixture to sugar mixture; mix until thoroughly combined. Add vanilla extract, coconut and nuts; mix well. Stir in bran flakes by hand. Spoon rounded teaspoonfuls of cookie dough onto prepared baking sheet. Bake for 8 to 10 minutes, until edges brown and center of cookie is soft and light in color. (Do not overbake.) Allow cookies to cool completely on baking sheet before removing.

Note: Cookies continue to bake outside of oven and will be deliciously chewy.

Yield: Approximately 4 dozen
                              Bernadine Bonessa

Triple Chocolate Biscotti

4¾ cups flour
1 cup cocoa powder
1 tablespoon baking powder
2 cups sugar
1 cup butter, softened
4 tablespoons Crème de Cocoa liqueur
2 tablespoons water
2 cups coarsely chopped walnuts, optional
6 eggs, at room temperature
1 cup semi-sweet chocolate chips
6 ounces semi-sweet or sweetened (white or dark) baking chocolate

In a large bowl, mix together the flour, cocoa and baking powders; set aside. In a large mixing bowl, using an electric mixer, cream together the sugar, butter, liqueur and water. Add nuts. Add eggs to sugar mixture, one at a time, beating well after each addition. Slowly add flour mixture into sugar and egg mixture. Stir in the chocolate chips. Cover prepared dough with plastic wrap and refrigerate for 3 hours. Preheat oven to 375 degrees. Line 2 baking sheets with parchment paper. Divide dough into 4 equal portions. Place 2 dough portions on each baking sheet. Coat hands with oil or nonstick vegetable oil cooking spray and shape dough portions into long loaves, ½-inch high and 3-inches wide. Allow 3 inches between each loaf on baking sheets. Bake for 16 to 20 minutes, until firm to the touch. Cool on baking sheets for 15 minutes. Cut loaves diagonally into ½ to ¾-inch slices. Place slices, cut-side down, on baking sheets. Return to oven and bake 5 to 7 minutes on each side, until lightly browned. Allow biscotti to cool completely before removing from baking sheets. Using a double boiler, over medium heat, melt the baking chocolate. Remove from heat when chocolate is smooth and easily drips off a spoon. Rearrange biscotti slices into loaf form. Drizzle chocolate over each loaf. *This biscotti makes a beautiful presentation for any occasion.*

Note: Baking sheets may be greased if parchment paper is not available.

Variation: Pecans, macadamia nuts or almonds may be used in place of the walnuts.

Yield: 4 loaves; approximately 40 biscotti

Joanne Redondo

"Must Try" Peanut Brittle

1 cup raw Spanish peanuts
1 cup sugar
Dash of salt
½ cup light corn syrup
1 teaspoon vanilla extract
1 tablespoon butter or margarine,
    softened
1 teaspoon baking soda

Line a baking sheet with heavy-duty aluminum foil and coat with nonstick vegetable oil cooking spray; set aside. In a large microwaveable bowl, mix together the peanuts, sugar, salt and corn syrup. Cover with plastic wrap and microwave on high for 5 to 6 minutes. Using oven mitts, carefully remove bowl from oven. Stir in the vanilla extract and butter. Re-cover and microwave on high for an additional 1 minute and 20 seconds. Carefully remove from oven; quickly stir in the baking soda. (Mixture will bubble.) Quickly pour mixture onto prepared baking sheet, spreading into a thin layer. Let cool completely on baking sheet. Pull brittle off of foil as 1 large piece. Break into smaller pieces. Store brittle in a sealed container to prevent it from becoming tacky.

Note: Microwaves vary in intensity. These cooking times are suited to a 1200-watt microwave oven.

Variation: Almonds or cashews may be substituted for the Spanish peanuts.

Yield: Approximately 1 pound

Cathy Van Wassen

Mint Brownies

Brownie Layer
1 (16-ounce) can chocolate syrup
½ cup butter, softened
1 cup sugar
4 eggs
1 cup flour

Mint Layer
½ cup butter, softened
4 cups powdered sugar
4 tablespoons milk
1½ teaspoons peppermint extract
Food coloring, optional

Icing
½ cup butter
¾ cup chocolate chips

Preheat oven to 350 degrees. Lightly grease a 15x10x1-inch jelly-roll pan; set aside. To prepare the brownie layer, in a large bowl, mix together the chocolate syrup, butter and sugar. Add eggs; mix well. Stir in flour until well combined. Spread mixture evenly onto prepared pan. Bake for 25 to 35 minutes, or until center springs back when touched lightly. (Top of brownies will look moist.) Remove from oven and allow to cool for 15 minutes. Place pan in refrigerator and cool for an additional 20 minutes. To prepare mint layer, in a large bowl, mix together the butter and powdered sugar. Add milk and peppermint extract, mixing until smooth. Add food coloring, if desired. Spread mint layer evenly over cooled brownie layer; refrigerate for an additional 20 minutes. To prepare the icing, in a double boiler, melt the butter and chocolate chips. Spread icing over cooled mint layer. Refrigerate brownie until serving. Cut into 2-inch squares.

Note: Brownies freeze well.

Yield: Approximately 3 dozen

Jill O'Connor

Biscotti Di Regina

Queen's Cookies

1½ cups flour
⅔ cup sugar
¾ teaspoon baking powder
6 tablespoons butter, melted
1 egg, beaten
1½ teaspoons vanilla extract
¾ cup sesame seeds

Preheat oven to 350 degrees. In a medium bowl, mix together the flour, sugar and baking powder; set aside. Using a wooden spoon, blend in the butter, egg and vanilla extract. Using your hands, press the dough firmly together. Divide dough into approximately ½-cup portions. Shape dough portions into ¾-inch thick ropes, approximately 3 to 4 inches in length. Cut each rope length into 1 to 1½-inch pieces. Roll pieces in sesame seeds to completely coat. Place on ungreased baking sheets ½ inch apart. Bake for approximately 18 minutes until lightly golden. Cool completely on wire racks. *Delicious with a hot beverage.*

Note: Store biscotti in airtight containers.

Variation: Add 2 tablespoons of grated orange peel or ¾ teaspoon of anise seed to the dough.

Yield: 3 to 4 dozen

Terry Laskowski

Pumpkin Gobs

Cookie
2 cups brown sugar
1 cup vegetable or canola oil
2 large eggs
2 cups unseasoned pumpkin
1 teaspoon vanilla extract
3 cups flour
1 teaspoon baking soda
1 teaspoon baking powder
1 teaspoon salt
1 teaspoon ground cloves
1 teaspoon ground cinnamon
1 teaspoon ground ginger

Icing
1 (3-ounce) package vanilla
  instant-pudding mix
1 cup sugar
1 cup shortening
1 cup milk
1 teaspoon vanilla extract

Powdered sugar

Preheat oven to 350 degrees. Grease 2 large baking sheets; set aside. To prepare cookie dough, in a large mixing bowl, using an electric mixer, cream together the brown sugar, oil and eggs. Mix in the pumpkin and vanilla extract; set aside. In a small bowl, mix together the flour, baking soda, baking powder, salt, cloves, cinnamon and ginger. Slowly add dry ingredients to the pumpkin mixture, beating until thoroughly combined (mixture will be thick). Spoon dough by rounded tablespoonfuls onto prepared baking sheets to make 48 cookies. Bake for 12 to 15 minutes. Set aside to cool completely. To prepare icing, in a small bowl, cream together all of the icing ingredients. Spread a generous amount of icing atop 1 cookie. Top with a second cookie to create a gob. Repeat for all remaining cookies. Sprinkle tops of the *Pumpkin Gobs* with powdered sugar.

Yield: 2 dozen gobs

Hannah and Alaire Chybrzynski

Brutzel Bars

Cracker Candy

**35 plain salted cracker squares
(approximately 1 sleeve)**
½ pound butter
½-1 cup sugar, to taste
**1 (12-ounce) bag semi-sweet
chocolate chips**
2 cups chopped walnuts, optional

Preheat oven to 350 degrees. Line a jelly-roll pan with heavy-duty aluminum foil. Place crackers side by side to cover entire bottom of pan; set aside. In a medium, heavy saucepan, over low heat, melt the butter. Add sugar; cook over medium to high heat, stirring, until mixture comes to a boil. Decrease heat and allow mixture to come to a *Brutzel boil* (a gentle, lazy surface bubbling). Immediately remove from heat and pour mixture over crackers. Spread the chocolate chips and walnuts evenly over top. Bake for 15 minutes, or until chocolate chips are melted. Allow to cool to room temperature. Refrigerate until hardened. Peel foil from back of *Brutzel Bars.* Break into cracker-size squares.

Note: Number of crackers used may vary depending on pan size.

Variation: White chocolate chips may be used in place of the chocolate chips.

Yield: Approximately 35 bars

Diane Norkus and Lisa Granata

Luscious Lemon Squares

Crust
1 cup butter, softened
2 cups flour
½ cup powdered sugar

Filling
4 eggs, lightly beaten
6 tablespoons freshly squeezed lemon juice (approximately 2 lemons)
½ teaspoon lemon zest, optional
2 cups sugar
4 tablespoons flour
½ teaspoon baking powder

Powdered sugar

Preheat oven to 350 degrees. To prepare the crust, in a medium bowl, mix together the butter, flour and powdered sugar. Press mixture into an ungreased 13x9x2-inch baking pan to evenly cover bottom. Bake for 25 minutes. While crust is baking, prepare the filling. In a medium bowl, whisk together the eggs, lemon juice, zest, sugar, flour and baking powder. Pour lemon mixture over baked crust; bake for an additional 25 minutes. Allow to cool before cutting into 2x2-inch squares. Dust the tops with powdered sugar.

Yield: 28 squares

Marie Malczak

Shoo Fly Cookies

Pastry
2 cups flour
½ pound butter, softened
1 (8-ounce) package cream cheese, softened

Filling
2 eggs
2 teaspoons butter, melted
½ teaspoon vanilla extract
1½ cups brown sugar
½ cup ground walnuts or pecans

Crumb Topping
¼ cup butter, softened
¾ cup flour
½ cup brown sugar

Preheat oven to 375 degrees. To prepare the pastry, in a medium bowl, mix together the flour, butter and cream cheese until a soft dough forms. Shape dough into 1-inch balls. Place 1 dough ball in each tin of 3 mini-muffin pans. Using a wooden tassie press or fingers, form each dough ball into a dough cup; set pan aside. To prepare the filling, in a medium bowl, mix together all of the filling ingredients. Add 1 teaspoon filling to each dough cup; set aside. To prepare crumb topping, in a small bowl, using a pastry blender, cut together the butter, flour and brown sugar until crumbly. Place equal amounts of crumb topping over top of each filled dough cup. Bake for 15 minutes.

Note: A prepared boxed pie crust mix may be substituted for the pastry.

Yield: 36 cookies

Darlene Fertig

Mom's Apple Dumplings

Dumplings
½ teaspoon baking powder
2 tablespoons sugar
Dough for 2 uncooked pie crusts
   (homemade or box mix),
   prepared using milk in place
   of water
6-8 baking apples, peeled, cored

Syrup
¾ cup brown sugar
2 cups water
2 tablespoons butter

Preheat oven to 375 degrees. Butter an 8x8 or a 9x13-inch baking dish; set aside. To prepare dumplings, add the baking powder and sugar to pie crust dough; knead lightly to thoroughly combine. On a lightly floured surface, roll pie crust dough into a large square or rectangle. Cut dough into 6 or 8 squares, depending on number of apples used. Place 1 apple on each dough square. Fold dough square edges up over sides of apple to cover. Crimp edges together to seal. Using a fork, prick through the dough into apple in numerous spots. Repeat with remaining apples. Place dough-covered apples in prepared baking dish. To prepare the syrup, in a small saucepan, over medium heat, mix together the brown sugar, water and butter until boiling and slightly thickened. Pour ½ of the syrup over the apples. Bake for 30 minutes. Pour remaining syrup over apples; bake for an additional 10 to 15 minutes. Serve dumplings warm. *Delicious with vanilla ice cream.*

Yield: 6 to 8 dumplings

Frances Flannagan

Scottish Shortbread

1 cup butter, softened
1 cup sugar, and to taste
3 cups flour

Preheat oven to 350 degrees. In a large bowl, cream together the butter and 1 cup of sugar. Add flour gradually. On a lightly floured surface, knead dough briefly. (If dough is difficult to handle, refrigerate for 20 minutes.) Press dough into an 8-inch round cake pan or form an 8-inch round on a baking sheet. (Dough should be ½ to ¾-inch thick.) Using a fork, prick entire depth of dough round at 1-inch intervals. Bake for 25 to 30 minutes until lightly browned. Sprinkle additional sugar over top of shortbread. Slice into pie-shaped wedges while still warm.

Yield: 16 shortbreads

Maura Petrone

Fred Deever's Fudge

1½ teaspoons butter, softened
¾ cup butter, melted
1 (7-ounce) package semi-sweet chocolate chips
1 (7-ounce) package milk chocolate chips
1 (7-ounce) package peanut butter chips
1 (14-ounce) can sweetened condensed milk
3 tablespoons whole milk
1 cup butterscotch chips
1 (7-ounce) jar marshmallow cream
½ teaspoon almond extract
½ teaspoon vanilla extract
1 cup chopped walnuts, optional

Line a 13x9x2-inch pan with heavy-duty aluminum foil. Grease the aluminum foil with the 1½ teaspoons butter. Place the melted butter, the semi-sweet chocolate, milk chocolate and peanut butter chips in a double boiler. Add the condensed and whole milks; stir over medium heat until smooth and melted. Remove from heat. Add the butterscotch chips, marshmallow cream, almond and vanilla extracts; mix well. Stir in the walnuts. Spread batter evenly in the prepared pan. Let cool until firm; cut into bite-size pieces.

Yield: 16 to 20 servings

Dubblebbees Dog Grooming Studio,
Highland Park neighborhood,
Pittsburgh, PA

Regent Square

*R*egent Square, a tree-lined neighborhood on the eastern edge of Pittsburgh, is nestled between Swisshelm Park, Squirrel Hill, Point Breeze, Wilkingsburg and Edgewood. Its border to the west is Frick Park, which was once known as Frick's Woods.

Regent Square was originally part of the Wilkins Place Plan of Lots. Wilkins, an engineer, designed the street plan in 1901. George Westinghouse became the major developer of the neighborhood as he sought to create a welcoming and comfortable area for his executives and their families. In 1907, Regent Square was said to have houses of every architectural type, as Westinghouse Company executives and engineers insisted on unique one-of-a-kind homes.

In 1913, the Harmon Company re-planned the neighborhood and named it Regent Square. Smaller homes began to be built in a square-like configuration and in the shadow of the large executive's residences that were considered to be "regent-like." The smaller houses were actually large three-story structures with stained glass windows and interesting architectural features.

In 1919, Pittsburgh industrialist Henry Clay Frick donated Frick's Woods to the City of Pittsburgh to be used as a park. His initial intent was to build a home on the 150-acre property. Upon his death, his will instructed that a million dollar trust fund be established for maintenance, capital improvements and additional land acquisition for the park. The will also stipulated that if the park was not maintained, the property and trust would revert to his trustees. As a result, between 1919 and 1942, over 300 additional acres were purchased to enlarge the park. Frick's daughter Helen also donated a large parcel of land bringing the total park area to 476 acres.

Regent Square has a vibrant business district along South Braddock Avenue. Pittsburgh Filmmakers operates the Regent Theatre. Flowering trees and broad sidewalks frame floral shops, restaurants, dentist and doctor offices, an art gallery, and bakery. Outdoor café seating adds to the neighborhood charm.

An active Regent Square Civic Association, proximity to downtown Pittsburgh, attractive and well-maintained housing stock, Frick Park with its ball fields, tennis courts, walking paths, and children's playground make Regent Square a thriving community and a showcase for city living. ♥♥

Peach Chiffon Pie

2 cups sliced fresh peaches
¾ cup sugar
1 (1-ounce) envelope plain gelatin
¼ cup cold water
½ cup hot water
1 tablespoon lemon juice
Dash of salt
1 cup whipping cream
1 (9 or 10-inch) pie crust, baked

In a small bowl, combine the peaches and sugar; let stand for 30 minutes. In a separate small bowl, stir the gelatin into the cold water. Let stand for 5 minutes until thickened. Add the hot water to gelatin; stir well. Set aside to cool. In a large bowl, combine the gelatin with ½ cup of the peaches; blend well. Add the remaining peaches, lemon juice and salt; blend well. Chill the peach mixture until partially set, approximately 5 minutes. In a chilled mixing bowl, whip the cream until slightly stiff. Do not overbeat. Using a spatula, gently fold ¼ of the whipped cream into peaches. Continue folding in the whipped cream, in batches, until completely incorporated. Gently spread the peach mixture into baked piecrust; chill until firmly set.

Yield: 6 to 8 servings

Alexandra Davides

Kathy's Cranberry-Raisin Pie

Filling
2 cups uncooked cranberries
1½ cups golden raisins
1½ cups sugar
¼ cup maple syrup
2 tablespoons butter, softened
1-2 tablespoons brandy, to taste
1 teaspoon vanilla extract
Grated rind of 1 orange

1 (9-inch) unbaked pie shell

Preheat oven to 450 degrees. In a large mixing bowl, combine all filling ingredients; mix well. Pour filling into unbaked pie shell. Bake for 15 minutes. Reduce temperature to 350 degrees; bake for an additional 30 to 40 minutes until set. *This rich pie is an attractive holiday dessert.*

Yield: 6 to 8 servings

Patty Just

Little Fellow Lemon Pies

Pastry for 2 (9-inch) pies,
  rolled thin

Filling
½ cup butter, softened
2 cups sugar
4 eggs
1 tablespoon flour
⅓ cup lemon juice

Powdered sugar, optional

Preheat oven to 350 degrees. Using a knife, cut pastry dough into 2½-inch squares. Line 4 dozen mini-muffin tins with dough squares; set aside. To prepare filling, using an electric mixer, cream together the butter and sugar. Add the eggs, one at a time, beating well after each addition. Add the flour; mix well. Stir in the lemon juice. Spoon filling into pastry shells to ⅔ full. Bake for 30 minutes or until golden. Let pies cool. Sprinkle with powdered sugar.

Note: The pastry may also be cut into 2¾-inch circles using a biscuit cutter.

Yield: 4 dozen

Darlene Fertig

Blueberry Crumb Cake

1 tablespoon dry unseasoned
  breadcrumbs

Crumb Topping
⅓ cup flour
½ cup sugar
1 teaspoon cinnamon
¼ cup butter, softened

Cake
2 cups flour
2 teaspoons baking powder
½ teaspoon salt
2 cups fresh blueberries, rinsed,
  drained
¼ cup butter, softened
¾ cup sugar
1 teaspoon vanilla extract
1 egg
½ cup milk
Zest of 1 lemon, approximately
  1 teaspoon

½ cup finely chopped walnuts,
  optional

Preheat oven to 375 degrees. Butter a 9-inch square baking pan; dust with the breadcrumbs; set aside. To prepare crumb topping, in a small bowl combine the flour, sugar and cinnamon. Using a pastry blender or fork, cut the butter into the flour mixture until crumbly. Set crumb topping aside. To prepare the cake, in a medium bowl, sift together the flour, baking powder and salt. In a small bowl, combine the blueberries with 1½ tablespoons of the sifted flour mixture; set aside. In a large mixing bowl, using an electric mixer, cream the butter with the sugar. Beat in the vanilla extract and egg until fluffy. Stir in the remaining sifted flour mixture and milk, alternately, starting and ending with the dry ingredients. Gently fold in the blueberries and lemon zest. (Batter will be stiff.) Spread batter evenly in prepared pan. Sprinkle with the walnuts and crumb topping. Bake for 50 minutes. Let stand for 10 minutes before serving.

Yield: 12 servings

Sarah Chybrzynski

Elaine's Excellent Chocolate Cake

2¼ cups flour
3 teaspoons baking powder
1 teaspoon baking soda
¼ teaspoon salt
½ cup butter, softened
2 cups sugar
2 eggs, separated
1 cup milk
⅔ cup unsweetened cocoa powder
    (imported Dutch cocoa
    preferred)
1 cup boiling water
1 teaspoon vanilla extract
1 tablespoon chocolate extract,
    optional

Bittersweet Chocolate Glaze
6 ounces semi-sweet chocolate
6 tablespoons fresh, strong coffee
6 tablespoons unsalted butter,
    chilled

Preheat oven to 350 degrees. Grease and flour a 13x9x2½-inch baking pan; set aside. In a small mixing bowl, sift together the flour, baking powder, baking soda and salt; set aside. In a large mixing bowl, using an electric mixer, cream together the butter and sugar until fluffy. Beat in the 2 egg yolks, one at a time. Add the dry mixture alternately with the milk, beating well after each addition. Dissolve cocoa powder in the boiling water; stir into batter. Add the vanilla and chocolate extracts. In a separate bowl, beat the 2 egg whites until stiff; gently fold into batter. Pour batter into prepared pan. Bake for 40 to 45 minutes, or until a cake tester inserted into center of cake comes out clean. (Do not over bake.) To prepare the glaze, in a double boiler, over medium heat, melt the chocolate while stirring in the coffee. Remove from heat. Whisk in the butter, 1 to 2 tablespoons at a time. Continue until butter is melted and emulsified into chocolate. Glaze will have a smooth consistency. Pour glaze over cooled cake. *Your company will love this chocolate cake.*

Variation: Once the glaze is set, spread apricot or raspberry preserves over the glaze for a European-style chocolate cake.

Yield: 12 to 16 servings

Elaine Light

Harvest Peach Coffee Cake

2 eggs
½ cup vegetable oil
1 cup milk
3 cups flour
1½ cups brown sugar
4 teaspoons baking powder
½ teaspoon salt
3 cups peeled, cubed fresh peaches

Streusel Topping
2 tablespoons butter, melted
½ cup brown sugar
⅓ cup flour, and to taste
1 tablespoon cinnamon
1 teaspoon allspice

Preheat oven to 375 degrees. Butter a 13x9-inch glass baking dish; set aside. In a large mixing bowl, using an electric mixer, combine the eggs, oil and milk; mix well. Slowly add the flour, brown sugar, baking powder and salt; beat until smooth. Pour batter into prepared pan; top with the peaches. In a separate bowl, combine all topping ingredients. If needed, add more flour, 1 tablespoon at a time, until topping is crumbly. Sprinkle topping evenly over peaches. Bake for 40 minutes or until a cake tester inserted in center of cake comes out clean. Serve warm.

Note: Out of season, substitute 1 (1-pound) bag of frozen unsweetened peaches. Thaw peaches at room temperature before use.

Yield: 12 servings

John Marthens

Gazebo Cheesecake

½-¾ cup crushed Graham
 crackers, approximately
 4 whole crackers
2 (8-ounce) packages cream
 cheese, softened
¾ cup sugar
3 medium eggs, lightly beaten
⅓ cup flour
3 tablespoons milk
3 tablespoons sour cream
1-2 teaspoons vanilla extract,
 to taste
1-2 teaspoons lemon extract,
 to taste

Preheat oven to 340 degrees. Grease an 8 or 9-inch springform pan or coat with a nonstick vegetable oil cooking spray. Press the graham crackers evenly onto bottom of pan and ¼ inch up the sides. Using an electric mixer, combine the cream cheese and sugar on low speed until smooth. Slowly add the eggs; blend until well combined. Scrape down the sides of bowl. Add the flour, milk, sour cream, and extracts; mix well. Pour batter into prepared pan. Place the pan inside a larger pan and add 1-inch of water to create a water bath. Bake for 1 hour. Allow cake to cool completely before removing sides from pan. *Many Pittsburghers will fondly remember eating this delicious cheesecake at the "Gazebo", a former Shadyside establishment.*

Yield: 8 to 10 servings

Melvin Hackman

Danielle and Kristen's Dreamed-Up Cake

1¾ cups flour
3 teaspoons baking powder
1 teaspoon salt
2 teaspoons cinnamon
2 ounces unsweetened chocolate
5 tablespoons boiling water
½ cup butter, softened
1½ cups sugar
4 egg yolks
1 cup milk
1 teaspoon vanilla extract
4 egg whites
Apples, peeled, cored, thinly sliced
Powdered sugar, optional

Preheat oven to 350 degrees. Grease a 13x9x2-inch pan; set aside. In a small mixing bowl, combine the flour, baking powder, salt and cinnamon; set aside. Using a double boiler, melt the chocolate. Mix 5 tablespoons of boiling water into the melted chocolate; set aside to cool. In a large mixing bowl, cream the butter. Add the sugar; cream until light and fluffy. Beat the egg yolks into the sugar mixture, one at a time. Add the chocolate; mix well. Alternately, add the flour mixture and milk, mixing well after each addition. Add the vanilla extract. In a separate bowl, whip the egg whites until stiff, but not dry. Gently fold egg whites into cake mixture. Pour into prepared pan and bake for 35 to 40 minutes. Cool cake in pan on a wire rack. Sprinkle lightly with powdered sugar. Serve cake with freshly cut apple slices. *A delicious variation of an old-time favorite.*

Yield: 12 to 16 servings

Danielle Fine and Kristen Raffensperger

Vanilla Butternut Pound Cake

½ cup shortening
1 cup butter, softened
3 cups sugar
¼ teaspoon salt
5 large eggs
3 cups flour
1 (4-ounce) can evaporated milk
   mixed with ½ cup water
2 tablespoons vanilla butternut
   flavoring
1 cup chopped nuts, optional
1 (10-ounce) jar maraschino
   cherries, drained, quartered
Powdered sugar, optional

Do not preheat oven. Grease and flour an 8 or 9-inch tube or Bundt pan; set aside. In a large mixing bowl, using an electric mixer, cream together the shortening, butter, sugar and salt. Add the eggs, one at a time, beating well after each addition. Alternately add the flour and evaporated milk to the shortening mixture, ending with flour. Mix in the flavoring and nuts. Gently fold in the cherries. Spread batter evenly into prepared pan. Place in cold oven. Heat oven to 300 degrees. Bake for 1 hour and 45 minutes. (Do not open oven door while cake is baking.) Immediately remove cake from pan; cool on a wire rack. Sprinkle powdered sugar over the top of cooled cake.

Yield: 12 to 16 servings

Betty Moyer

One-Step Pound Cake

2¼ cups flour
2 cups sugar
½ teaspoon salt
½ teaspoon baking soda
1 teaspoon vanilla extract
1 cup butter or margarine,
   softened
1 cup sour cream
3 eggs
Powdered sugar

Preheat oven to 325 degrees. Grease and flour a 10-inch bundt or tube pan; set aside. Place all ingredients, except powdered sugar, in a large mixing bowl. Using an electric mixer, blend on low speed until thoroughly combined. Beat on medium speed for 3 minutes. Pour batter into prepared pan; bake for 65 to 75 minutes or until a cake tester inserted in center of cake comes out clean. Let the cake cool in pan for 15 minutes. Remove cake from pan; cool completely on a wire rack. Before serving, sprinkle top of cake with powdered sugar. *A very moist pound cake everyone will love.*

Note: To prepare a simple glaze, combine 1 cup of powdered sugar and 1 to 2 tablespoons of lemon juice. Drizzle over the cake in place of the powdered sugar.

Variation: Substitute 1 (8-ounce) container pineapple yogurt for the sour cream.

Yield: 12 to 16 servings

Francine Marthens

Chocolate Zucchini Cake

½ cup milk
1 teaspoon vinegar
½ cup butter or margarine,
    softened
½ cup vegetable oil
1¾ cups sugar
2 eggs
1 teaspoon vanilla extract
2½ cups flour
4 tablespoons cocoa powder
½ teaspoon baking powder
1 teaspoon baking soda
½ teaspoon cinnamon
¼ teaspoon salt
2 cups grated peeled zucchini
½ cup chocolate chips

Preheat oven to 325 degrees. Grease a 13x9-inch baking pan; set aside. In a small bowl, combine the milk and vinegar to create sour milk; set aside. In a large mixing bowl, cream together the butter, oil and sugar. Add the eggs, vanilla extract and sour milk. In a separate bowl, combine the flour, cocoa powder, baking powder, baking soda, cinnamon, and salt. Add the dry ingredients to wet; mix well. Add the zucchini; stir gently to combine. Spread batter evenly into prepared pan. Sprinkle chocolate chips over top. Bake for 55 minutes or until a cake tester inserted in center of cake comes out clean. *A great alternative for using up the zucchini harvest.*

Yield: 12 servings

Deborah McCarthy

Chocolate Intrigue Cake

3 cups flour
2 teaspoons baking powder
½ teaspoon salt
1 cup butter, softened
2 cups sugar
3 eggs
1½ teaspoons vanilla extract
1 cup milk
¾ cup chocolate syrup
¼ teaspoon baking soda
Powdered sugar

Preheat oven to 350 degrees. Grease and flour the bottom of a 10-inch tube pan; set aside. In a medium bowl, sift together the flour, baking powder and salt; set aside. In a large mixing bowl, using an electric mixer, cream the butter. Gradually add the sugar; cream until smooth and fluffy. On medium speed, add the eggs one at a time, beating well after each addition. Add the vanilla extract to the milk. On low speed, alternately add the dry ingredients and milk; beginning and ending with dry ingredients. Pour ⅔ of the batter into the prepared pan. Blend the chocolate syrup and baking soda into the remaining batter. Pour batter into pan. Do not mix. Bake for 65 to 70 minutes, until cake springs back lightly when touched in the center. Remove cake from oven; let cool completely before inverting tube pan. Before serving, sprinkle with powdered sugar. *A fun cake to make with children.*

Yield: 12 to 16 servings

Kelly Runco

Nana's Ultimate Chocolate Cake

2 cups sugar
¾ cup shortening
2 eggs, beaten
2½ cups flour
¾ cup cocoa powder
2 teaspoons baking soda
1 cup buttermilk
1 teaspoon vanilla extract
1 cup boiling water

Icing
2 cups sugar
⅔ cup cocoa powder
1 teaspoon salt
8 tablespoons butter, softened
½ cup milk
2 teaspoons vanilla extract

Preheat oven to 350 degrees. Grease and flour a 13x9x2-inch pan; set aside. In a large mixing bowl, cream together the sugar and shortening. Add the eggs; mix well. In a separate bowl, sift the flour and cocoa powder together. Stir the baking soda into the buttermilk. Alternately, add the flour mixture and the buttermilk to the creamed mixture. Add the vanilla extract. Mix in the boiling water. Pour batter into prepared pan. Bake for 40 to 45 minutes or until a cake tester inserted into center of cake comes out clean. Let cake cool in the pan. To prepare icing, in a medium saucepan, combine all ingredients. Bring to a boil. Cook, stirring, for 1 minute. Remove from heat. Using an electric mixer, beat icing until thickened; spread evenly over cooled cake.

Yield: 12 to 16 servings

Pam Giardina

Cream Cheese Pound Cake

¾ cup margarine, softened
1 (8-ounce) package cream cheese, softened
1½ cups sugar
4 eggs
1½ teaspoons vanilla extract
2 cups flour
1½ teaspoons baking powder
Powdered sugar

Preheat oven to 325 degrees. Grease and flour a 10-inch Bundt pan; set aside. In a large mixing bowl, using an electric mixer, blend together the margarine, cream cheese and sugar. Add eggs one at a time, mixing well after each addition. Add the vanilla extract. Gradually add the flour and baking powder. Spread batter evenly into prepared pan. Bake for 50 to 60 minutes or until a cake tester inserted in center of cake comes out clean. Sprinkle top of cake with powdered sugar.

Note: For a thicker, crispier crust, grease Bundt pan with butter and use sugar in place of the flour.

Variation: For a delicious variation, reduce vanilla extract to ¾ teaspoon and add ¾ teaspoon lemon extract.

Yield: 12 to 16 servings

Francine Marthens

Pumpkin Chocolate Chip Cake

3 cups flour
2 cups sugar
2 teaspoons baking powder
2 teaspoons baking soda
½ teaspoon salt
½ teaspoon cinnamon
⅔ cup vegetable oil
4 eggs
1 (15-ounce) can pumpkin
1 cup chocolate chips

Powdered sugar, optional
Cinnamon, optional

Preheat oven to 350 degrees. Grease a 10-inch bundt pan; set aside. In a large mixing bowl, combine all cake ingredients. Mix well. Pour batter evenly into prepared pan. Bake for 1 hour, or until a cake tester inserted in center of cake comes out clean. Let cake cool for 20 minutes before removing from pan. Sprinkle with powdered sugar and cinnamon.

Yield: 12 to 16 servings

Cathy Rosfeld

Lorraine's Coffee Cake

1½ cups sifted flour
2 teaspoons baking powder
½ teaspoon salt
¾ cup sugar
¼ cup shortening, softened
1 egg
½ cup milk

Streusel
½ cup brown sugar
2 tablespoons flour
2 teaspoons cinnamon
2 tablespoons butter, melted
½ cup chopped nuts

Preheat oven to 375 degrees. Grease and flour an 8-inch square baking pan; set aside. In a small bowl, combine the flour, baking powder and salt; set aside. In a large bowl, mix together the sugar, shortening and egg. Stir in the milk. Gently fold in the flour mixture. To prepare the streusel, in a small bowl, combine all streusel ingredients; mix well. Spread ½ of the batter into prepared pan. Sprinkle ½ of the streusel evenly over top of batter. Spread the remaining batter evenly over streusel layer. Cover top of batter with the remaining streusel. Bake for 20 to 30 minutes or until a cake tester inserted in center of cake comes out with moist crumbs attached. Do not overbake.

Yield: 8 to 10 servings

Lorraine Raffensperger

Cranberry Pie Cake

2 cups cranberries, rinsed and
    drained
1½ cups chopped walnuts
1½ cups sugar, divided
2 eggs
1 cup butter, melted, cooled
1 cup flour
¼ teaspoon salt
¼ teaspoon almond extract

Preheat oven to 350 degrees. Grease a 10-inch springform pan or 10-inch deep-dish pie plate; set aside. In a medium bowl, combine cranberries, walnuts and ½ cup of the sugar. Spread cranberry mixture evenly over bottom of prepared pan. In the same bowl, mix together the eggs, butter, remaining 1 cup of the sugar, flour, salt and almond extract. Stir until smooth; pour over cranberry layer. Bake for 40 minutes or until a cake tester inserted in center of cake comes out clean. *A perfect holiday or winter dessert.*

Note: If using a springform pan, place a baking sheet with sides under pan in oven to catch possible drips.

Yield: 8 to 10 servings

Diane Norkus

Hotmilk Shortcakes

4 eggs
2 cups sugar
2 cups flour
2 teaspoons baking powder
1 teaspoon vanilla extract
1 cup milk
½ cup butter, softened
Powdered sugar

Preheat oven to 375 degrees. Place paper liners in 24 cupcake tins; set aside. In a large bowl, mix together the eggs, sugar, flour, baking powder and vanilla extract; set aside. In a small saucepan, over medium to low heat, bring the milk to a boil. Remove from heat. Add butter to milk; stir until melted. Add to egg mixture in bowl; mix well. Pour ¼ cup of the mixture into each cupcake tin, approximately ½ to ¾ full. Bake for 20 minutes or until a cake tester inserted in center comes out clean. Let shortcakes cool in tins. Sprinkle with powdered sugar or top with your favorite jam.

Note: The shortcakes also make a delicious base for strawberry shortcakes.

Yield: 24 shortcakes

Karen Mitchell

Crazycakes with Ice Cream Frosting

Cakes
3 cups flour
2 cups sugar
½ cup cocoa powder
2 teaspoons baking soda
1 teaspoon salt
2 teaspoons vanilla extract
2 tablespoons white vinegar
¾ cup vegetable oil
2 cups water

Frosting
2 cups powdered sugar
½ cup shortening
1 tablespoon flour
2 tablespoons milk
1 egg white
1 tablespoon butter, softened
1 teaspoon vanilla extract

Powdered sugar

Preheat oven to 350 degrees. Place paper liners in 30 cupcake tins; set aside. To prepare the cakes, in a large mixing bowl, combine all cake ingredients. Using an electric mixer, beat until well blended. Pour batter into each cupcake tin, approximately ½ full. Bake for 15 to 20 minutes or until a cake tester inserted in center of 1 cake comes out clean. Allow cakes to cool completely. To prepare frosting, in a large bowl, using an electric mixer, cream together all frosting ingredients until smooth. To assemble crazycakes, cut out quarter-size round holes, ½ to ¾-inch deep, from tops of each cake. Remove cake pieces; set aside. Place frosting into holes. Place cake pieces back onto frosting-filled crazycakes. Sprinkle tops of cakes with powdered sugar.

Note: For even more festive crazycakes, add food coloring to the frosting.

Yield: 30 crazycakes

Karen Mitchell

Marge's Cheesecake

1 cup plus 2 tablespoons sugar, divided
3 (8-ounce) packages cream cheese, softened
¾ teaspoon almond extract
¼ teaspoon salt
5 eggs
1 cup sour cream
½ teaspoon vanilla extract

Preheat oven to 325 degrees. Butter a round 9-inch nonstick cake pan or glass pie plate; set aside. Using an electric mixer on the lowest speed, mix together 1 cup of the sugar with the cream cheese, almond extract and salt. Add the eggs one at a time, mixing well after each addition. Pour the cream cheese mixture into prepared pan. Bake for 45 to 50 minutes, until set. Remove from oven and let cool for 20 minutes. In a small mixing bowl, stir together the sour cream, vanilla extract and the remaining 2 tablespoons sugar. Spread sour cream mixture over top of cooled cake. Bake for an additional 15 minutes. Serve plain or topped with fresh berries. *This easy-to-make cheesecake forms a crust as it bakes.*

Yield: 6 to 8 servings

Marge Runco

Orlando Orange Cake

**5 eggs, separated, at room
   temperature**
1 cup sugar, divided
2 tablespoons fresh orange juice
1 teaspoon grated orange rind
½ teaspoon pure lemon extract
1 cup flour
½ teaspoon salt

Syrup
2 egg whites
½ cup sugar
¾ cup fresh orange juice
2 tablespoons grated orange rind

½ pint whipping cream, whipped
Grated rind of 1 orange

Preheat oven to 325 degrees. Grease and flour a 13x9-inch baking pan; set aside. In a large bowl, using an electric mixer, beat 5 egg yolks until they become pale yellow. Gradually add ½ cup of the sugar beating until mixture thickens. Add the orange juice, orange rind and lemon extract. Gradually add the flour (mixture will be stiff); set bowl aside. In a separate mixing bowl, beat the 5 egg whites and slowly add the remaining ½ cup of sugar and salt. Beat until egg whites form soft peaks, approximately 2 to 3 minutes. (Do not overbeat egg whites.) Using a spatula, fold ¼ of the egg whites into flour mixture until well combined. Fold in remaining egg whites. Pour batter into prepared pan. Bake for 30 to 35 minutes or until a cake tester inserted in center of cake comes out clean. Let the cake cool in pan. To prepare the syrup, in a small mixing bowl, beat the 2 egg whites and sugar together until stiff. Gradually add the orange juice and rind; blend well. Cover the cooled cake with syrup; refrigerate. Once cake has chilled and syrup has hardened, slice entire cake in the pan. Cover top of cake with the whipped cream. Garnish with orange rind. Refrigerate any uneaten cake.

Note: For the most flavorful cake, use Temple oranges or tangerines. The syrup recipe includes uncooked egg whites.

Variation: Omit the syrup and whipped cream topping. Serve the cake topped with fresh fruit.

Yield: 16 to 18 servings

Alexandra Davides

Coconut Bundt Cake with Roasted Apricot Sauce

1¼ cups canned cream of coconut
1 cup sweetened flaked coconut
⅔ cup plain yogurt
⅔ cup canola oil
½ cup fresh lemon juice
1½ teaspoons grated lemon peel
4 cups flour
2½ cups sugar
2 tablespoons baking powder

Roasted Apricot Sauce
16 apricots, peeled, halved, pitted
⅔ cup packed brown sugar
¼ cup water
3 tablespoons sliced almonds

Preheat oven to 350 degrees. Butter and flour a 12-cup bundt pan; set aside. In a large bowl, whisk together the cream of coconut, flaked coconut, yogurt, oil, lemon juice and lemon peel. In a separate large bowl, combine the flour, sugar and baking powder. Whisk flour mixture, one cup at a time, into the coconut mixture. (Batter will be thick.) Spoon batter into prepared pan. Bake for 70 to 80 minutes or until a cake tester inserted in center of cake comes out clean. Cool cake in pan on a wire rack for 15 minutes. Remove cake from pan and continue to cool completely on rack. To prepare sauce, preheat oven to 400 degrees. Mix all sauce ingredients together in a 13x9x2-inch glass baking dish. Bake, stirring occasionally, until sugar melts and apricots are heated through, approximately 20 minutes. Slice cake and drizzle sauce over individual servings. *This cake, crisp on the outside, has the texture of a macaroon inside.*

Note: Jarred or canned apricots may be used in place of fresh; peeling optional. Cake may be made 1 day ahead. Store, covered, at room temperature.

Yield: 8 to 10 servings

Diane Norkus

Apricot Torte

Nut Filling
1 pound ground walnuts,
    approximately 4 cups
2 tablespoons cinnamon
1 cup sugar

Dough
1½ cups butter or margarine,
    softened
4 egg yolks
4 cups flour
½ cup milk
1½ (¼-ounce) envelopes dry yeast,
    dissolved in ¼ cup warm water

3 (10-ounce) jars apricot filling
4 egg whites
8 tablespoons sugar

Preheat oven to 350 degrees. Lightly grease a 15x10x1-inch baking pan; set aside. To prepare the nut filling, in a small bowl combine the walnuts, cinnamon and sugar; set aside. To prepare the dough, in a large mixing bowl, combine the butter and egg yolks. Stir in the flour, milk and yeast mixture; mix well. Knead the dough slightly. Divide the dough into 3 equal parts. On a lightly floured surface, roll 3 dough portions to approximate size of prepared pan. Place one rolled dough portion in pan. Press to edges and up sides of pan. Spread ¾ of the nut filling over the dough; set remainder aside. Place second dough portion on top of nut filling. Press down gently along the edges. Spread the apricot filling over the second dough layer. Place third rolled dough portion on top of apricot filling. Bake for 35 minutes, or until browned. While torte is baking, beat the 4 egg whites until stiff. Add the 8 tablespoons of sugar and beat until dissolved. Remove torte from oven. Spread egg white mixture over top of torte. Sprinkle with the remaining nut filling. Return to oven and bake for an additional 10 minutes. Let cool; cut into diamond shapes for serving.

Variation: Substitute cherry or pineapple filling for the apricot filling.

Yield: 10 to 12 servings

Marie Malczak

Aunt Celina's Lekker Koeken

Belgian Sweet Cake

1 tablespoon butter, softened
¾ cup sugar
1 egg
¼ teaspoon ground cloves
¼ teaspoon cinnamon
¾ cup honey
1 teaspoon baking soda dissolved
    in 1 cup buttermilk
2¼ cups flour, sifted

Preheat oven to 325 degrees. In a large mixing bowl, using an electric mixer, cream together the butter and sugar until crumbly. Add the egg, beat until light and creamy. Add the cloves, cinnamon and honey; beat to combine. Gradually add baking soda-buttermilk mixture. Slowly add the flour, beating after each addition. (Batter will be thick.) Spread batter in a 9x5-inch loaf pan. Bake for 1 hour and 15 minutes or until a cake tester inserted in center of cake comes out clean. Cake will rise in the center and crack on top. *Enjoy this bread-like cake with butter and hot tea or coffee.*

Variation: May substitute light corn syrup for the honey.

Yield: 8 to 10 servings

Henrietta Van Huffel

Rum Cake

½ cup chopped pecans
1 (18-ounce) package (pudding-in-
    the-mix) yellow cake mix
4 eggs
½ cup vegetable oil
½ cup cold water
½ cup rum

Sauce
½ cup butter
1 cup sugar
¼ cup rum
¼ cup water

Preheat oven to 325 degrees. Grease a 10-inch bundt pan. Sprinkle the pecans over bottom of prepared pan; set aside. Using an electric mixer, beat together the cake mix, eggs, oil, water and rum. Pour the batter over nuts in pan. Bake for 55 to 60 minutes or until a cake tester inserted in center of cake comes out clean. Approximately 10 minutes before cake is done, begin sauce preparation. In a small saucepan, combine all sauce ingredients. Bring mixture to a boil; stir continuously for 2 minutes until sugar dissolves and sauce thickens. Remove cake from oven and leave in pan. Slowly pour the sauce evenly over cake. Allow cake to cool completely before inverting onto serving platter.

Yield: 10 to 12 servings

Marge Runco

English Trifle

Sponge Cake
1 cup flour
1 teaspoon baking powder
2 eggs, separated
1 cup sugar
1 teaspoon vanilla extract
½ cup boiling water

Custard
1 cup sugar
3 tablespoons cornstarch
½ teaspoon salt
4 cups whole milk
8 egg yolks
2 teaspoons vanilla extract

1 cup cream sherry, or to taste
2 (10-ounce) packages frozen
   raspberries, thawed, drained
6 tablespoons slivered, toasted
   almonds
½ cup whipped cream

To prepare sponge cake, preheat oven to 325 degrees. Grease and flour 2 (8-inch) round nonstick cake pans; set aside. In a small bowl, combine the flour and baking powder; set aside. In a large bowl, beat the egg whites to medium stiff peaks. In a separate bowl, lightly beat the egg yolks. Add the egg yolks, sugar and vanilla extract to egg whites. Alternately, add the flour with the boiling water to the egg mixture. Pour batter into prepared pans. Bake for 50 to 60 minutes or until a cake tester inserted in center of cakes comes out clean. Let cakes cool completely in pans on wire racks. To prepare the custard, combine sugar, cornstarch and salt in a medium, heavy saucepan. Over medium heat, slowly add the milk, stirring continuously until thickened. Bring to a boil and stir for one additional minute. Remove saucepan from heat. In a medium bowl, lightly beat the 8 egg yolks. Slowly add approximately 1 cup of the hot milk mixture to the egg yolks, beating well so eggs do not congeal. Stir egg mixture into saucepan with remaining hot milk mixture. Return saucepan to heat and bring to a boil, stirring continuously. Remove from heat; add the vanilla extract. Let custard cool. To assemble, place one cake in a glass trifle dish, cutting to fit if necessary. Pour ½ cup of the cream sherry over cake. Spread ½ of the raspberries and 3 tablespoons of the almonds evenly over cake. Spread ½ of the custard over top. Place remaining cake over custard; repeat layering. Serve chilled trifle in individual bowls topped with whipped cream.

Note: In season, replace the frozen raspberries with farm-fresh.

Yield: 8 servings

Lila Decker

Troy Hill

*M*ajestically perched on a plateau above other North Side communities, Troy Hill has the look and feel of an old European village. The neighborhood of proud row houses and lovingly preserved single family homes possesses one of the most spectacular views in the city of Pittsburgh.

Sitting on a narrow mile-long bluff, Troy Hill overlooks the Allegheny River and picturesque Washington's Landing, formerly Herr's Island. Standing on Troy Hill, one can look down the river to view the Pittsburgh skyline.

Troy Hill is still identified with its German ties. Its sizable churches are populated by German Catholics and Lutherans, a popular Oktoberfest is held annually at the Penn Brewery and the distinctive Teutonia Mannerchor is the cultural center for Pittsburgh's German population. With more than 2,000 members, the club continues to embrace its German heritage with singing, food and dance.

In 1880, Father Suibertus Goddfried Mollinger's devotion to St. Anthony of Padua resulted in the construction of St. Anthony Chapel, one of Troy Hill's most prominent historical landmarks. The chapel houses more than 5000 relics of saints, making it the world's largest collection of relics outside of the Vatican.

Troy Hill is the site of the oldest firehouse in Pittsburgh and the only firehouse in the city to have a bell. It is named "Die Glocke Sarah," German for "The Bell Sarah." The old firehouse was automated in the early 1900's. When the alarm bell rang, the horses ran to their places in front of the fire engine and harnesses dropped on top of them. At the same time, a gas jet in the floor was firing up the steam engine.

Many stories about the Troy Hill firehouse are part of local lore. Older residents reminisce how, as children, they followed the firefighters as they walked the horses through the streets to exercise them. Others recall the firehouse as the place to go when you needed any kind of help. Local firefighters insist that the firehouse is haunted, saying that ghosts of past firefighters have been spotted in the basement playing cards just as they did in the old days! Today, the firehouse serves as host to the Western Pennsylvania Firefighters Memorial, which is located down the street in the neighborhood's scenic and historic Voegtly Cemetery.

The red brick firehouse still sits in the center of Troy Hill, a welcoming sight in a tight-knit community of active citizens, narrow winding streets, cobblestone sidewalks and charming old-world streetscapes. ♥♥

Pittsburgh Irish Festival, Inc. was created to contribute to the city's rich cultural expression of Irish history and tradition. Since 1991, the nonprofit organization has hosted a three-day event each September called the "Halfway to St. Patrick's Day Festival." At the festival, visitors view cultural displays, national and local Irish entertainment, instrumental demonstrations and have the opportunity to meet Irish authors. A Sunday mass in Gaelic, lively Irish step dancing, and tastings of fish and chips, Dublin Coddle, boxty pancakes, scones and tipsy cake turns everyone into an Irishman.

Pittsburgh Irish Festival, Inc. strives to create a greater awareness of the richness and significance of Irish and Irish-American culture and its presence in the city from both an historic and contemporary perspective. The organization's "Education Outreach Program" serves as a year-round resource for Irish education and culture.

Colcannon is Ireland's best-known traditional potato dish. At Halloween, a ring and thimble were hidden in the colcannon. The ring denoted marriage, but the person who found the thimble was to be a spinster for life.

Colcannon

An Irish Potato Dish

2½-3 pounds baking potatoes, unpeeled, scrubbed
1 small spring or Savoy cabbage
Salt and freshly ground black pepper, to taste
4-5 tablespoons butter, divided
1 cup boiling milk

Place potatoes in a large pot filled with cold water. Add a pinch of salt; bring to a boil. When potatoes are half-cooked, approximately 20 minutes, strain off ⅔ of the water. Cover and continue cooking over low heat, steaming potatoes until fully cooked. Drain; set aside to cool slightly. Remove and discard the dark outer leaves from the cabbage. Quarter, core and rinse the cabbage; finely chop. Place the cabbage in a pot filled with salted boiling water. Cook until soft, approximately 15 minutes. Drain the cabbage well; season with salt, pepper and 1 tablespoon of the butter; set aside. Pull skins off of the warm potatoes and discard. In a large mixing bowl, mash the potatoes, mixing in enough of the boiled milk to make a fluffy purée. Mix in an equal amount of cabbage; season with additional salt and pepper. Serve the colcannon immediately, in a warmed dish, with a lump of the remaining butter melting in the center. *Irish grandmothers made a special treat by forming left over colcannon into potato cakes and frying them in butter until crisp and brown on both sides.*

Note: Colcannon may be prepared ahead. Reheat in a 350 degree oven for 20 to 25 minutes.

Yield: 8 servings

Pittsburgh Irish Festival, Inc.
Maura and Nan Krushinski, directors

**Engine & Truck Company #4,
Pittsburgh, PA**
Uptown

Pittsburgh's Engine and Truck Company #4 is located in the Uptown section of the city between Mercy Hospital and Duquesne University. The building also houses the office of the Deputy Chief. Prior to the 1950's, Engine Company #4 was located on Webster Avenue in the Lower Hill District. The earlier building dated from the era when horses were used to take men and equipment to the fires. In fact, during the summer, hot and tired firemen would refresh themselves by creating a swimming pool in the room that was originally designed for bathing the horses. The earlier building was demolished to make room for the Civic Arena. Today, in addition to Uptown, Engine Company #4 also answers calls for downtown, the lower Hill, Oakland and the South Side flats. The 40 firefighters, including officers, work in shifts with 8 firefighters on duty at all times to serve the city.

Although firefighters are known for enjoying hearty, abundant meals, they, along with the general population, have started to eat lighter and healthier. This is one of Engine Company #4's favorite summer dishes.

Grilled Chicken Salad

Marinade
3 cups olive oil
1 cup soy sauce
4-5 cloves garlic, minced

Salad
**12-15 skinless, boneless chicken
    breast halves**
1 head of iceberg lettuce
1 head of red leaf lettuce
**1 (12-ounce) bag of spinach, stems
    removed**
**2 large cucumbers, peeled, seeded,
    sliced**
3-4 carrots, peeled, sliced or grated
**2-3 large ripe tomatoes, cut into
    wedges**
**1 (5½-ounce) can pitted black
    olives, drained**
¾ cup thinly sliced red cabbage
**1 red bell pepper, seeded, sliced,
    optional**

In a medium bowl, whisk together all of the marinade ingredients. Place chicken in a large roasting pan; coat with the marinade. Cover pan and refrigerate for at least 2 hours or overnight. Clean the lettuce and spinach; drain well and tear into bite-size pieces. In a large serving bowl, toss together all of the salad ingredients except the chicken; set aside. Drain the chicken; discard the marinade. Heat an outdoor grill. Grill the chicken until thoroughly cooked. Slice the chicken; add to salad. Top with your favorite salad dressing. Serve with French or Italian bread.

Variation: The firefighters sometimes add penne, ziti or farfalle pasta to the salad.

Yield: 8 to 10 hungry firefighter servings

*Engine and Truck Company #4,
Pittsburgh, PA*

Stephen Collins Foster
Lawrenceville & Oakland

American composer Stephen Collins Foster (1826-1864) was born and raised in Lawrenceville. Foster, who lived nearly all his life in Pittsburgh, worked at songwriting. He rented a second floor office in downtown Pittsburgh on Wood Street and a piano to go in it. Foster was a true musical pioneer. There was no music business then as we know it today. There were no performing rights fees, no way of earning money except through a 5 to 10 percent royalty or through the outright purchase of songs by a publisher. In today's music industry, Foster would be worth millions of dollars, but at the time of his death he had only 38 cents in his pocket.

While he may not have left a financial legacy, Foster did leave us with an extraordinary musical legacy. In his 37 years, he wrote over 285 songs, many of which continue to be sung today including "Oh Susanna," "Camptown Races," "Jeanie with the Light Brown Hair," "My Old Kentucky Home" and "Way Down Upon the Swanee River." To learn more about Foster, visit the Stephen Foster Memorial and the Center for American Music at the University of Pittsburgh in Oakland.

This recipe for apple fritters was adapted from an 1860 recipe in *Godey's Lady's Book and Magazine*. *Godey's* was the most popular woman's magazine in the 19th century. It is likely that Foster's wife and mother were subscribers. In addition to providing sewing patterns, advice, recipes, fiction and regular columns, each issue included a new song. Several of Stephen Foster's songs were featured.

Apple Fritters

1 pint of milk
3 egg yolks, lightly beaten
3 egg whites, lightly beaten
2 cups flour
½ teaspoon salt
Lard for frying
2-3 apples, peeled, cored, sliced ¼-inch thick to create donut shapes

In a large mixing bowl, beat together the milk and egg yolks. Add the egg whites, flour and salt; mix to create a thick batter. In a large, heavy skillet, heat the lard to 275 to 300 degrees. (Level of lard should be approximately ½-inch deep.) Spoon ⅛ to ¼ cupfuls of batter into the skillet. Lay 1 apple slice in center of each dollop of batter. Do not crowd the fritters. Fry, in batches, until lightly browned, approximately 2 to 3 minutes. Turn and fry for 1 additional minute. Drain on paper towels. Serve apple fritters warm with butter and cinnamon-sugar. Also delicious topped with maple syrup.

Yield: 12 to 18 fritters

Center for American Music,
University of Pittsburgh Library System

Spigno Saturnia is a town located in the Lazio region of Italy. The Spigno Saturnia Italo-American Society of Pittsburgh is located in Morningside, a neighborhood in the East End of the city. All members of the society trace their heritage to Spigno Saturnia. The society was formed in 1927 when the first generation of 35 families bonded together in Pittsburgh. The families that had immigrated to America after World War I realized the importance of unity and how it could help them to overcome the many difficulties of settling in a new country. The society helped the members with language as well as with understanding American customs and laws.

Today, the Spigno Saturnia Italo-American Society of Pittsburgh has 135 members. Many are third generation Spignese. The society not only provides support for its members, but its hall continues to serve as a meeting place for social events that promote a strong Italian-American heritage. Menus prepared for social events include an abundant array of homemade Italian dishes. Manicotti, always a favorite, is prepared with delicate crêpes in this traditional recipe.

Manicotti

An Italian Entrée

Crêpes
4 eggs
2 cups water
2 cups flour, sifted
1 teaspoon salt
Vegetable oil

Ricotta Cheese Filling
2 pounds ricotta cheese
⅓ cup freshly grated Parmesan cheese
2 cups shredded mozzarella cheese, approximately 8 ounces
2 egg yolks, lightly beaten
1 teaspoon dried parsley
Salt and freshly ground black pepper, to taste

Meat Filling
1 pound ground veal
1 pound ricotta cheese
½ cup shredded mozzarella cheese
1 cup chopped fresh spinach
2 tablespoons seasoned breadcrumbs
1 tablespoon dried parsley
1 egg

2-3 cups tomato sauce, divided, to taste
Freshly grated Parmesan cheese, to taste

Manicotti (continued)

To prepare the crêpes, in large mixing bowl, beat together the eggs and water. Gradually add the flour and salt, mixing until smooth. Heat a 6 or 7-inch crêpe pan or skillet over medium heat. Lightly coat pan with the vegetable oil. Pour ¼ cup of the batter into heated pan, swirling to coat bottom. Cook until lightly browned on both sides, approximately 1 to 1½ minutes per side. Stack with waxed paper placed between the crêpes. Cover stack with aluminum foil to keep warm. To prepare ricotta or meat filling, in a large mixing bowl, thoroughly combine all filling ingredients. Preheat oven to 350 degrees. To assemble manicotti, cover bottom of a 3-quart baking dish with 1 cup of the tomato sauce. Spoon ricotta or meat filling into center of each crêpe. Roll each crêpe up and place, seam side down, into baking dish side by side. Spoon remaining tomato sauce over top of crêpes. Top with Parmesan cheese. Bake, uncovered, for 30 minutes.

Yield: 6 to 8 servings; 14 to 16 crêpes

Spigno Saturnia Italo-American
Society of Pittsburgh, PA

Pack & Troop #373,
Boy Scouts of America
Shadyside

Boy Scout Pack and Troop #373 serves Sacred Heart School and the Shadyside community by providing the scouting program to boys in first through twelfth grades. The aims of boy scouting are character development, citizenship training and both mental and physical fitness. These aims are achieved by applying the ideals of scouting to daily life and by providing outdoor programs for the scouts while under the supervision of adult role models. Ongoing opportunities are given for personal growth, leadership development and advancement in the scouting program.

The boy scouts enjoy bicycle hikes in Ohiopyle and along the C & O Canal. They have also gone spelunking. The younger cub scouts take many local field trips including visits to fire stations and trips to the airport. All of the scouts camp regularly at Camp Guyasuta and Heritage Reservation in the Laurel Highlands.

The following recipe is a mainstay of the troop and a perennial favorite of both the boys and adult leaders. It is never the same twice, yet always tasty and satisfying after an active day of scouting.

373's One Pot Meal

2 tablespoons olive oil
4 boneless, skinless chicken breast halves, cut into cubes, seasoned with salt and ground black pepper
1 teaspoon cayenne pepper, or to taste
1 teaspoon garlic powder
1 onion, chopped
4 cups chicken broth
1 tablespoon chopped fresh parsley
1 (10-ounce) bag frozen mixed vegetables
1 (12-ounce) bag wide egg noodles

Heat a large campfire Dutch oven over very hot coals. Add the olive oil. When the oil is hot, add the chicken and brown. Add the cayenne pepper, garlic powder and onion. Sauté until the onions are soft and translucent. Add the chicken broth and parsley; cover and bring to a simmer. Add the mixed vegetables; re-cover and simmer until vegetables are tender. Add the noodles; cook until the noodles are tender. Add water or additional chicken broth, if necessary, to maintain a stew-like consistency.

Note: Recipe may be prepared on a stovetop using a conventional Dutch oven.

Yield: 6 to 8 servings

Boy Scouts of America
Pack and Troop #373, Pittsburgh, PA

Benkovitz Seafoods, Pittsburgh's well-known fish and seafood retailer, provides customers with the finest fresh fish and seafood year round. Located in Pittsburgh's historic and colorful "Strip District," Benkovitz is a family-owned and operated business now in its fourth generation. Their famous fish sandwiches, known far and wide, are a Pittsburgh tradition. The business provides elegant party fare, including raw seafood bars, imported caviars and smoked salmons. Benkovitz will also bring an authentic New England clambake to the home.

Walking into Benkovitz Seafoods to choose fish, order lunch, or to purchase a prepared seafood salad is a real treat. The following recipe is just one of the delicious dishes served at this Pittsburgh landmark.

Mrs. B's Famous Crabcakes

¼ cup vegetable oil
1 rib of celery, diced
½ small onion, diced
¼ green bell pepper, diced
¼ red bell pepper, diced
2-3 cloves of garlic, minced
1 cup mayonnaise
2 tablespoons fresh squeezed
   lemon juice
1 tablespoon Old Bay seasoning
1 tablespoon dry mustard
¾-1 cup fresh white breadcrumbs,
   divided, to taste
2 pounds Nordic backfin
   crabmeat or jumbo-lump
   crabmeat, drained, picked
   through for shells

Preheat oven to 375 degrees. In a large skillet, heat the oil over medium heat. Add the celery, onion, bell peppers and garlic. Sauté until the vegetables are soft. Remove from heat; allow to cool. In a large mixing bowl, combine the cooled vegetables, mayonnaise, lemon juice, Old Bay seasoning, dry mustard and ½ of the breadcrumbs. Gently fold in the crabmeat being careful not to break up the lumps. Use a 4-ounce ice cream scoop to form 8 evenly-sized crabcakes. Pat gently into shape. Lightly coat each crabcake with the remaining breadcrumbs. Place on an ungreased baking sheet. Bake for 20 minutes or until golden brown. Serve the crabcakes with Benkovitz Seafoods' creamy tartar, zesty homemade cocktail, or robust mustard sauce.

Yield: 8 crabcakes; 4 servings

Benkovitz Seafoods
Evelyn and Bernard Benkovitz,
Joe Benkovitz, owners; Tony Gratter, chef

Carnegie Library of
Pittsburgh-Homewood
Homewood

In 2003, the Carnegie Library of Pittsburgh-Homewood was restored to its original grandeur. The beauty of the original design was retained while the library was updated to meet the needs of today's East End community. Dedicated in 1910, the library was designed by Pittsburgh architectural firm Alden & Harlow. It features an ornate Gothic entrance and English brown brick with stone trim. The leaded glass skylights as well as the original windows flood the 3-story library with light, enhancing its beauty.

In addition to the regular collection, the library houses a unique African-American Collection. This collection, the largest in the Carnegie system, contains over 12,000 items including a large selection of children's materials. Patrons find both popular and historical information in magazines, books, videos and reference materials. The collection also includes jazz, blues, gospel and symphonic compact discs.

A *Mad Hatter's Tea Party* is held annually the first Sunday of June. It is a major fundraiser hosted by the Friends of the Carnegie Library-Homewood. The library serves the community in many ways. There are meeting rooms, story times, family nights, after-school activities and a popular Teen Corner. The library also serves as a resource for book clubs. Book clubs are known for both lively discussions and potluck dinners. In the summertime, this cold fruit soup is refreshing served as either a first course or as a dessert.

Peach and Melon Soup

8 ripe peaches, peeled, sliced
8 tablespoons fresh squeezed
   lemon juice
1½ tablespoons honey
¼-½ teaspoon cinnamon, to taste
1 ripe cantaloupe, seeded, roughly
   chopped
½ ripe honeydew melon, seeded,
   roughly chopped
1½ cups orange juice
Fresh blueberries
Fresh mint leaves

In a saucepan, over medium heat, bring the peaches, lemon juice, honey and cinnamon to a boil. Lower the heat. Cover and simmer for 10 minutes. Remove saucepan from heat; cool to room temperature. Using a food processor, purée the peach mixture. Transfer to a large bowl. Purée the melons and orange juice together. Transfer to the bowl with the peaches; mix well. Cover and chill. To serve, ladle the soup into individual serving bowls; garnish with blueberries and a mint leaf.

Note: For a smoother texture, strain soup through a chinois or cheesecloth. For a coarser texture, reserve 1 cup of each melon. Finely mince or chop and add to the soup with the puréed melon.

Variation: A dollop of crème fraîche or vanilla yogurt with fresh raspberries is another nice presentation.

Yield: 6 to 8 servings

Diane DeNardo and Antonia DeNardo Piccoli, appreciative visitors to the Children's Room at the Carnegie Library of Pittsburgh-Homewood

St. Nicholas Cathedral
Greek Food Festival
Oakland

Like many Pittsburgh religious congregations, St. Nicholas Greek Orthodox Church traces its roots back to the turn of the century when immigrants came to America looking for work. Many of Pittsburgh's Greek immigrants were employed to paint the smokestacks and buildings of iron and steel mills. The congregation bought its Oakland church in 1923. It was fitting that the facade reflected Greek architecture with a large pediment and Ionic columns. A World War II memorial in front of the church attests to the large contribution of manpower the congregation made toward the war effort. In 1955, St. Nicholas Church became a Cathedral.

St. Nicholas hosted its first Greek Food Festival in 1962 serving a few hundred diners. Today, the six-day festival serves lunch and dinner to over 25,000 guests every May. The members of St. Nicholas prepare all of the food and pastries for this fundraiser. The cooking and baking begins in January and doesn't end until the week of the festival.

Guests attending the Food Festival dine on traditional Greek dishes including souvlakia, pastitsio, moussaka and spanakopeta. Regulars know to leave plenty of room for the pastry selection. Tables are laden with galatoboureko, baklava, diples, finikia, and loukoumades, to name but a few of the sweet selections. Musicians play bouzouki music and the children of St. Nicholas perform lively Greek dances in traditional costume.

Psari Plaki

Baked Fish with Vegetables

4 halibut, striped bass, sea bass or tilefish fillets
Salt and freshly ground black pepper, to taste
Juice of 1 lemon
½ cup olive oil, divided
3 medium onions, thinly sliced
1 (12-ounce) can whole tomatoes, drained, chopped
½ cup chopped fresh parsley, divided
1 cup seedless raisins, marinated in 1 cup white wine for 1 hour
4 lemon slices

Preheat oven to 350 degrees. Rinse fish fillets and pat dry. Season with the salt, pepper and lemon juice; set aside. In a large skillet, over medium heat, heat 3 tablespoons of the olive oil. Add the onions; sauté until soft and lightly brown. Add the tomatoes, ¼ cup of the parsley, remaining olive oil, raisins and wine; cook over low heat for 10 minutes, stirring occasionally. Spread ½ of the onion mixture evenly over bottom of a 13x9-inch baking dish. Lay fish fillets side by side over the onions. Top fillets with the remaining onion mixture. Place 1 lemon slice on top of each fillet. Bake, uncovered, for 30 to 40 minutes or until fish is tender and flakes easily with a fork. Garnish with the remaining parsley.

Yield: 4 servings

St. Nicholas Cathedral Greek Food Festival

Pilafi

Rice Pilaf

6 tablespoons butter
1 cup long-grain rice
4 cups hot chicken broth
1 teaspoon salt
Dash of freshly ground black
    pepper

Preheat oven to 350 degrees. Prepare pilafi in a large ovenproof skillet with a fitted lid. In the skillet, on the stovetop, melt the butter over medium heat. Add the rice; stir for 3 to 5 minutes or until rice is light in color. Add the broth, stirring, until broth begins to boil. Season with salt and pepper. Cover skillet tightly; transfer to oven and bake for 25 minutes. Remove skillet from oven and fluff rice lightly with a fork. Serve immediately. *Rice is a staple in Greek cooking and accompanies both meat and fish dishes.*

Yield: 4 to 6 servings

St. Nicholas Cathedral
Greek Food Festival

Bidwell Training Center, Inc.
Manchester

Bidwell Training Center, Inc., located on Pittsburgh's North Shore, is a post-secondary career and academic training institution. The nonprofit organization was established in 1968 as a means to make training opportunities available to people in Pittsburgh regardless of race, religion, ancestry or national origin. Bidwell students choosing to study culinary arts gain first-hand experience while working with Bidwell Catering. Many of the students who graduate from Bidwell go on to work in Pittsburgh restaurants and hotels and for catering companies. Others obtain work in hospital and corporate kitchens or on cruise ships.

Along with courses in food preparation, nutrition and menu writing, Bidwell students learn to cook foods from many different cultures. *Mulligatawny Soup* is an anglicized version of a southern India soup meaning "pepper water." The rich curried soup was traditionally made with hot peppers and coconut milk.

Mulligatawny Soup

1½ cups peeled, diced eggplant
2 tablespoons butter
1 small or medium onion, finely diced
1 large carrot, peeled, finely diced
2 ribs of celery, finely diced
¼ cup plus 1 tablespoon flour
1½ tablespoons curry powder
Salt and ground white pepper, to taste
1 quart hot chicken stock or broth
1 apple, peeled, cored, diced
2 cups milk or heavy cream, scalded
1 cup cooked rice
½ pound cooked turkey, diced

Place the eggplant in a large pot of boiling water for 5 minutes to blanch; drain well. In a large soup pot, over medium heat, melt the butter. Add the onions, carrots and celery; sauté until tender. Add the flour, curry powder, salt and pepper. Cook, stirring, over low heat, for 5 to 6 minutes. (Do not brown.) Add the chicken stock; increase heat to medium-high. Stir until thickened and smooth, approximately 10 minutes. Add the eggplant and apples; simmer just until eggplant is tender, approximately 5 minutes. Blend in the milk. Add the rice and turkey; stir well to combine. Serve hot.

Yield: 6 to 8 servings

Bidwell Training Center, Inc.
Cindy Tuite, director,
Culinary Arts Program

The Society for the Preservation of the Duquesne Heights Incline
Duquesne Heights

Pittsburgh was once home to 19 inclines climbing the steep hills, or "slopes," that define the city's topography. Because of the hard work and dedication of the nonprofit Society for the Preservation of the Duquesne Heights Incline, one of two of these unique forms of transportation remains to this day. The Duquesne Incline, originally steam powered, now electric driven, opened in 1877. Along with the Monongahela Incline, the Duquesne Incline is a reminder of how engineering and ingenuity overcame the rugged terrain surrounding the Monongahela, Allegheny and Ohio Rivers. In the early days, incline rides cost one nickel. Mill workers would often walk down the "city steps" at the beginning of their shift and pay the nickel to ride up the steep hillside after their long day's work. The Duquesne Incline continues to transport workers, although today, that transport takes them to jobs in a modern metropolis.

The Society for the Preservation of the Duquesne Heights Incline was formed in 1963. The dedicated volunteers are responsible for saving the incline from an uncertain future. They then raised the funds for its restoration and operation. The incline cars still retain the original handcarved cherry panels with birds-eye maple trim, the amber glass transoms and the original handsome hardware. In 2004, an interior platform opened. This allows visitors the opportunity to view the massive machinery that operates the incline, including the original cable drum and the unique wooden-toothed drive gear.

When Linda Hillenburg first visited Pittsburgh, her sister took her to the historic Duquesne Incline for an unrivaled view of the city. Like all visitors to Pittsburgh, she marveled at the unusual cars that have been climbing Mt. Washington for over 125 years. A panoramic vista of Pittsburgh would not be the same without the Duquesne Incline's red cars gliding up and down the hillside. They are truly a Pittsburgh treasure.

Caribbean Seafood Salad

2 tablespoons butter or margarine
1 pound bay scallops
1 pound cherry tomatoes, halved
1 pound frozen, precooked small
   shrimp, thawed, drained
1 (6-ounce) can pitted ripe olives,
   drained
1 (5-ounce) can sliced water
   chestnuts, drained
½ head of cauliflower, cut into
   bite-size pieces

Dressing
2 cups mayonnaise
½ cup prepared horseradish, well-
   drained
2 teaspoons dry mustard
2 teaspoons lemon juice
½ teaspoon salt

Green bell pepper slices, optional

In a large skillet, over low heat, melt the butter. Sauté the scallops just until cooked through, approximately 3 to 5 minutes. Drain on paper towels. Transfer to a covered bowl and refrigerate. In a large bowl, combine the tomatoes, shrimp, olives, water chestnuts, cauliflower and chilled scallops. In a medium bowl, combine all dressing ingredients; mix well. Pour dressing over salad; toss gently to coat. Cover tightly and refrigerate salad overnight or for a minimum of 4 hours. Garnish with bell pepper slices.

Yield: 8 servings

Linda Hillenburg

Linden Garden Club
East End

The Linden Garden Club was founded in 1924 with Mrs. William H. Mercer serving as the first president. The mission of this long-lived organization is to "stimulate the knowledge and love of gardening, to aid in the preservation of native plants and birds, and to encourage interest in civic beauty and its preservation." To see firsthand the work of this dedicated group, visit their *Daffodil Garden* in Pittsburgh's Mellon Park. This, their most recent civic project, is enjoyed by all that visit the urban park.

The Linden Garden Club has been serving *Ham Loaf* at its luncheon meetings for many years. After a busy morning of planting or organizing, it is a favorite dish of the gardeners.

Ham Loaf

1 pound ground ham
1¼ pound ground pork
1 teaspoon brown sugar
1 teaspoon dry mustard
2 cups Wheaties
1 cup milk
2 eggs

Sauce
½ cup water
1½ cups lightly packed brown sugar
½ cup vinegar
1 tablespoon dry mustard

Preheat oven to 350 degrees. Evenly coat a 9x5-inch loaf pan with nonstick vegetable oil cooking spray; set aside. In a large mixing bowl, combine all of the ham loaf ingredients, mixing well by hand. Spread evenly into prepared pan; set aside. To prepare the sauce, place all ingredients in a small saucepan. Cook over medium heat, whisking gently until sauce is well mixed and smooth, approximately 3 to 5 minutes. Lightly coat the ham loaf with the sauce. Bake for 2½ hours, basting every 20 minutes with additional sauce. Discard leftover sauce. *A delicious alternative to the traditional meatloaf.*

Note: Ham loaf may be served cold as lunchtime fare.

Yield: 8 to 10 servings

Linden Garden Club

Bloomfield-Garfield Corporation
Garfield

Bloomfield-Garfield Corporation is a community development organization dedicated to revitalizing the physical, economic and social environment of Garfield, Friendship and other surrounding city neighborhoods. The nonprofit organization has over 300 members. Activities focus on youth education and employment, public safety, and housing and commercial development projects along the Penn Avenue corridor and elsewhere in Garfield and Friendship. The organization is working hard to re-ignite the private market in a section of Pittsburgh that was hit hard by the city's decline in population beginning 35 years ago. *The Bulletin,* a newsletter published by the organization, keeps residents, business owners and interested citizens informed about the vigorous efforts being made to improve city life in the Garfield and Friendship areas.

Bloomfield-Garfield Corporation works hard to strengthen the community. Every June, the entire city is invited to celebrate at the "Penn Avenue Arts Festival." In July, the organization sponsors a community picnic. Block Watch type programs organized by the group emphasize "neighbors looking out for neighbors." In Pittsburgh, sitting out on the porch remains a great way to spend an afternoon or evening. Whether chatting with long time neighborhood friends or making new acquaintances, *Fresh Pear Cake* and a glass of iced tea are a delicious treat for the occasion.

Fresh Pear Cake

2¼ cups flour
1 teaspoon baking soda
½ teaspoon salt
¾ cup margarine, softened
1½ cups sugar
2 large eggs
1 heaping teaspoon instant coffee
    dissolved in ¾ cup hot water,
    cooled to room temperature
3-4 ripe medium pears, unpeeled,
    cored, cut into small pieces,
    approximately 3 cups

Streusel Topping
½ cup packed light brown sugar
3 tablespoons flour
1 teaspoon cinnamon
2 tablespoons margarine, softened
½ cup finely chopped walnuts

Preheat oven to 350 degrees. Grease a 13x9-inch baking pan; set aside. In a small bowl, combine the flour, baking soda and salt; set aside. In a large mixing bowl, cream together the margarine and sugar. Beat in the eggs. Gradually add the flour mixture alternately with the coffee. Using a spatula, fold in the pears. Spread batter evenly in prepared pan. To prepare the streusel topping, in a small bowl, combine the brown sugar, flour, cinnamon and margarine to a crumb-like consistency. Stir in the walnuts. Sprinkle streusel topping over top of batter. Bake for 45 to 50 minutes or until a cake tester inserted in center of cake comes out clean.

Yield: 10 to 12 servings

*Catherine Curry, Garfield resident and
Bloomfield-Garfield Corporation board member*

**The Old Allegheny West
Victorian Christmas House Tour**
Allegheny West

The nonprofit Allegheny West Civic Council has conducted house tours in this historic district for over ten years. The *Christmas House Tour,* which takes place the second weekend in December, is a personally guided tour featuring seven restored Victorian homes and the historic Calvary United Methodist Church. It affords a rare opportunity to glimpse a by-gone era, and to experience the warmth of the season in a truly "old-fashioned" style. Lavishly decorated for the holidays, the homes recall the late 19th century birth of the traditional American Christmas—elaborately decorated mantels, towering Christmas trees, as well as stairs and chandeliers adorned with pine, holly and mistletoe.

The organization also hosts an annual house and garden tour. Flowers vie with garden statuary and classic Victorian exteriors reflecting each homeowner's personal taste and style. Antique car displays, artisan demonstrations, wine tasting, and delicious food adds to the festive event.

The Allegheny West house tours feature elegant menus. The food is provided by "Linda Iannotta Catering", a business located in this historic district. *Eggnog Muffins* add to the festive holiday fare.

Eggnog Muffins

3 cups flour
3 teaspoons baking powder
½ teaspoon nutmeg
¼ pound butter, softened
¾ cup sugar
2 eggs
2 cups dairy eggnog
½ cup chopped pecans
½ cup chopped craisins (dried cranberries)
½ cup golden raisins

Icing
½ cup powdered sugar
Dash of nutmeg
Eggnog

Preheat oven to 325 degrees. Place paper liners in 24 muffin tins or spray with nonstick vegetable oil cooking spray; set aside. In a medium bowl, sift together the flour, baking powder and nutmeg; set aside. In a large mixing bowl, using an electric mixer, cream together the butter and sugar. Beat in the eggs. Alternately, add the flour mixture and eggnog. Using a spatula, fold in the pecans, craisins, and raisins. Fill muffin tins ¾ full. Bake for 25 minutes; allow to cool. To prepare the icing, mix together the powdered sugar, nutmeg and enough eggnog to create a drizzling consistency. Drizzle icing over cooled muffins. Store in an airtight container.

Yield: 24 muffins

Linda Iannotta Catering

St. Basil's Christian
Mothers & Guild
Carrick

St. Basil Parish, celebrating it's 99th year, is centrally located in Carrick on Brownsville Road. The Christian Mothers and Guild was established in 1921. This 83-year-old organization has faithfully served the parish for almost a century. The guild hosts an annual reception after the "Anointing of the Sick" mass. Every spring, the First Holy Communion participants are invited to take part in the annual May Crowning. The guild, which meets monthly, also holds two card parties each year. St. Basil is next door to the Carnegie Library-Carrick and close to the community's senior citizen high rise. Other parish organizations include the Ladies of Charity, Ushers, Golden Agers, Youth Group, and Boy Scouts. The parish continues to be very involved in the surrounding community.

Like all parish guilds, St. Basil's Christian Mothers and Guild is known for its bake sales. *Italian Nut Cookies* are a delicious addition to dessert trays, Christmas cookie exchanges, and a favorite Pittsburgh tradition, the wedding "cookie table."

Italian Nut Cookies

4 cups flour
1½ cups sugar
½ cup cocoa powder
4 teaspoons baking powder
2 teaspoons cinnamon
1 teaspoon allspice
½ teaspoon ground cloves
Pinch of salt
1 cup milk
1 cup vegetable oil
1 teaspoon vanilla
1 cup chopped nuts

Mocha Cream Icing
1½ cups powdered sugar
2 tablespoons cocoa powder
Pinch of salt
½ cup butter, softened
3 tablespoons strong fresh coffee
1 tablespoon cream or half & half
1 teaspoon vanilla

Preheat oven to 375 degrees. In a large mixing bowl, combine the flour, sugar, cocoa powder, baking powder, cinnamon, allspice, cloves and salt. In a separate bowl, mix together the milk, oil, vanilla and nuts. Pour the nut mixture into the dry ingredients. Mix well to thoroughly combine. Roll teaspoonfuls of dough into balls. Place on ungreased baking sheets 1 inch apart. Bake for 15 minutes. Let the cookies cool on wire racks. To prepare the icing, in a small bowl, sift together the powdered sugar, cocoa powder and salt; set aside. In a mixing bowl, using an electric mixer, beat the butter until creamy. Gradually add the sugar mixture. Add the coffee, cream and vanilla; beat until smooth and creamy. Top cookies with the icing.

Yield: 5½ dozen

St. Basil's Christian Mothers and Guild
Kathy Poljak, guild president

Troy Hill sits on a high ridge overlooking the Allegheny River. It is a small but active community. The houses cling to the hillsides, steeples pierce the sky and narrow streets lead into the town square. Six registered historic landmarks keep alive the neighborhood's pride in its German heritage. In 1971, Troy Hill Citizens, Inc. was formed to give the residents a voice in deciding what future development would come to their neighborhood. In the 1980's, the organization established the Troy Hill Citizens Community Park, which is maintained entirely by volunteers. Every September, the organization holds its "Day in the Park," celebrating with ethnic music, dancing, and food.

Mary Wohleber, a lifelong Troy Hill resident, recalls her father saying that on Sunday's, the "Hill" was enveloped in the scent of sauerkraut, all homemade of course. Like sauerkraut and sauerbraten, red cabbage is a traditional German dish. Each family adapts the recipe to their own taste.

Red Cabbage

A German Side Dish

1 onion, finely chopped
3 tablespoons of bacon grease
1 medium head of red cabbage, outer leaves removed, cored, sliced or chopped
½ cup water
½ cup cider vinegar
½ cup brown sugar
2 apples, peeled, cored, chopped
Salt and ground black pepper, to taste

In a large skillet, over medium heat, sauté the onion in the bacon grease until soft and translucent. Add the cabbage. Cover the skillet. Cook, stirring occasionally, until slightly softened, approximately 10 to 15 minutes. Add the water, vinegar, brown sugar, and apple. Season with salt and pepper. Bring to a boil. Turn off heat. Stir the cabbage and re-cover. Let stand for 10 minutes. Serve warm.

Yield: 10 to 12 servings

Mary Wohleber,
Troy Hill Citizens, Inc.

A

Asparagus

B

F

Fish (also see Seafood)

Frostings, Icings and Glaze (see Desserts)

Fruit (see individual listings)

G

Garlic

Grains and Cereals

Grilling Recipes

H

ℐ

ℐ

𝒦

ℒ

Lamb

Leeks

Lemon

Lobster (see Seafood)

ℳ

Mushrooms

𝒩

Nuts

Almonds

S

Salad Dressings

Salads

Salmon (*see Fish*)

Sandwiches

Sauces and Marinades

Sauerkraut

Sausage (*see Pork*)

Seafood

Clams

Crab

Sacred Heart Elementary School PTG
325 Emerson Street
Pittsburgh, PA 15206

Please send _____ copies of *The Heart of Pittsburgh* II   @ $17.95 each

Please send _____ copies of *The Heart of Pittsburgh*   @ $17.95 each

Plus postage and handling   @   3.50 each

Total _____

Pennsylvania residents add 7% sales tax of $1.26 for each book

Name _____

Address _____

City _____ State _____ Zip _____

Make checks payable to Sacred Heart Elementary School PTG

- -

Sacred Heart Elementary School PTG
325 Emerson Street
Pittsburgh, PA 15206

Please send _____ copies of *The Heart of Pittsburgh* II   @ $17.95 each

Please send _____ copies of *The Heart of Pittsburgh*   @ $17.95 each

Plus postage and handling   @   3.50 each

Total _____

Pennsylvania residents add 7% sales tax of $1.26 for each book

Name _____

Address _____

City _____ State _____ Zip _____

Make checks payable to Sacred Heart Elementary School PTG